DUBLIN ZOO

An Illustrated History

DUBLIN ZOO

An Illustrated History

CATHERINE DE COURCY

The Collins Press

FIRST PUBLISHED IN 2009 BY
The Collins Press
West Link Park
Doughcloyne
Wilton
Cork

in association with

© Catherine de Courcy 2009

Catherine de Courcy has asserted her moral right to be identified as the author of this work.

British Library Cataloguing in Publication Data
De Courcy, Catherine.
  Dublin Zoo - an illustrated history.
  1. Dublin Zoo (Dublin, Ireland)—History.
  I. Title
  590.7'341835-dc22

ISBN-13: 9781848890084

Design and typesetting by Anú Design, Tara
Typeset in Bembo
Printed in Italy by Printer Trento

Contents

Preface

When I was about five years old, Mr Kenny, the famous elephant keeper, allowed me to take a ride on Komali, the young Asian elephant. I have never forgotten the feel of her prickly skin as I held on to her neck while she walked around the yard of the elephant house. Dublin Zoo was the zoo of my childhood and I was a frequent visitor, but as a teenager, the idea of keeping animals in zoos apparently for entertainment purposes unsettled me and I avoided them. In 1988, when Melbourne Zoo invited me to write their history, I accepted the invitation because it linked into my academic interest in nineteenth-century institutions. Before long, however, I was drawn in by the animals and the work of the staff and the more I learnt, the more I was impressed by the important role zoos play in the modern world.

The World Association for Zoos and Aquariums is a global organisation for over 1,000 zoos, which receive over 600 million visitors annually.[1] In 2008, Dublin Zoo attracted more than 930,000 visitors. Through international networks, the zoos cooperate to preserve and conserve species that are in danger of extinction through human encroachment, climate change and other threats to their natural habitats. At the same time, zoos are introducing new generations of children to the magic of close encounters with animals and they are finding ways of drawing attention to small animals such as meerkats, squirrel monkeys and stick insects. Lifelong concern for the well-being of species can come from a simple childhood encounter with an animal in a zoo.

Over the past twenty-one years, I have visited numerous zoos and enjoy being in those zoos where standards of animal accommodation, education and professional work are evidently high. In April 2008, I visited Dublin Zoo's Kaziranga Elephant Trail and watched two-month-old Budi playing with his sister, Asha, and half-sister, Anak; when I was invited to write a history of Dublin Zoo shortly afterwards, I willingly accepted the challenge.

And challenge it was. Dublin Zoo's history is enormous with many exciting and surprising avenues to explore. A comprehensive history of the Zoo merits a multi-volume work in which a variety of writers tell the stories about the animals who lived in the Zoo, the staff, the council members, the visitors, the parties, the people who donated or acquired animals for the Zoo, the relationship with governments, the social and political context, and so on. I have taken the approach of presenting a chronological history that focuses on the animals and the visitors and presents the major themes of its evolution. I have limited the number of stories about staff and council members but only because of the restrictions set by the length of this book.

Over the past year I have received help, information, stories, photographs and insights from a great many people. Dublin Zoo staff, current and retired, were of immense assistance. They helped me to get to know the Zoo and the animals, explained their work to me and, on several special occasions, brought me close to the animals. Gerry Creighton (senior), who retired in April 2009, provided information and entertained me with memories of his past fifty-one years in the Zoo. Former staff members, including Pam McDonough, Michael Clarke and Tom McGrath walked around the Zoo with me, showing me hidden corners and telling me stories that stretched back through the decades. Family members of former staff related tales and supplied me with photos, including Betty Murphy, Michael Ward, who lived in the Zoo during the Second World War, and Paul Kenny, the son and grandson of two generations of elephant keepers. Current council members gave me insights into the workings of this dedicated group of people who belong to the body that has been managing the Zoo since 1831. I wish to thank everyone who took the time to talk to me and many of these valuable conversations are identified in the endnotes.

Practical help came from a range of sources. In the Zoo, Kathleen Molloy, Veronica Chrisp, Suzanne O'Donovan, Sandra Devaney, Dan Mahony and the staff in the Dublin Zoo offices were vital in helping me draw together this complex project. Staff in Dublin's major institutions were generous with advice and information including Dr Marie Bourke, Dr Brendan Rooney and Leah Benson in the National Gallery, Robert Mills in the College of Physicians, Dr Martyn Linnie in the Trinity College Zoological Museum, Dr Nicole Marples in Trinity College Zoology Department, Nigel Monaghan in the Natural History Museum, Alex Ward, curator of costume in the National Museum who helped me to date photographs in Dublin Zoo's collection, and the staff in the National Photographic Archive. The staff in Trinity College Dublin Manuscripts Department, where the early Zoo records are held, were unfailingly helpful in meeting my frequent requests for access to the material.

Gathering images for the book was made significantly easier by the generous help I received from photographers and archivists including Chris Corlett in the Department of Heritage and Environment, who scanned glass slides for me; Douglas Duggan, who provided photographs from his substantial collection of images of the Zoo in the mid-twentieth century; Mark Hogan, Neil McShane and Frank Malone who took photographs specially for this book; Maureen Gillespie in the *Sunday Tribune* and Irene Stevenson in *The Irish Times*, who made photographs from their respective newspapers available to me; Gay McCormack in the Irish Professional Photographers Association, Frank McGrath and Robert Allen in helping to trace photographers; and Eoin Cooney who created the charts of annual visitor numbers. I am particularly grateful to Damien Maddox, who was immensely generous and patient in scanning images and taking hundreds of photographs of the staff, visitors, animals and scenes around the Zoo for this history. I am also very grateful to the photographers who allowed me to use their pictures, and to the current and former staff members, visitors and families of former staff who provided photographs. All the photographs, except where otherwise stated, were taken in Dublin Zoo and photographers, where known, have been identified in the credits at the end of the book.

I would like to thank several people for their kindly assistance and advice on the text, including Stephen Butler, Michael O'Grady, Mary de Courcy, Helen Clarke, Professor Gabriel Cooney, Noeleen Behan, Sally Hayden and Ann Stewart. I would especially like to thank Leo Oosterweghel who invited me to write this history; over the past year, he has provided insights, information and encouragement at critical moments that helped me to manage the vast amount of information available to me and complete this book within the timeframe. Any errors and omissions are my responsibility alone.

All of these stories and insights have been drawn into this history directly and indirectly to bring life to the records of Dublin Zoo. Throughout the text I have used the word 'zoo' although this truncation of 'zoological gardens' was not commonly used until the mid- to late-nineteenth century. It first appeared in print in 1847 to describe Clifton Zoo in Bristol and became popular with the music-hall song 'Walking in the Zoo on Sunday'.[2] In Ireland, newspapers used the word 'zoo' in inverted commas until the early twentieth century when the inverted commas were gradually dropped.

It has been a pleasure and a privilege for me to work on the history of one of our important institutions and I hope that it will prompt other writers and researchers to develop some of the very many themes and stories that I can only touch on in this book.

Introduction

Dublin Zoo was opened in 1831 to allow members of the Zoological Society to view exotic animals on land made available by the Lord Lieutenant. Although it was a private organisation, the public were allowed in for a small fee and it quickly became one of Dublin's more popular institutions.

The story of the Zoo told in this entertaining book shines a light on important aspects of our modern history. The founders of the Zoo were a remarkably liberal and diverse group who defied contemporary attitudes to open the Zoo's gates to the working classes on a Sunday for a penny in 1840. Samuel Haughton, secretary of the Society whose name is immortalised in the Zoo's Haughton House, emerges as a provocative Home Ruler who declared at an annual general meeting of the Society that he was not a law-abiding Englishman but an Irish man who had sufficient influence to set up a riot if necessary! In the early twentieth century, the mood of the Zoo's council changed perceptibly and loyalty to the British throne became so pronounced that the king was named as patron of the Society until 1935. In 1938, when the council learnt that several keepers had joined a trade union, the staff were at last given a paid half-day's leave per week and paid annual holidays.

Yet despite political differences and social tension, Irish people in their tens, then hundreds of thousands visited the Zoo, ensuring that it survived the Famine, the 1916 Rising, the War of Independence, the Civil War, economic recessions and the two World Wars to provide a place of 'peaceful resort' where families could experience the wonders of the animals.

The ownership of the Zoo remained private and relied largely on admission fees and sponsorship to keep going. In 1854, the government gave them an annual grant of £500 in recognition of the penny admission on Sundays and free entry to charity groups. By the 1980s, the Zoo was still receiving a modest annual grant from the public purse of £10,500 and needed help to grow. As Lord Mayor of Dublin, Minister for Labour, Minister for Finance and then as Taoiseach, I was glad to be able to assist this national institution that had been – and still is – a source of joy to me and my family.

I am proud to watch as the staff and council work together to continue the development of a world class zoo that attracts nearly one million visitors a year. This beautiful book captures succinctly the stories of the animals and the visitors and reveals the fascinating history and philosophy that shaped one of our most important institutions.

Bertie Ahern T.D.

CHAPTER I

FOUNDATION
1830–1860

Foundation

'If there ever was a moment more propitious than another for commencing such an undertaking, it is the present,' said Philip Crampton at the first meeting of the Zoological Society of Ireland in May 1830. 'The public mind and time are comparatively disengaged . . . We have now leisure to be wise; I trust we shall apply it to the advancement of knowledge, and the maintenance of peace.'[1]

And so, Philip Crampton, the surgeon-general, and Whitley Stokes, a physician, together with an influential body of supporters founded the Zoological Society of Ireland. The Duke of Leinster chaired the foundation meeting, the Earl of Longford proposed the first resolution, while the Earl of Leitrim and the Earl of Howth sat on the foundation committee along with eminent doctors, academics and scientists. The Lord Lieutenant, Duke of Northumberland, invited the Society to establish their zoological gardens by a lake[2] in the Phoenix Park not far from his own residence, the Vice Regal Lodge. On 1 September 1831, Dublin Zoo opened to the public.

The motivations behind this ambitious undertaking ranged from self-interest to altruism. At the foundation meeting in the Rotunda, Parnell Square, Philip Crampton spoke passionately about the practical value of having animals available for study: when they were alive, they could be used for comparative analysis between species; when dead, they would be dissected and analysed and, therefore, further the knowledge of 'the healing arts'. Using the example of the liver, he noted that,

> The liver is the largest in the animals that breath the least, (as fishes and amphybiae) . . . and that the liver is totally wanting in the animals whose respiration is the most complete, as in the insect tribes, who are as it were all lungs.[3]

From this he suggested that a study of the relationship between the lungs and liver in each of these animals would be helpful in understanding diseases of the liver and lungs in man: 'when the liver becomes hardened and obstructed, (too often by intemperance) the lungs, performing a double labour, soon become inflamed and disordered.'[4]

Crampton also spoke about the role of the Zoological Society in promoting the popular study of natural history and the value that a visitor could derive from the study of animal nature in a zoo. With reference to the controversial sport of bear-baiting, he said:

Left: Sir Philip Crampton, 1777-1858, surgeon-general and co-founder of the Zoological Society of Ireland.
Right: Whitley Stokes, (1763-1845), physician, co-founder of the Zoological Society of Ireland.

'The boy who, day after day, shares his cake with the bear who runs up a pole to receive it, with the activity and almost the gestures with which a sailor climbs a mast, will scarcely go out of his way to see such an animal baited and torn to pieces by infuriated dogs, set on by . . . the most abandoned of men'.[5]

The bear pit, London Zoo. Hand-coloured lithograph by G. Scharf, 1835.

Crampton identified several other reasons for creating a zoo, including the potential use of some animals to assist in industry. He suggested, for example, that a wapiti might be used to increase the speed of horse-drawn transport, but this objective was soon forgotten.

In 1830, there were three other zoos of a similar nature in existence. The Tiergarten Schönbrunn in Vienna was established in 1752 when Emperor Joseph II opened his imperial menagerie to the public. The zoo in the Jardin des Plantes in Paris dates from 1793, when exotic animals were sent to the Muséum National d'Histoire Naturelle during the French Revolution. London Zoo had been created in 1828 by the Zoological Society of London; its combination of scientific resource to support the study of live and dead animals, and its rapidly acquired fashionable status with elegant gardens was the prototype that the Irish emulated.[6] However, Dublin Zoo differed in one critical aspect from London Zoo. From the very first day, in September 1831, Dublin Zoo was open to the general public on payment of an entrance charge; London Zoo was open only to the society's members and their guests.[7]

The Site

There was a delay in the Zoological Society of Ireland taking over the four-and-a-half-acre site in the Phoenix Park when the Department of Woods and Forests in London claimed that the Lord Lieutenant had no authority to grant the land to the Society. In March 1831, Crampton wrote to the Lord Lieutenant's office asking for permission to occupy the land; in his letter he mentioned that the King and the London Zoological Society had donated some animals to Dublin Zoo, which were currently waiting to be transferred. In the course of the discussions, Crampton agreed that the Society would vacate the site in the Park with two months' notice should the Lord Lieutenant ask it to do so. On these terms, the land 'near the pond' and the six-room lodge on the site were granted.[8]

Dublin, from the Phœnix Park.

Dublin from the
Phoenix Park, 1832.

Two families in Phoenix Park were disrupted by the arrival of the Zoological Society. The Goddens, who lived in the lodge, were the family of the park keeper. Godden the father and Godden the son, as they were referred in the Society's records[9] agreed to look after the wild boar for a small fee, which was the only animal in the Zoo's collection in the summer of 1831.[10] While the Goddens waited for another house to be built for the family, they were obliged to let the Society's committee use the large downstairs room for meetings; the family was also compensated for the loss of their orchard and vegetable gardens.[11] George Godden, the son, continued to work for the Zoo for a number of years.

The Rourke family was also affected by the arrival of the society. They lived in a cottage close to the south entrance of the Zoo but Mrs Rourke, who communicated with the Society on behalf of the family, was told that she did not have to move because the Society did not need her house yet. In 1832, access between her house and the Zoo was cut off. A year later she was cautioned against hanging any more of her linen in sight of the visitors to the gardens. Another year on and the impoverished Society was now so desperate to get rid of her that they offered her an annual sum of money to live somewhere else; eventually, in 1835, she was told to leave immediately or forfeit any goodwill on the part of the Society. Miles Rourke, who was employed by the Society for periods during the 1830s, may well have been a relation of Mrs Rourke.[12]

The Early Days

In August 1831, George Godden went to London Zoo to collect the first of several consignments of animals, including deer, macaws, cockatoos, and a pair of emus. Crampton and the committee rushed to prepare cages and paddocks for the animals. A row of open sheds was built along part of the northern wall of the old orchard, sections of the pond were enclosed by stakes below and a 3-foot trellis above, paddocks were created using rough timber uprights and bars, the deer houses were built and a warm house with glazed windows and a stove was prepared.[13] Dr Arthur Jacob, a member of the committee, prepared accommodation for the bear, the raccoon and the fox at his own expense.[14]

Dublin Zoo opened on Thursday 1 September 1831 at 9.00 a.m. For a lengthy description of a visit to the Zoo, we have to wait until the following summer when the first issue of the *Dublin Penny Journal* in June 1832 devoted two pages to stories about the Zoo. The writer started by entering Phoenix Park from the Chesterfield Gates and 'taking the Irish-like way' across the fields rather than along the formal Chesterfield avenue, arrived at the Zoo:

Can we not fancy ourselves in Paradise, and removing the idea of cages and barriers, think we see Adam and Eve walking in innocence amongst the creatures, while they sported and frisked about them? It would be rather difficult indeed to set down this whiskered exquisite, with a cigar in his mouth, who is throwing nuts to the monkey for old father Adam, or this decayed and venerable maiden, whose monstrous bonnet expands over her spare bust, for good mother Eve – but a truce to criticism – here are two grave, philosophic young men, whose remarks must be very instructive; and though we would not be guilty of the rudeness of intruding on any one, we may, without a breach of politeness, follow in rear and listen to their observations.

Stuffed passenger pigeon in the Zoological Museum, Trinity College Dublin. The passenger pigeon is now extinct.

After eavesdropping on a comparison of the toes of the ostrich and those of the emu, and a discussion about the wapiti and its horns, the grave, philosophic young men spotted the scarlet macaw.

Do you not think that this scarlet macaw resembles old cross hook-nosed General Slowfoot who owes his elevation to an improvement he suggested in officers' epauletts or this cockatoo to our cousin ensign Johnny Newcome![15]

Such is our first account of a visit to Dublin Zoo. Six months later, a visitor from Belfast wrote a long letter to the *Dublin Penny Journal* expressing concern about the conditions in which the animals were kept, and this provides a rare description of what the Zoo was really like in the 1830s. The visitor, who signed himself I. D. M. expressed pleasure at the establishment of the Zoological Society in Dublin, and praised the beauty of the location and its proximity to the city. However when he observed the crowded conditions, he expressed the sincere hope that the homes for the animals were only temporary, as they could not possible thrive in those conditions. He was particularly distressed by the shed, which was 25 feet long and 12 feet wide, and housed the leopard and leopardess, a hyena, several monkeys, a squirrel, a pelican, parrots, macaws, a kestrel hawk, herons, birds, tortoises and others. He was also worried that the boxes used by the ostriches and emus at night were so low that the birds had to stoop if they were to take shelter inside and he was unhappy about the way the buzzard and peregrine falcons were chained to trees without access to branches for perches.[16]

ZOOLOGICAL SOCIETY.

THE Zoological Garden, in the Phœnix Park, under the patronage of his Excellency the Lord Lieutenant, will be opened for Visitors on THIS DAY, THURSDAY, SEPTEMBER 1st, at Nine o'Clock in the morning, and will not be closed until a late hour in the day.

All persons are to be admitted for Six Pence each.— They are to write their names at the gate.

A member who has paid his subscription, and two of his friends coming with him, are admitted free of expense.

Members are also allowed to purchase transferable tickets.

The Committee request that visitors may leave their stick and umbrellas at the gate.

And that children may be kept from approaching too near to the bars which confine the animals.

J. Fim, Esq., 41, Dame-street, continues to receive subscriptions and donations.

The first day's receipts will be given to the Mendicity Association.

Advertisement from *Saunders's News-Letter*, 1 September 1831.

A pelican was purchased in 1832 for £14 14s; it was the first large expenditure on an animal in Dublin Zoo. Image from the *Dublin Penny Journal*, 1836.

A bear: image from
the *Dublin Penny
Journal*, 1832.

At this point, in November 1832, Dublin Zoo had fifty-six mammals including fifteen monkeys, and seventy-two birds, among them two passenger pigeons.[17] The carnivorous animals included the wolf, the raccoons, the hyena, the leopard, foxes and the bear. Mr R. Drewitt, a former animal keeper from London, who was experienced in looking after carnivorous animals, was employed as the Zoo's first superintendent.[18]

The Design

Crampton and the committee were aware of the shortcomings of the animal accommodation and had engaged Decimus Burton to design the layout of Dublin Zoo. Burton had designed London Zoo and, in his work for Dublin, he included some designs for animal houses based on his experience in London. The small plot of land occupied by the Zoo was on the east side of the lake, close to where the Haughton House and the Roberts House now stand. The lake formed the border on the west side, and a small, irregular wall formed the border on the east. The only existing building was the Godden's lodge.

Burton's design used the lake as the focus of the Zoo and he incorporated the west side of the lake, ignoring the fact that the land was not occupied by the Society.[19] He placed the

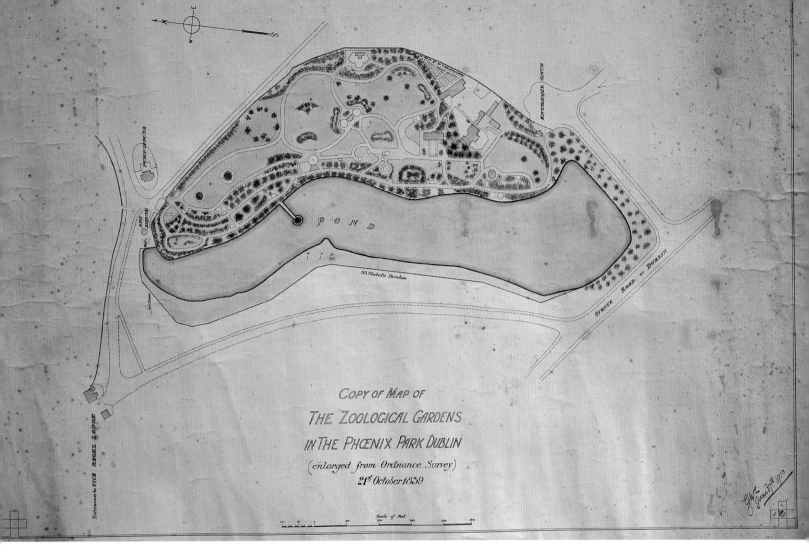

COPY OF MAP OF

THE ZOOLOGICAL GARDENS

IN THE PHŒNIX PARK DUBLIN

(enlarged from Ordnance Survey)

21ˢᵗ October 1839

Scale of Feet

entrance in its current position on the south side because it was convenient to the city. Most of the animals were to be kept on the higher ground, which was about 26 feet above the level of the lake. The shrubs and undergrowth around the lake were to be cleared, allowing visitors beautiful views down the hill and across the water to the park beyond. He suggested that small ponds be formed at the north side of the lake, where it was shallow, so that water-fowl could be displayed in different categories. He also suggested incorporating the spa or spring, which was contiguous to the Society's grounds, because it was already an attraction to the public.[20]

Over winter and spring 1832–33, the committee organised, planned and supervised the construction of enclosures, cages, and fences. William Deane Butler, a member of council and

Copy of map of the Zoological Gardens in the Phoenix Park Dublin, 21 October 1839.

GATE-HOUSE OF THE ZOOLOGICAL GARDENS, PHŒNIX PARK.

Entrance Lodge in
Dublin Zoo, 1835.

an architect, did a lot of the design work, including the famous entrance lodge, which was completed in early summer 1833. The intention was to complete the small lodge for under £30; by way of comparison, the council offered £60 for a camel a month later.[21] The lodge has remained an icon of Dublin Zoo, despite plans over the years to demolish and replace it.[22]

Restructure 1833

All of the effort so far had gone into creating the Zoo and in 1833, the founders turned their attention to the academic aspect of their Society, which was intended to support scientific study by the physicians and surgeons and other interested members. Their model, the Zoological Society of London, was holding regular lectures, had created a museum and was publishing papers on zoological matters.[23] The Zoological Society of Ireland began by restructuring its management on the lines of the Geological Society of London and introduced the office of president. The president was to be appointed on an annual basis in an effort to ensure that the interests of one individual did not dominate the Society for a lengthy period of time. It proved an impractical arrangement and most of the early presidents held the position for several years. Other officers already in existence included the honorary secretary and the honorary treasurer. The body of the council was to consist of fifteen members, several of whom were to be replaced each year. The basic organisational structure of the Zoological Society of Ireland, designed in 1833, remains in place today with some modifications. The rules governing ordinary membership of the Society, by which the applicant had to be proposed by one member, seconded by another and accepted by council was relaxed in the late twentieth century[24]. Lectures and an essay competition were also arranged but neither became a significant activity of Dublin Zoo.

P. Dixon Hardy, the editor of the *Dublin Penny Journal*, often included articles on zoological matters based on animals in the Zoo. Referring to specific animals, the articles discussed

'The puma and the camel'. Image from the *Dublin Penny Journal*, 1836.

the variety in their anatomy, their instincts and the behaviours that fitted them 'to fill the various stations in which they are placed by nature'. For example, in an article in 1836, the different shapes of mouths were discussed:

> The mouth of the man, or of the monkey, who have hands to lift their food, recedes, and is thus only fitted for the reception of what is placed into it. The projecting jaws and sharp teeth of the dog enables it to snatch and seize the object of its pursuit. The full lips, the rough tongue, and broad teeth of the ox, or of the horse, qualify them for browsing upon an herbaceous pasturage . . . Thus, not only are all the species of the same kind peculiarly adapted by their structure to their respective stations, whether it be mountain or plain, trees, marsh, or water, but each individual species is placed in that particular climate which is best suited to the supply of its peculiar wants.'[25]

The day out, recreation

Perhaps one of the reasons why the academic side of the Zoological Society of Ireland was struggling to gain a foothold was because Dublin Zoo was open to the general public and, therefore, the council's efforts were focused on providing a place of recreation and education to the populus. By the mid 1830s, when the city's population was about 200,000[26], over 40,000 people were walking, riding or taking carriages out to the Zoo each year. Dublin Zoo now had a bear pit with a pole up which a bear could climb to reach for buns. Sticks and umbrellas had to be checked in at the gate; the reason for this was not declared but it was probably to stop the visitors from tormenting the animals by poking them. How a Dublin visitor fed buns to a bear balanced at the top of a post is not on record. Entertainments were laid on in the Zoo and military bands played regularly, in summer and occasionally in winter. Summer fetes were arranged and the Lord Lieutenant was sent an invitation. The keeping staff were given dark green, velveteen waistcoats and jackets, and the two ground staff were given coats and waistcoats with buttons adorned with a harp.[27]

It was critical for the success of the Zoo that it should be seen as a place of genteel recreation. Traditionally, exotic animals were exhibited in temporary fairs and circuses amid scenes of alcohol consumption and rowdy behaviour. Donnybrook Fair was the most famous of the Dublin fairs; it was an annual carnival, the licence for which dated back to the thirteenth century. Trading livestock and selling were the main purposes for the fair but

View of the
Entrance Lodge,
Dublin Zoo, 1833.

by the 1830s, it was a major, if notorious, event in Dublin held every August, with food and alcohol to suit every pocket and taste, and dancing, music and entertainment going through the night. Sideshows and menageries, mostly from England, were attracted to the fair. In 1819, for example, an elephant was part of Polito's menagerie and in 1830, lions cubs reputedly born in Navan were exhibited.[28]

Dublin Zoo's founders were determined that their collection of animals would not become the focus for an alcohol-fuelled party for the working classes, hence the patronage of the Lord Lieutenant and other aristocrats was critical to their structure. In 1831, a list of subscribers was deliberately placed by the gate and, for those socially conscious, it was attractive company. By 1833, there were forty-eight titled members including bishops,

LAMAS.—VIEW IN THE ZOOLOGICAL GARDENS.

Llama in Dublin Zoo, 1836.

dukes, earls, lords, and sirs along with army officers, doctors and academics among its 283 members. There were a few women, including the Countess of Glengall and a Miss Edworth, the only single woman on the list and one of the few people whose street address was not included.[29]

The involvement of landed gentry in nineteenth-century zoos was often motivated by an interest in securing deer, cattle, llamas, partridges, pheasant, waterfowl and other animals with potential economic value, which might be released on their properties. In the late 1830s, when Dublin Zoo was going through a financial crisis, there was discussion about focusing more on propagating useful animals but no systematic effort was made to support this suggestion, although such animals, particularly the waterfowl, remained an important part of the stock.[30] In fact, the Irish landed gentry were more inclined to provide deer and fowl to augment the collection in Phoenix Park than the other way around.

The yellow-crested cockatoo. Image from the *Dublin Penny Journal*, 1836.

British Association for the Advancement of Science Conference 1835

Despite the scientific aspect of the Irish Zoological Society being relatively weak, the Zoo took part in the important British Association for the Advancement of Science Conference when it was held in Dublin in 1835. The Association had been founded in 1831 to encourage dialogue about science in Britain and Ireland and its meetings drew together 'middle-class spectators and provincial and metropolitan scientific elites.'[31] In August 1835, up to 600 members attended scientific meetings while the social occasions associated with the conference attracted hundreds and, in the case of the Zoo function, thousands of guests.[32] On Tuesday, 13 August, the delegates and friends of the council were invited to *déjeuner* at the Zoo. It was an exclusive occasion: only those with a ticket received from a member of the Zoological Society were permitted to enter during the day, and this was also on payment of a shilling. After four o'clock, a greater number of people were allowed in, but they also needed a special ticket for the privilege. However, the number of people with such tickets was enormous and on this beautiful summer afternoon, there was chaos at the gate. The *Evening Freeman* described the scene:

Wapiti. Image from the *Dublin Penny Journal*, 1832.

> For a considerable time after four o'clock, the crowd of persons outside the gate suffered much inconvenience from the gradual accumulation which took place from the arrival of people from the city. The gate was only open at intervals, and many were obliged to wait for nearly two hours before they could procure ingress. After some time, indeed, a second gate was thrown open higher up, but not until a good degree of actual annoyance had been undergone, particularly by ladies who were unavoidably crushed most unmercifully at the door. The number of persons of all sexes in the gardens at six o'clock was immense; and they had not ceased pouring in from Dublin until after seven. The Lord Lieutenant walked through the grounds for a couple of hours. There were two fine bands in attendance . . . Our fellow citizens would have passed a most delightful afternoon had the entrance been better regulated.[33]

Crampton and the wapiti

With meetings held at least once a week, the core group of the Zoological Society council visited the Zoo regularly. How much they studied the animals while they were alive is conjecture, however, the following story gives a glimpse into Philip Crampton and his involvement with the Zoo. In June 1835, he was visiting the Zoo with two colleagues, surgeons Palmer and Campbell, when they spotted a wapiti in trouble, apparently having difficulty breathing. Palmer and Campbell helped the keepers to restrain the animal, putting her head in a noose, getting her to the ground and placing boards across her body. Crampton performed a tracheotomy and at once, it was reported, she relaxed and her breathing eased. Crampton put two fingers in the aperture and the deer breathed easily for fifteen minutes. Then he had to leave so he placed a keeper's fingers in the aperture. The animal breathed 'until all effects of the accident had ceased to be perceptible'. Fifteen minutes later she was up and eating grass once more. An earlier story about Crampton performing an emergency tracheotomy in the Richmond Tavern on a waiter who was choking on a piece of beef was well known in Dublin. Now the story about his emergency tracheotomy on the wapiti, a large deer originally from North America, spread and hundreds of visitors thronged to see the subject of his attention.[34]

Elephants and rhinoceros

In 1835, a ten-year-old elephant arrived in Dublin Zoo, on loan for £100 a month from a travelling animal keeper called Atkins. In the hope of buying it from him, the Society had

THE ELEPHANT.

Elephant in Dublin Zoo, 1835.

Nelson, del.

THE RHINOCEROS.

R.CLAYTON. S⁵

Rhinoceros in Dublin
Zoo, 1835.

organised a collection to purchase the elephant and Atkins was offered £600. Perhaps this was not sufficient, or the animal was not for sale, but this elephant did not remain in Dublin Zoo for very long. The Society had also rented an Asian rhinoceros[35], which was described in the *Penny Journal* as having skin so hard that it resisted 'sabres, lances, javelins, and even musket balls, the only penetrable parts being the belly, the eyes and about the ears. Hence hunters generally attack them when they lie down to sleep.'[36]

In spring 1836, Dublin Zoo received an Asian elephant from London Zoo. London Zoo had received an elephant from the King and now it was glad to be able to help 'the sister Society in Dublin, by lending to that institution the female elephant which was previously in the Gardens'.[37] The loan involved giving the live elephant to Dublin on condition that the skeleton of the animal would be returned to London when it died. This elephant died in 1842 and Dublin was allowed to keep the skeleton. After a series of public demonstrations of the elephant's anatomy, the skeleton was presented to the Royal Dublin Society for its natural history museum.[38]

Coronation day

In November 1837, the young Queen Victoria agreed to become patroness of the Zoological Society of Ireland.[39] At the annual general meeting in May 1838, the council made the announcement and said that, in 'a minor change', the Society would henceforth be called 'The Royal Zoological Society of Ireland'. On the Queen's coronation day, 28 June 1838, the Zoo was opened from twelve o'clock until six in the evening with free admission. It was estimated that 20,000 people came to visit the animals.[40] By then the membership privileges had been relaxed and members' children under twelve were being admitted free of charge. Sixpence was still prohibitive to the general public, although it was possible that they were able to see the animals from the perimeter fence, or by crossing the lake where it was shallow. The Zoo was particularly vulnerable on Sunday mornings as the gardens did not open until 2.00 p.m. at this stage and there were few staff around to stop people entering the Zoo illegally.

Finance

Opening the Zoo free of charge put a dent in the admissions fee income for that year but the loss was more than met by the increase in the number of members. Aside from being permitted to use the land rent-free, the Zoological Society was entirely self-funding through subscriptions, donations and, when it opened, admission fees. In 1830 the Society had attracted over 140 members, some of whom had joined as life members for a fee of £10

The great Deambulatorium or exercising Cage 36 Feet long for Carnivorous Animals erected at the Gardens of the Royal Zoological Society of Ireland

The Deambulatorium, financed by Philip Crampton in 1838 to provide the lions, tiger and leopard with space to take exercise. The big cats did not take to it and, after they were sold, up to seventeen eagles were put into it.

while annual membership cost a guinea.[41] By 1838, there were 615 members but during the 1840s, income from membership dropped steadily, even as visitor numbers were increasing. Finding enough money to keep the Zoo going was a constant problem and the council members were lending money to pay wages and food bills.

By 1838, the Society was under severe financial pressure and the honorary secretary, Robert Ball, wrote to London Zoo about the situation in Dublin:

> I regret to say that with all efforts we can make (save converting our Garden with a puppet show or place of carousel) we cannot gain sufficient public support to enable us to add to our collection to any great extent. It not infrequently happens that at this time of the year that our receipts at the door do not exceed £3 in the week.[42]

In July 1839, as the financial pressure continued, Ball wrote to London Zoo asking if they would be interested in purchasing Dublin's carnivora; at this stage, the Zoo was feeding beef to the lioness and tigress, puma and leopard, rather than the cheaper horseflesh, which they were feeding other carnivora:

> It is believed [the sale] will not only effect a very considerable reduction of expenditure but prove acceptable to the public, who perhaps find their curiosity with respect to carnivora sufficiently gratified by the more frequent exhibitions at theatres and other places . . . our stock of carnivora is small but it is particularly healthy, we have a very fine tigress, a lioness, jaguar, pumas and leopard (all save the jaguar extremely gentle).[43]

London Zoo agreed to buy the jaguar only.

Strife

By now the council had established a particular style of management in running the Zoo: despite the presence of an experienced superintendent, the council made all of the decisions on the design, construction, modification and planning of fences, cages, paths, paddocks and buildings. They met at least once a week and issued instructions on the basis of their discussions. Mr Drewitt, the superintendent, was finding it difficult to work with their level of micro-management. In 1834, he had challenged them on their insistence that they hire,

The lion. Image from the *Dublin Penny Journal*, 1834.

fire and fine all staff. Drewitt had claimed it diminished his authority but he had been told firmly that all staff employment issues rested with the council. He had withdrawn his resignation on that occasion. Periodically an animal would escape or die due to perceived neglect on the part of one of the keepers. For example, two parakeets in Miles Rourke's care died and the council reduced his wages; two months later, his wages were increased for good conduct. Daniel Gorman was fined 2/6, or nearly two days' wages, for permitting a jackal to escape. A man called Culagh was dismissed for allowing the bears to escape. And when, in July 1838, the keepers were 'refusing to wear the frocks provided for them,'[44] Drewitt was told to deduct 1/- per week from each man until a sufficient sum was raised to purchase other suitable clothes for them.

In 1837 the council decided to hold its weekly, Saturday morning meetings in the parlour in Drewitt's house in the Zoo and breakfast was to be served to them by a keeper. Drewitt resigned in protest at the intrusion but withdrew his resignation again a few months later

20 DUBLIN ZOO – AN ILLUSTRATED HISTORY

and accepted the council's right to use as much of the house as it required in the future. In July 1839, Drewitt was given his notice. When he left, he purchased the lioness and tigress that London Zoo would not buy. According to Ball:

> We have sold the lioness and tigress for £200, no other offer having been made, and our late superintendent the purchaser, urging that if he got them he would not send them out of this city, but erect a large house for the larger carnivora at the 'Vesuvius Gardens', he set up some time since here, such Gardens have been the upsetting of our funds.[45]

A new superintendent was appointed and it was made clear to him that he was the servant of the council and that the parlour in his house was to be made available to the council as required. That pattern of management between council and superintendent continued well into the twentieth century. Superintendents were usually accorded the courtesy of being referred to as 'Mr' while the keeping and gardening staff were referred to by surname only. Periodically the first name of a staff member was recorded, usually in the case of a death, injury, age increase or dismissal.

JACKALS—VIEW IN THE ZOOLOGICAL GARDENS.

Left: Robert Ball, (1802–1857), secretary of the Zoological Society of Ireland from 1837 until his death. 'With him the prosperity of the Zoological Gardens was a personal concern … His motives for this exertion were a pure love of science … and a benevolent desire to make that science as available as possible to the widest circle of the public.' *Saunders News-Letter*, 6 May 1857. Right: Jackals in Dublin Zoo, 1836.

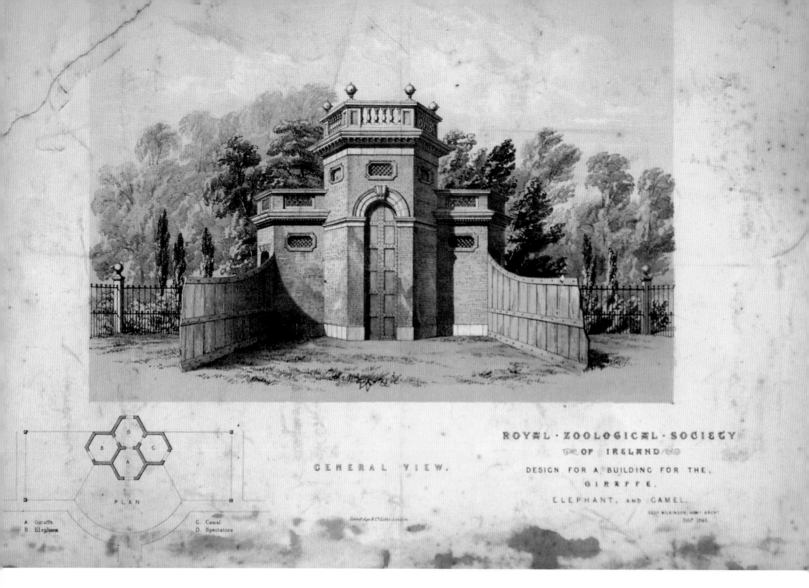

ROYAL · ZOOLOGICAL · SOCIETY
OF IRELAND

GENERAL VIEW.

DESIGN FOR A BUILDING FOR THE
GIRAFFE,
ELEPHANT, AND CAMEL.

PLAN

A Giraffe
B Elephant

C Camel
D Spectators

Penny Sundays

In 1840, James Haughton, a corn merchant and social reformer, and Robert Ball, 'co-operating heartily' are credited with reducing the entrance charge to the Zoo on a Sunday to one penny. They argued that this would benefit the funds of the Society and provide 'healthy and instructive recreation for the well-conducted people who are busily occupied during the week.'[46] From 1 May 1840, the working classes, who worked six days a week, were more likely to be able to afford a visit to the Zoo; at the time, a major newspaper, such as the *Saunders's News-Letter*, cost four pence[47]; the publication of the *Dublin Penny Journal* made newspapers

Design for Albert Tower, the combined giraffe and elephant house built in 1845.

available, so clearly one penny was affordable to many. Sunday opening to the masses was a radical move at the time and the behaviour of the Sunday visitors was constantly monitored. From May 1840 to April 1841 81,404 people took advantage of this cheap entry and 'The Council have further pleasure in stating that although on many occasions upwards of 3,000 persons have been in the Gardens at a time, no injury has resulted to the grounds or animals'. The following year, the report of the council said: 'Though the majority of visitors to the Gardens were admitted at the low rate of one penny . . . the Council believe that this, so far from lessening the value and importance of the Society, shows it . . . as a valuable aid to the enlightenment of the people and a powerful contributor to the maintenance of the improved and temperate habits.'[48] Soon afterwards, the council began to reduce the entrance charge to a penny on selected public holidays, especially around Christmas and Easter.

The giraffe

London Zoo had purchased three male and one female giraffe in 1836 from a French trader in the Sudan and, in 1839, a giraffe was born but died soon afterwards. Another, a male, was born in May 1841 and named Albert. When Robert Ball requested a giraffe in 1844, London Zoo decided to send Albert because he was considered the most portable and hardiest of their stock despite his great popularity as being the first ever reared in London. In exchange, Ball sent a two-toed sloth and a new species of tiger cat.[49] Dublin Zoo had nowhere to keep the young animal and George Wilkinson, the society's honorary architect and a member of council, designed a building that could house a giraffe, an elephant and a camel in separate compartments, and put a look-out tower on the top. A scaled-down version of Wilkinson's plan was built and opened with an elegant ceremony. The president of the society, the Duke of Leinster, in the presence of the Lord Lieutenant, laid the foundation stone on 24 May 1845. The stone was hollow and two glass jars were placed in

Above and opposite: Coins struck in 1831; Below: 'The cameleopard or giraffe.' Image from the *Dublin Penny Journal*, 1836.

it with a series of items, including an illustration of the building, admission tickets for a lecture in the Royal Dublin Society's premises in Leinster House, Kildare Street, and for a promenade in the Zoo. Newspaper reports of the Society's annual general meeting were also included, as were twenty-one white metal and two copper admission tickets embossed with the head of a giraffe and issued by the Society to allow admission to the giraffe house, which cost extra. The stone with its contents emerged in May 1962 when Albert Tower, as the giraffe's new home became known, was demolished to make way for a hippo house.

The giraffe was an instant success and 132,000 people visited the gardens in 1844-1845, more than half the estimated population of Dublin at the time. Nearly 99,000 were penny visitors, and it was not until 1857 that that number of visitors was again recorded.

The Famine years

The presence of the giraffe cushioned the early effects of the Great Famine on the fortunes of the Zoo but by 1847, the impact was unmistakable as income and visitor numbers receded and the cost of feeding the animals escalated. The council announced that they were no longer using food that could be consumed by humans, and horsemeat and rough barley took the place of bread, oats and butchers' meat. Biscuit, beans, bran and wheat appeared on the list of food purchased during the late 1840s. Presumably, given the council's announcement, much of this was unsuitable for human consumption. Milk, eggs and turnips were purchased occasionally, as was cabbage for the ostrich, and onions, rock salt and clover for the giraffe. Potatoes had been part of the diet of several animals in the 1830s, including the bears, but vanished from the list of food purchased at this time. Ordinary animal food continued to be purchased, such as canary seed and hemp seed. Small quantities of poor quality Indian corn were fed to the fowl, and the price of hay and straw was of major concern. Francis Buckley, the superintendent, was instructed to be very careful to get the best price when he went to the market and to ensure he was not overcharged.[50]

During the Famine years, many animals died but only a black bear was recorded as having died for want of food. Other animals died from distemper, heart disease, or 'decline'. The goat was destroyed by the bison, young bloodhounds died at birth, a golden eagle on loan was killed by an otter, an arctic fox was 'destroyed by the others', a kangaroo had a swollen face and died, baboons died from diarrhoea, an African eagle escaped when the roof was

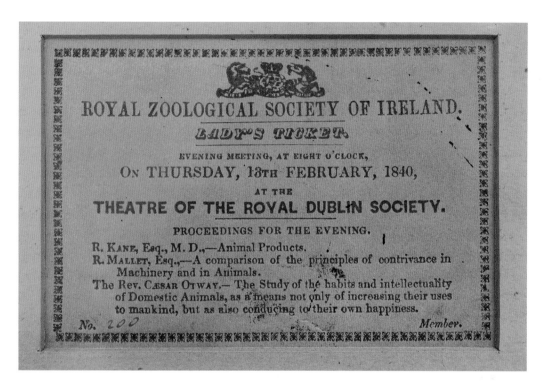

ROYAL ZOOLOGICAL SOCIETY OF IRELAND.

LADY'S TICKET.

EVENING MEETING, AT EIGHT O'CLOCK,

On THURSDAY, 13TH FEBRUARY, 1840,

AT THE

THEATRE OF THE ROYAL DUBLIN SOCIETY.

PROCEEDINGS FOR THE EVENING.

R. Kane, Esq., M. D.,—Animal Products.

R. Mallet, Esq.,—A comparison of the principles of contrivance in Machinery and in Animals.

The Rev. Cæsar Otway.— The Study of the habits and intellectuality of Domestic Animals, as a means not only of increasing their uses to mankind, but as also conducing to their own happiness.

No. 200   Member.

Lady's ticket, found in the time capsule created when Albert Tower was being constructed in 1845.

blown off his cage, an otter escaped through the weir while another otter was killed by his mates, and an Egyptian goose got into the bear cage and was killed. The cause of death of a dromedary was listed as 'long sick' and the elephant died quickly and unexpectedly from an inflammatory disease. A high mortality rate in a nineteenth-century Zoo was not unusual and, in the cases where cause of death was noted, the ways in which animals died during the Famine years were not markedly different from the way they died in other periods of the Zoo's history. Robert Ball, in his capacity as director of the Zoological Museum in Trinity College, was a frequent purchaser of carcasses of animals, and this provided a small income for the Zoo: and, as the highly active honorary secretary to the council, he had the advantage of receiving the animals quickly after they died. Such was the value of a carcass to the medical community, a rattlesnake was donated to the Zoo on condition that the owner received the animal as soon as it died; however, it was burnt to death and was therefore of no use to the donor.

Besides the giraffe, the stock of animals in the 1840s included black bears, raccoons, a sloth bear, otters, hedgehogs, silver partridges, swans, geese, and a pair of bloodhounds which

THE KANGAROO.

THE CASSOWARY.

Images from Dublin Zoo in the *Dublin Penny Journal*, 1836.

produced large litters frequently, most of which did not survive. Seals, monkeys, a cassowary, a fox and a squirrel were among the very few animals purchased during these years. In 1847, the council warned that if it could not liquidate the debt of the society, they would have to decide whether they could face another winter when the expenses increased due to cost of fuel but gate income was reduced to almost nothing. They pleaded with members to pay their subscriptions and, with the help of the penny entrance fees, the Zoo survived. In 1849, the council congratulated itself on keeping the Zoo going during those difficult years. By then, its staff consisted only of the superintendent, a clerk who also worked as the gatekeeper and watchman, two keepers and two gardeners.

Rebuilding in the 1850s

Despite their threat to close, the council members continued to carry the debt of the society by lending sums of money to keep the Zoo open and, when the country began to recover in the 1850s, the Zoo recovered with it. In 1853, the International Exhibition on Leinster Lawn attracted nearly 1 million visitors between May and October, including Queen Victoria. The Zoo 'shared from the influx of strangers brought hither,'[51] and recorded 114,000 visitors in its reporting year, 1853–1854, a number surpassed only in 1844 when the giraffe arrived. With the help of the consequent rise in income, the council was able to clean up the Zoo, rebuild structures which were decaying, including stables, offices, sheds and other structures.

In 1854, an aquarium was opened in Dublin Zoo. London had opened their aquarium, known at the time as the Marine and Fresh Water Vivarium, the previous year. Created by the naturalist, Philip Henry Gosse, London Zoo's aquarium incorporated the latest knowledge in keeping fish and aquatic plants together in a tank and aerating the water to ensure that both stay alive. Dublin Zoo's aquarium, or Aquatic Vivaria, was built close to the perimeter fence near what is now the reptile house; it was fitted with a forcing pump, tanks and pipes to supply water to the fish tanks as well as supplying water to the two other houses. A 'horizontal windmill' aerated the water in the several fish tanks, fifteen of which were brought into action in mid-1854. Plants and rocks were used to furnish the fish tanks, and mirrors were concealed in one of the larger tanks to throw light on the fish and the rock-work from below. Frost caused some difficulties the following winter but overall the system of aerating the water proved very successful. The aquarium remained fairly well stocked with many varieties of seawater and freshwater fish, and with sea anemones, zoophytes and crustaceans procured from the coasts of Howth and Dalkey.[52]

Government support

In 1854, the Society received an annual government grant in response to yet another plea for assistance. The council had justified its request by explaining that crowds of people 'bearing the marks of weekly toil' were provided 'with a resource from which they go home refreshed and with quiet minds, fitting them to work happily for the next week at their several occu-pations.'[53] The government pledged an annual grant of £500 a year to the Society. The following year, the council announced that governesses and other female 'inmates' of the houses of members should be allowed in with members and the members' children. Members could fill in a form identifying the female member of staff who might bring the children to the Zoo in the absence of the member or their wife. The council came up with this scheme

THE ZEBRA.—VIEW IN THE ZOOLOGICAL GARDENS.

Image from the *Dublin Penny Journal*, 1836.

to 'avoid the demoralising effect of children being introduced [into the Gardens] by nurses and others [who were using] false names; and it is hoped the present plan will, with the cooperation of the members, prevent the evil referred to.'[54] Further concessions were made, including evening entry during the summer months after six o'clock at one penny, and after two o'clock on Sundays. Art students were to be admitted free of charge, as were charitable groups. The tradition of admitting groups of children associated with charitable organisations free of charge continued until well into the twentieth century, while a small charge was levied for groups of schoolchildren from fee-paying schools.[55]

The Treasury Commission tried to complicate this annual grant ten years later by suggesting that it would be convenient if the Royal Dublin Society made all representations to the government on behalf of the Zoological Society and other scientific societies. In rejecting this suggestion out of hand, the council stated that, had the Royal Dublin Society been in a position to control the Zoological Society, 'the precedent of the admission of the public on Sundays . . . might have been seriously interfered with.'[56]

Seal of the Royal Zoological Society of Ireland.

The beginning of the Irish lion industry

With the success of 1854 and 95,000 people visiting in 1855, the council felt confident that they could afford the initial cost and ongoing expense of keeping lions once more and they

Group photograph taken 1855. (L–r): Sir Dominic Corrigan, Dr George Hatchell, Jacob Owen, Dr Robert Ball, Sir Francis Brady, Professor George Allman, Patrick Supple, James Lowe (superintendent), Welsh (Carpenter), John Supple, Patrick Rice.

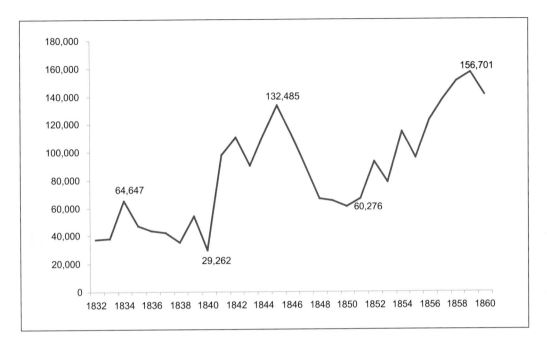

180,000

160,000 — 156,701

140,000 — 132,485

120,000

100,000

80,000

64,647

60,000 — 60,276

40,000

29,262

20,000

0

1832 1834 1836 1838 1840 1842 1844 1846 1848 1850 1852 1854 1856 1858 1860

Visitor numbers
1832–1860. The peak
in 1859 was owing to
the popularity of the
polar bear, lion cubs,
the arrival of the
Bengal tiger, and
good weather.

purchased a pair of young lions for £285, which was more than their entire income from subscriptions in 1854. The council was satisfied that their staff had the skills to keep these animals and, in telling their members of this development, pointed out that a leopard had lived in the gardens for over ten years and a puma and jaguar had been living there for four years. The pair of lions were reportedly taken at Natal, in southern Africa, and were named Natal and Natalie. In 1857, Natalie had a litter and this marked the beginning of what became known as the 'Irish Lion Industry'. Before he died in 1864, Natal had had a total of forty-two cubs, ten of them with Natalie. In 1858, a terrier dog was purchased as a playmate for a young lioness, 'with whom it still lives in the strictest friendship,' we were told.[57] The lions became a sizable source of income for the Zoo as the cubs could be sold or exchanged. In 1860, one lioness was exchanged for a rhea, a king vulture, a peccary, four monkeys and an additional '£10-worth of good, healthy monkeys' within six months of the transaction. In 1861, four young lioness cubs were exchanged for a lioness, a polar bear, a black bear, a Nilgai, a boa constrictor, a rhea, and several smaller quadrupeds and birds. As the first generation of the Dublin Zoo's council moved towards retirement, all the elements required to keep this institution going were in place.

CHAPTER 2

CONSOLIDATION
1860–1895

Dublin Zoo in 1860 was a very popular venue for all classes of Dubliners. Dukes, earls, lords and ladies mixed with government officials, doctors, lawyers and other members at the promenades and on the sixpenny days. The working classes turned up on Sundays and summer evenings when the entrance fee was a penny. In 1860, there were over 140,000 visitors, not including the number who managed to get into the Zoo by making their way across the shallow part of the lake or hopping over the fence or even squeezing through the turnstile.

The area occupied by the Zoo was still confined to the east side of the lake and the Society was still on two months' notice to vacate it. There was a carnivore house, an aquarium, several aviaries, cages, small paddocks, the entrance lodge, the superintendent's house, the imposing Albert Tower and a tent-like structure, which housed the valuable plesiosaurus fossil.[1] The substantial collection of animals, gathered by donation, purchase and exchange, was looked after by the superintendent, Mr Lowe, and four keepers, Patrick Rice, Thomas Flood, John Supple and James Gorman. William Flanagan, a gardener, was also employed, and a carpenter named Walsh was mentioned periodically. The council members who had steered the Zoo since its foundations were retiring and, fortunately, the next generation was just as enthusiastic as the first. The Reverend Professor Samuel Haughton was the most influential member of the council during this period.[2]

Entrance to the Zoo,
c. 1860s.

The collection in 1860

In 1860, the collection of animals was large and varied enough to appeal to paying visitors, who looked at them, studied them, drew them and used every opportunity to interact with them, mostly by feeding them but unfortunately also by teasing, poking or even throwing stones at them. The most popular mammals were the African lions and their cubs, a pair of Bengal tigers, black bears, polar bears, the dog-faced baboon and the many monkeys. The aviaries in the Zoo contained a variety of native and exotic birds including cockatoos, parakeets and peafowl. Ostriches, emus and rheas were kept in paddocks, while ducks, geese and swans were encouraged to nest on the lake. The aquarium contained cuttlefish and pike, and the reptile collection included small tortoise, salamanders and green lizards. Mammals and birds, such as llamas, cashmere goats, Indian goats, grouse, partridge, guineafowl and quails suggest that the

Left: The superintendent's lodge *c.* 1865. It was demolished in 1868. Right: Image from the Royal Zoological Society of Ireland visitors' notebook, 1859–1866. Samuel Haughton signed the first entry and Dr S. Gordon signed the second entry in which he drew attention 'to the condition of the porcupines which in my opinion will not live much longer without fresh air. I have had a plan . . . made out and find that an excellent cage suitable for them can be made for £10. The value of the animals is almost £10 each.'

Zoological Society may have been catering to some small extent to the interests of landed members who perhaps wished to learn more about potential new stock for their own properties. Of course, the physicists, surgeons, anatomists and other scientists continued to receive the animals when they died.[3]

During the week, at least one council member would visit the gardens to monitor the health of the animals, ensure the visitors were behaving themselves and check on the staff. They recorded their observations in a notebook: 'Visited the gardens and found everything in order. Several visitors were present and seemed to take much interest in the various animals,' said one.[4] 'Visited the gardens, found all things regular and all the keepers actively engaged,' said another.[5] 'Visited the gardens; gave Mr Lowe general directions which he has since attended to,' reported a third.[6] 'Visited the Gardens on Thursday last and found everything in good order and found several visitors amongst whom was the Lord Chancellor,' said a fourth visitor.[7]

The health and condition of specific animals was sometimes noted. One reported that the lions' cage needed new flooring because an accident to the lion's foot may have arisen from a splinter of the old floor penetrating his foot. Another suggested that the straw in the kangaroos' paddock was injurious: '[the kangaroos'] claws are growing abnormally long for want of hard walking.' Yet another noted that the bison was not well and ordered a warm mash of bran and oats, with some chalk. He returned to check on the animal: 'Bison is all

Cartoon of Samuel
Haughton from
Ireland's Eye, 1874.

right today. Warm mash and chalk stopped the purging'. Dr S. Gordon expressed concern about the conditions in which the porcupines resided and purchased them a cage that would allow them fresh air. A few months later Joseph Beete Jukes said that the porcupines would not survive the winter in their new cage as it was too cold for them.[8]

The state of the grounds was also commented upon. Lt Col Leach suggested that the pile of manure be reduced as soon as possible as it was now visible from the Park. Another member referred to the state of the thatched roofs which were used on several animal houses at the time: 'Roof of wapiti deer stable very nearly destroyed by rats, thatch unsuitable for roof where rats find so much food.'[9]

Sir Dominic Corrigan (1802–1880), physician and president of the Royal Zoological Society of Ireland. In the early 1820s when attending an anatomy school, Corrigan robbed graves to acquire fresh cadavers for analysis. He went on to study at Edinburgh University. A Catholic with no connections or family money, his marked ability and hard work earned him successive promotions through the exclusive Irish medical profession.

In the early 1860s, Robert Montgomery, a barrister with a keen interest in animals, was employed as assistant secretary to the Society.[10] He wrote letters, travelled to England to purchase animals for the Zoo, followed up donations and purchases and, in 1862, began to visit the Zoo regularly. He made reports on the minutiae of daily management of the staff and animals in the visitors' notebook, which was then examined by the council each week.[11] The meetings started with breakfast in the ground floor parlour of the superintendent's house. The council discussed the health of the animals, the condition of their cages and enclosures and the financial position, which was invariably poor. When an issue arose that needed further investigation or management, a committee or subcommittee was set up to do the job. Acquisition of animals by purchase, donation or exchange formed a significant part of the agenda. By 1860, zoos had been established in numerous cities around the world, including Amsterdam, Antwerp, Berlin, Marseille, Calcutta, Melbourne and New York. The potential for using this network for the exchange of animals and information had not yet been realised and the council continued to work largely with animal dealers.

The visitors

About three-quarters of the people visiting the Zoo in the early 1860s came in on Sundays for a penny. The council was proud of their inclusiveness yet the behaviour of Sunday visitors was constantly monitored. In 1861, Dominic Corrigan proposed that admission to the Zoo after five o'clock each evening would be one penny, because of the 'continued general good conduct of the people.'[12] Not everyone agreed with him. Dr John Kinahan, a member, complained that he had seen 'several instances of misconduct in teasing the animals, breaking the branches of the trees, and cutting the flowers and, he noted, the policeman on duty did not prevent the bears from being teased. Reverend Professor Galbraith of Trinity College, an annual member, seconded Kinahan's motion. Galbraith said that the access to the delicate plesiosaurus fossil had to be closed on Sundays because of bad behaviour. Corrigan responded, saying that these complaints were exaggerated.[13] In summer 1861, Dr Robert McDonnell recorded:

> I heard a stranger (apparently a Yankee captain) make an observation to a friend who was with him about the general good humour and good conduct of the people. I also heard a lad asking, 'what are the police here for?' I saw no accident except a boy's cap fall into the bear pit.'[14]

Joseph Beete Jukes reported that all was well on a crowded Sunday in June 1861.

> There were persons of almost all classes, a number of ragged boys among them, but they seemed to be kept in check by the respectable persons about. Some boys attempted to get in from the park through the flags growing out of the mud but were sent back by Mr Lowe and a police officer.'[15]

In 1863, James Haughton, who had been instrumental in introducing the penny opening, asked why there was nothing in the annual report about the good conduct of 'their fellow citizens in the humbler walks of life'. Corrigan replied that 'it was not necessary to be always praising them for their good conduct'. The following year, Haughton raised the question again, concerned that 'silence on the subject ... might be construed into something like there being cause for complaint.' Corrigan reassured him saying, 'It was, to his mind, paying but a poor compliment to the citizens to say that they behaved themselves'.[16]

Robert Montgomery, the assistant secretary, occasionally reported incidents in the visitors' notebook, and made decisions on what action to take about them. On one summer day in 1863 he reported, 'The police took a young male, a carpenter, into custody for giving Lucifer matches to the monkeys. They very nearly set the cages on fire. As he seemed very penitent and *very innocent*, I let him off having given him a bad fright.'[17] He must have been very innocent, because, a year later, Montgomery was deter-

A bear on the pole in the bear pit, which was originally built in 1832 and located on the site of the current waldrapp ibis exhibit. Undated photograph taken *c.* 1908.

mined to ensure that a conviction against a Christopher Farrelly for throwing stones at the bear was recorded. Farrelly was let off the twenty-shilling fine because, Montgomery reported, no one believed he could pay, but the conviction remained. The bears were one of the more popular animals in the Zoo but they also attracted the wrong sort of attention. In 1865, Patrick Rice retrieved a wheelbarrow-full of stones from the bear pit. One of the stones had hit the male bear in the eye and the bear subsequently lost the sight in that eye. On another occasion, Rice told some young men told to stop teasing the lion cubs. They threatened to report the experienced keeper to a council member. Periodically keepers were formally admonished for rudeness to visitors, an admonishment that carried the threat of dismissal, reduction in wages or a fine.

IN THE ZOO. DUBLIN. 6098. W L

Albert Tower, designed for the elephant, giraffe and camel. Undated photograph taken in the late nineteenth century.

Promenades

Sixpenny visitors and subscribers continued to visit the Zoo from Monday to Saturday and it is from reports of the promenades that we learn more about them. The practice of holding summer promenades in the Zoo began in the 1830s. By the 1860s so many members of the 'walking community of the city'[18] arrived for the popular events in carriages that mounted police were on hand to ensure there was no congestion outside the Zoo. Once inside the gates, it was reported that:

> [The] tastefully laid out grounds [were] thronged by a fashionable assembly of ladies and gentlemen, the former having doffed their winter costumes and put on those light textures which look so gracefully charming beneath a brilliant summer's sun.[19]

Bands from the military, the police or the Hibernian School would play lively music while the visitors watched the monkeys. Sometime in the mid-afternoon, the Lord Lieutenant and his entourage would arrive to be met by the president of the society and members of the council. A band would strike up the national anthem and then, for the next two hours or so, depending on the weather, the party would be guided along the tended walks to view the lions and their cubs and other prize animals of the day. The lions would be fed so that the party could witness 'the voracity with which his majesty (the father) and her ladyship (the dam) devoured the flesh thrown to them.' The 'throngs of fashionable promenaders' would remain until after seven o'clock, again depending on the weather.[20]

The lake and ice skating

Since the 1830s, the council had made several attempts to get permission to erect a fence on the west side of the lake and, therefore, incorporate it fully into its jurisdiction.[21] Phoenix Park deer often swam across the water, upset the animals and ate the expensive young shrubs and plants in the Zoo's formal gardens. Superintendent Lowe once reported that up to a

The lake in the Zoo c. 1865. The fence erected in 1864 is visible on the far side of the lake.

dozen deer had crossed the lake and caused distress to the lions and hyenas when they went close to their dens. On another occasion, the day before a promenade in June 1861, the deer came over and cropped the flowers and shrubs. Human predators and their dogs were also a problem, particularly as they raided and otherwise interfered with the waterfowl nests on the lake.[22] And of course, it was possible for non-paying visitors to wade across the shallow part of the lake at the northern end and gain access to the Zoo.

When the lake froze, it became a perfect skating rink but, unless it was enclosed, the council could not control the crowds nor could they charge an entry fee. Samuel Haughton, who was constantly looking for ways to increase the Zoo's income sought permission from the government once more to fence it in. Eventually in 1864, the land was granted. Robert Montgomery informed the council: 'Mr Wilkie was lockspitting the ground on the opposite bank of pond. He has given us more space than I expected.'[23] A public appeal to support a 'fence fund' allowed the council to complete the iron-railed fence.[24]

By happy chance for visitors, the following winter was bitterly cold and the lake froze for two weeks. Penny entry on Sundays was suspended so all visitors, other than members, paid the full admission fee. At times there were up to 300 men, women and children skating on the ice. In January 1865, the ice cracked and five young men ended up in the water. One

Polar bears were in the Dublin Zoo collection from at least the 1850s. The caption on this print read: 'Old Deambulatorium removed and made into polar bear cages.' The keeper is referred to as 'Flood I', and is probably Thomas Flood, who was killed in the Zoo by a stag in 1880.

was the son of Dr William Steele of the Royal Dublin Society, 'and was very near being lost'.[25] He and his friends were saved by cork fenders attached to ropes and were hauled out safely. For the remainder of that skating season, the Zoo staff and ten policemen were on duty to sweep the ice and be ready in case of an accident.

Haughton and Arthur Foot became the 'Ice Committee' and researched 'the best means of saving life during the skating season'. After communicating with the Royal Humane Society in London, they purchased two folding ice ladders, two hand ladders, two cork belts and two stands marked 'dangerous'. The next ice season was not until 1866-67 but the rescue equipment was needed. After nearly four weeks of good skating conditions the ice became 'tender' and twenty-one people ended up in the water at the deep end of the lake, estimated to be about 17 foot deep at the time. The council reported that all were saved but 'two gave much trouble to restore them after being landed.' Superintendent Edward Carter and his wife who were living in the original lodge on the grounds looked after the unfortunate wet and cold skaters and a good profit was recorded from the skating season that year.[26]

The animals' living conditions

While the skaters enjoyed the freezing weather, the animals' accommodation was not adequate to care for them in such conditions. The following letter from Haughton to a meeting of the council sums up conditions for the animals in Dublin Zoo in the winter of 1863-64:

> A week of almost unexampled severity as to cold has just occurred during which some of the animals in our gardens have suffered severely from causes which it is in our power to remove … On Tuesday night … the house of the carnivora was very cold and its low temperature proved very injurious to our sick lion whose respiration was very rapid and labouring, 40 per minute. I therefore with Montgomery's concurrence ordered him two tumblers of punch and had the front of his den completely closed with straw and boards. Soon after his breathing became easier and he has been in a warm cage since Wednesday. On Thursday he was much better although today he seemed to fall back again. I strongly recommended the repetition of the dose of alcohol and the artificial warming of his den if possible.

He went on to describe the freezing conditions in which the seals, hawk, falcons, ostrich, monkeys and wolf were struggling to survive. He concluded, 'I sincerely trust that the council will spare no trouble to procure for the poor animals dependent on our care the comforts which they require during the continuance of the present frost.'[27]

Other problems faced by the animals in cramped conditions were reported to the council regularly. Many of the problems arose from pairs of animals being kept together. In 1865, Robert Montgomery observed that the old black female bear was very weak:

> She has been much cut and knocked about by the old male. Putting her in with the young bears.

Following a routine check, he reported that, 'due to rain, ostriches locked into house with half door open. The male chased the female, she jumped over the half door and broke her leg'. He pointed out at the end of the report that keeper Patrick Rice was not to blame. Even a keeper with Patrick Rice's skill and experience with the valuable lion cubs would not have been immune from sanction if it were judged that he had caused the death or serious injury of an animal.[28]

During the cold weather in December 1862, a Barbary ape was rubbed with fresh butter. She was in very poor condition and a few days later, the order came through to destroy her as 'her leg [was] absolutely rotten'. In January 1865, Montgomery reported, 'Boas torpid and stiff from cold, rolled in blankets and put by fire'; on another occasion, the boa constrictors had to be revived by placing them in warm water. That same winter,

Stuffed sacred or hamadryas baboon in the Zoological Museum, Trinity College Dublin. In November 1870 two 'Arabian baboons' were presented by Viscount Southwell to the Zoo; at a council meeting, Haughton said, 'These valuable animals have never before been exhibited in the gardens of the Society, nor have the naturalists of Dublin previously had an opportunity of examining them . . . The council are, therefore, of opinion that your lordship's donation will not only gratify the public of Dublin while living, but will also serve the cause of science after death.'

Montgomery noted that 'The big baboon is looking stupid and misses his hot tea morning and evening, Mrs Batho having hitherto given it at her own expense. I have given him a little ginger cordial.' A few days later, Montgomery gave the baboon laudanum for his digestive system but shortly afterwards the baboon died and was immediately sent to Haughton in Trinity College.[29]

Death of Natal

In 1864, Natal, the lion that had arrived in 1855 and sired so many cubs, died from a fever that lasted for fifteen days. During that time, every effort was made to keep him comfortable and he was given large draughts of beef tea and whiskey punch. On the Sunday before he died, the people from Dublin came out in large crowds to see him take his punch, which, they said, he did 'just like a Christian, only he wasn't handy at stirring it'. An elegy was composed by someone described only as 'one who has since earned substantial titles to fame':

Elegy on the death of our lion

Alas! Another heavy blow
Has added to the weight of woe
Already pressing on the Zoological Society

'Tis only one short month ago
(A fever 'twas that laid him low)
Death took the lion of the Zoological Society.

The keeper found him very low,
And sent a message for Pro-
fessor Haughton, of the Zoological Society.

The doctor came, with Foot not slow;
He found his patient but so-so,
And told the Council of the Zoological Society.

He wrote a grand prescription though:
'R. Kinahan's spir. oz. duo;
Aquae oz. sex; sumat leo;
S.H., physician to the Zoological Society.'

They tried to make him drink; but no
Teetotaler was ever so
Staunch as the lion of the Zoological Society.

In vain they sought to urge the no-
ble beast; that 'tumbler' was no 'go':
He thought that whisky-punch was low
For him, the lion of the Zoological Society.

They watched his every dying throe;
They rubbed him down from top to toe
So died the lion of the Zoological Society.

Some said it was the frost and snow
Others declared they did not know
But all agreed that, high or low.
Than this there ne'er was finer show,
This feast of reason, and this flow
Of whisky-punch, so promptly pro-
vided by order of the Zoological Society.[30]

The rhinoceros

In 1864, the Zoo purchased an Indian rhinoceros, which was transported from Calcutta to
Dublin via London, with the assistance of keeping staff from London Zoo. From the beginning, the rhino was 'very uneasy' and had 'a fit'. Haughton, Dr Dominic Corrigan and Dr
C. P. Croker recommended that the animal be given three pints of boiled rice with bran
and a gallon of milk, with some tonic power mixed in. But the fits continued and Haughton
ordered that his allowance be increased from three to four pints of boiled rice, morning and

evening. Cabbage was removed from the rhino's diet and, as his health improved, he was given potatoes in order to reduce his allowance of hay – which was expensive. For the next few months the rhino appeared to settle, although no one was surprised that he sometimes had little interest in food. In December he made a 'ferocious attack' on the keeper Patrick Rice. No injury was reported.[31]

On a Sunday the following March, Arthur Foot, a medical practitioner and an active member of council, caught a boy 'trying the thickness of the rhinoceros's skin with a pin' and threw him out. There were more reports of the rhino being unwell or agitated and then, on 5 April 1865 at about four o'clock in the afternoon, Montgomery found the animal showing indications of acute abdominal pain and having a prolapsed rectum 'to a frightful extent'. He immediately called Mr Murphy, a veterinary surgeon of Parkgate Street, who suggested puncturing the protruding matter. Montgomery could not authorise that and sent for Haughton, Professor Dr McDowell, Arthur Foot and Hugh Ferguson, also a veterinary surgeon. He also sent the following telegraph to Abraham Bartlett, superintendent of London Zoo: 'The rhinoceros has got prolapsus ani for some hours. What shall we do? The bowels were not out of order.'[32]

Haughton and his colleagues did not sit around waiting for a response. With great difficulty, they gave the rhino an enema of opium in three quarts of tepid water. Murphy said that he believed the inflammation had extended up the rectum and abdomen and gave up on him. With the rhino clearly in excruciating pain, a potion including castor oil, opium, aromatic spirits of ammonia, and spirits of turpentine to kill any worms, was administered with tepid water. As these measures were being taken, Bartlett's response arrived from London: 'Send for a veterinary surgeon. Let him treat the rhinoceros as he would a horse suffering from the same cause.'[33]

At eleven o'clock in the evening the rhino at last became quieter, although Montgomery suspected it was from exhaustion rather than any impact from the medication. Keepers John Supple, Thomas Flood and James Gorman stayed all night and at four in the morning, the rhino died. The Royal Dublin Society offered £15 for the carcase, another offer of £16 was received, while Haughton offered £19 and won the bid. The post mortem by Haughton assisted by Ferguson found,

> the stomach was filled to distension with a mixture of hay and whole Indian corn, both fermenting, and pervaded with an [aldehydic] smell, which overcame even the intolerable odour of the gases, with which the abdomen was distended almost to bursting point . . . Numerous tapeworms were found in the upper part of the intestines . . . I believe that death was caused by the improper administration of Indian corn . . . and I am further of the opinion that it is the duty of the council to institute the most searching inquiry into the manner in which Indian corn was given to this animal, as such food does not appear in the scale of dietary, formally presented by the council's order, to be used.[34]

Subsequently keeper Rice's wages were reduced from fifteen shillings a week to twelve shillings and sixpence per week for a year 'as a punishment for his disobedience of the council's orders, by means of which the death of the rhinoceros was caused.'[35]

Death of John Supple

In November 1867, John Supple was bitten by a reticulated python, which is not venomous. The reticulated python, which has been known to reach 10 metres in length, kills by strangulation. However fifty-five year old John Supple reacted fatally to the bite and died of congestion of the lungs, 'accelerated by alarm created on his having been bitten by a serpent' on the same day. The council contacted the superintendent of London Zoo to see if they had been at fault in believing that the snake was not venomous. Abraham Bartlett said both he and his keeper, Holland, were frequently bitten by a python but it only caused a smarting, unpleasant sensation. Bartlett did agree that someone could be frightened to death if bitten by the snake. The council paid the funeral expenses and employed his son, Patrick, who was then working for a lithographer in Middle Abbey Street. Patrick Supple continued to work in Dublin Zoo until his death in 1913.[36] His son, Jack Supple, started at the Zoo in 1902, and was known to many modern visitors as the man in charge of the chimpanzee tea parties; he retired from full time employment in 1961.

Capital works

In the late 1860s, the Zoo received substantial grants for capital works from the government.[37] A new superintendent's house was completed in 1868 and became known as 'Society House' because the ground floor contained a large room where breakfasts and council meetings were to be held. The superintendent and his family lived in the rest of the house. A new monkey house was also erected, the water supply was improved, and several cages were removed or replaced.[38] A further grant was made and a new aquarium and a carnivore house were built.[39] The carnivore house, often referred to as the lion house, was completed in 1869 and opened with a ceremony the modern reader can only marvel at. A newspaper described the scene of the lions being transferred from their old quarters to the new house:

> The usual method of transporting such animals was adopted on the occasion. Ladies as beautiful as Ariadne and as virtuous as Una, each holding a beefsteak on a toasting fork, preceded each leopard and lion to its new habitation. The leopards and lions followed as if in duty bound and are now on view in their new house.

Another procession involving beef, music and the lions, was scheduled for the following Thursday on the occasion of the first promenade of the season:

> At four o'clock precisely the band will strike up the 'Roast beef of Old England' and a procession headed by a wheelbarrow containing shins of beef will be

Top left: the aquarium, which was built in 1868 and formally opened by the Lord Lieutenant in 1869. It was demolished in 1992-93 and replaced by a new building, the facade of which was a replica of the original. Undated photograph taken in the 1890s. Top right: the lion house, which was opened with an unusual ceremony in 1869. Undated photograph taken in the 1890s. Left: dens of the lion house, opened in 1869.

formed, and proceed to open the new lion house in the gardens. The inhabitants . . . were successfully 'decanted' into their new residence on Monday last . . . The members of the Dublin public that had not the advantage of witnessing the striking procession of ladies and lions on Monday last are earnestly requested to favour the procession on to-morrow with their presence.[40]

The trams

For all the parties, bands and ice-skating, which attracted members and sixpenny visitors, the vast bulk of visitors to the Zoo during this period were the penny visitors. In 1871, when 167,000 people visited, 123,000 came on Sundays, bank holidays and during the summer evenings when entry was a penny. At that time, most would have made their way to the Zoo by foot, although records suggest that there was a bus company that came into the Phoenix Park.[41] In 1870, permission to construct tramways in Dublin had been submitted by various companies to the city engineer. Five main lines were proposed by one tram company. *The Irish Times* reported that the City Engineer recommended the submission adding, 'The Corporation, very properly for the interests of the citizens, have made it a condition that an additional route from Sackville Street to the Botanic Gardens and Glasnevin, and to the Park-gate and Zoological Gardens, by the North Circular-road, shall be established.'[42]

The tram line was operating by 1876 but the Zoological Society council was concerned that the tram stopped at the North Circular Road gate to the Phoenix Park. They put in a request to the Commissioners of Public Works to extend the line to the Zoo. By now, the cheap entry fee had been raised to twopence. The availability of the trams had no immediate impact on visitor numbers, in fact they dropped considerably in the mid 1870s and did not reach the high figures of the early 1870s until 1900.

Prince Tom and other elephants

The Zoo acquired an elephant on loan for the summer months in 1871 from a circus. The elephant had 'become foot sore and weary from acting at night, and travelling by day over the sloppy carbonate of lime on the roads of the country' and had been sent to rest in Dublin Zoo before going back to London.[43] It remained in Dublin until August, attracting huge numbers of visitors.

In August 1871, the Prince and Princess of Wales visited the Zoo where their attention was drawn to the lack of an elephant in the Dublin collection. Recently the Duke of Edinburgh had brought home an elephant from India. The Prince of Wales contacted the Duke of Edinburgh and soon the elephant, called Prince Tom, arrived in Dublin Zoo to take up residence in Albert Tower. Prince Tom learnt to behave like a true zoo elephant of the time. On one Sunday in September, 'he purchased and ate eight dozen and four buns and drank eight bottles of ginger beer'.[44] The following spring the 'Elephant howdah committee' purchased a howdah and devised a plan for collecting fees for riding the elephant. The following newspaper report was written in May 1872:

> Perfectly docile and harmless, [Prince Tom] is left almost to his own guidance and walks about the gardens with an apparent consciousness that he is the cynosure of the place. He generally keeps near the handsome kiosk where refreshments are dispensed, to which he is one of the best customers. If a visitor gives him a penny, which he receives with courtly grace, he at once enters the shop, at least he inserts his huge head and fore quarters, which nearly fill up the little place, hands the coin to the attendant and takes a bun in exchange. His greatest pleasure seems to be to receive a sixpence when, after purchasing his cake, he returns the change to the donor with a low salaam. A ride upon his back round the garden is a treat to the younger visitors.[45]

A month later, a different story emerged. When the Duke of Edinburgh was visiting Ireland, he asked if Prince Tom could be brought around to the Vice Regal Lodge so he could have a look at him. The council hesitated. Walking the elephant down the road to their next-door neighbour should have been no problem for either keeper or elephant, if the report in the newspaper about this docile animal walking among visitors was true. However, the council had it on record that Prince Tom had 'occasionally broken loose and endangered himself and others'. They told the Duke's representative that Prince Tom was 'not sufficiently tamed to be trusted outside the gardens but should his excellency think fit, they will incur the risk of sending the elephant'.[46]

Prince Tom continued to entertain the visitors inside the Zoo. A bathing pool was excavated for him and, during the summer months, he was scheduled to take a bath at four o'clock each day, an event that one newspaper said attracted 'a large and fashionable audience'. The large and fashionable audience, however, had to take care to avoid getting a shower of muddy water. One contemporary report described a bath in which Prince Tom filled his

Edward Carter, superintendent, with his wife, Maryanne (left), and eldest daughter, Maryanne, sitting outside the superintendent's house, which replaced the original lodge in 1868.

trunk with water and sprayed the crowd of visitors who had gathered around to watch: 'Pretty, delightful, and trembling the ladies dashed about where they could and what are called bonnets were mutually examined with intensest anxiety.' Prince Tom then walked into the pool and, 'Once in, he seemed happy, and taking almighty sniff, put his great head under water and began plunging, and rolling, and snorting in gigantic fashion'.[47]

In September 1873, however, a visitor, John Wall, instigated legal proceedings after he was injured by Prince Tom. He wanted medical and other expenses; he also recommended that the elephant be locked up when the gardens were open to the public.[48] The council rejected his claims. The following spring, Prince Tom attacked another visitor and then injured his keeper, who was trying to protect the visitor. The decision was then made to keep the animal inside his house on Sundays, when the Zoo was busiest. In September 1874, a keeper, who is not identified, was reported for being drunk and the elephant reported for behaving in a 'disorderly' manner at the same time. The outcome of that incident was that Prince Tom was placed on half rations for a week and confined to his house. From then until his death in 1882, it is likely that Prince Tom remained in his house with access to a small, enclosed space outside it.

The following report by Samuel Haughton to the Annual General Meeting in 1882 was recorded in a newspaper:

'[Prince Tom] is dying. He was a very ill tempered, ill conditioned elephant long before he left India, and killed his keepers on the way home and at home, and he had several times attempted to kill persons in the gardens. Greatly against their will, the council was therefore obliged to restrain his exercise and to lock him up. This affected his health, although they took the best care of him, and the animal had at last broken down in health and would not live long … He was being fed on every delicacy, sugar, rice balls, carrots and potatoes, all which he eat [sic] with pleasure (laughter). Some people thought they should take measures to kill him because he was dying. Now if any of themselves were dying (laughter), would he like his wife to enter the room and shoot him? Since he had got those delicacies, the elephant lay on his side resting himself and eating them and he (Dr Haughton) was beginning to think that maybe the animal would not die at all (laughter).[49]

The skeleton of the elephant, Prince Tom, in the Zoological Museum, Trinity College Dublin. Prince Tom died in the Zoo in January 1882.

Prince Tom died in January 1882. His body was drawn on a float to the Trinity College Department of Anatomy where, with shears, ropes and pulleys, he was studied and his skeleton placed in the Zoology Museum in the college. During his lifetime his ribs had been cracked and had healed over, the break and repair now clearly visible.

Irish lion industry

The lions continued to breed under the supervision of Patrick Rice and, between 1857 and 1876, ninety-two lions had been born in the Zoo, of which seventy-one had reached maturity.

QUEEN'S CUBS, BORN APRIL, 1885.

Many had been bred from Natal and Natalie or from their offspring. In 1876, 'Zoophilus' wrote that it was a popular belief in Dublin that the lions owed:

> their fecundity to the occasional use of boiled potatoes which in the opinion of many Irish women are believed to be efficacious in conferring offspring upon a barren woman. From my experience of lion breeding, I should be disposed to say that 'Pat' and 'Biddy' have something to do with the result as well as the potatoes for I find that of the ninety-two cubs born in the gardens, a single lioness produced fifty-four, of which she reared fifty, losing only four, or 8 per cent, instead of the average 23 per cent.[50]

Dublin's lion cubs had the reputation of being strong, healthy and a good size, and could therefore command high prices from animal dealers. As was normal practice for animal dealers at the time, Dublin Zoo took no responsibility for the cubs once they left the Zoo. But there

were few complaints about the quality of the cubs and they tended to travel easily to their new owners. Sales, swaps and partial swaps were arranged with dealers and other zoos, and the lion cub industry became an important factor in the solvency of Dublin Zoo in the nineteenth century.[51]

International tourists came to the Zoo especially to see the lions. In summer 1870, there was a report in the *Brooklyn Daily Eagle* about Dublin's lions, in which the author said that, 'I shall never see a lion again without pleasing remembrances, and the belief that I have patted his father or mother upon the neck in the Dublin gardens.'[52] Many American visitors came to see the lions and in December 1878, General Ulysses Grant, who had recently completed two terms as president of the United States, visited the Zoo and 'at length stood impassive, lighting a fresh cigar opposite the cage of the celebrated lion "Charlie" the gem of the collection'.[53]

Pygmy hippopotamus

Although Dublin Zoo could not afford some of the great 'stars' of the nineteenth-century zoos, such as the hippopotamus or the giraffe, occasionally it received very rare animals from an Irish person living abroad. In 1873, it received a pygmy hippopotamus, which had been captured in Sierra Leone after the death of its mother. At the time, Dublin Zoo's council claimed that it was 'hitherto an almost unknown animal.'[54] In March 1873, Patrick Supple was sent to Liverpool to collect the small creature, which was estimated to be about eight weeks old and weighing 25 lb. Unfortunately, the journey to Europe took its toll

Stuffed pygmy hippopotamus from Dublin Zoo in the Zoological Museum, Trinity College Dublin. The young animal died in 1873 shortly after arriving at the Zoo.

and despite the best efforts of Patrick Supple, the pygmy hippopotamus died a few hours after it arrived in Dublin Zoo. Alexander Macalister, director of the Trinity College Zoological Museum, acquired the remains and undertook a dissection, the results of which were published in the transactions of the Royal Irish Academy. The skin of the animal was preserved and stuffed and this extraordinary little creature is still on display in the Trinity College Zoological Museum.

Lectures and education

The council constantly referred to the educational side of Dublin Zoo on formal occasions. For example, in an address to welcome the new lord Lieutenant, Earl Cowper, in 1880, Haughton said:

> The objects of our society lie entirely outside the region of politics and are for the advancement of zoological science theoretical and practical and the education and instruction of the people. We aim at carrying out the first of these objects by the acclimatisation of foreign animals and by affording the scientific schools of the city an opportunity of studying their structure. Our second object is accomplished by opening our gardens to the humbler classes of the citizens at a nominal rate on Sunday afternoons.[55]

At the time the educational services for the general public did not extend beyond labelling and the occasional lecture series but occasionally an opportunity to introduce an international speaker arose. In 1862, when Paul du Chaillu and his stuffed gorillas visited Ireland, the council invited him to speak in the Zoo. Du Chaillu had returned to Europe from an expedition to West Africa with twenty stuffed gorillas, skins, skulls and skeletons of gorillas and claimed that he was the first European to have seen the animal. Charles Darwin's *On the Origin of Species* had been published in 1859, sparking widespread debate and controversy about the validity of his theory of evolution based on natural selection. The presence of du

Patrick Supple and cheetah, 1893.

Stuffed zebras in the Natural History Museum. The zebra on the right is the subspecies, the Burchell Zebra, which was probably purchased by the Zoo from Antwerp Zoo in 1874 and sent to the Museum after its death in 1895. The council noted that acclimatisation societies in France and Belgium were hoping to use this subspecies 'as a means of improving our breed of mules'. When it died, the council said that 'A Zoological collection without a zebra is something like a play of Hamlet without the Ghost', so they planned to purchase another quickly.

Chaillu's gorillas fuelled the debate with many claiming that the stuffed gorillas were fakes and that he was an impostor. The visit of du Chaillu to Dublin Zoo should have been cause for great excitement except that on the day of his talk it rained. A military band had been organised and a hired car brought du Chaillu and his stuffed gorillas to the Zoo but very few people turned up. Du Chaillu offered to waive his fee but the council insisted on paying him.

The presence of du Chaillu and his gorillas in Ireland did not stir up great debate, discussions or even jokes, as they had done in Britain. Periodically, over the following years, there was the occasional reference to the theory of evolution and the primates in the Zoo. In 1874 an *Irish Times* journalist, who was mourning the loss of his own pet monkey from respiratory infection, wrote:

> A party of my fellow creatures staring … at the antics of the caged monkeys in the
> Zoological Gardens is, to me, a pitiful and a painful spectacle; it is enough to persuade
> a man of the truth of Darwinism. Mr Gladstone, who, not long ago, deplored the fact
> that his special duties gave him no leisure to read Darwin and Wallace … might

Two famous images of gorillas as depicted by Paul du Chaillu.

perhaps now find time to spend an hour in front of the monkey-house in the Zoological Gardens. He would, I am sure, come away a strong believer in this fashionable doctrine.[56]

In 1878, Haughton organised six lectures, one of which he was to deliver. The news of the lecture series was greeted by one newspaper with the following frankness:

> There are many persons who would find a difficulty in determining which affliction is the greater, attendance on a scientific lecture or an exercise on the treadmill for the same length of time … The first lecture may be safely pronounced free from the danger of dullness, feebleness or pedantry. It is by Dr Samuel Haughton, and he has named his subject 'The large cats and their poor relations'.[57]

The lectures excited little interest. One newspaper said that while it was an excellent series, that they were not popular as claimed by the Society and presupposed a good deal of special knowledge on the part of the hearer.

Meanwhile, the Zoo's dead animals were still supplying comparative anatomists, physicians and directors of zoological museums with dead, exotic animals but, with Haughton on the council, the competition was stiff, especially for the primates and larger cats. Some animals were bid on before they died. In August 1885, the Zoo acquired an orang-utan in part exchange for four lion cubs. Patrick Supple was given charge of the valuable and delicate animal, named Sinbad, and told 'on no consideration whatever to feed the ourang-outan but at regular hours and on specified food and never to open the glass case for anyone, not even member of council'.[58] Three months after Sinbad arrived, Dr D. J. Cunningham of the Trinity College Department of Anatomy, offered £4 for the animal, provided it was sent to him the moment it died. Haughton countered this offer by bidding £5 for the remains 'in the improbable event of the death of the orang outan'.[59] On one occasion, in 1887, Sinbad fell ill and after an anxious time, his convalescence was announced and he was allowed 'to receive visitors from 1 to 3 o'clock p.m. daily.' He lived for nearly four years in the Zoo with the help of Patrick Supple's care and a glazed cage. He died of a disease that was similar to typhoid fever: 'His near kinship to ourselves was thus borne out to the end, seeing that he succumbed to a complaint which is supposed to be peculiar to man,' wrote an anonymous council member.[60] Samuel Haughton secured the body for the Trinity College Zoological Museum.

Death of Thomas Flood

Keeper Thomas Flood was attacked by a red deer stag in the Zoo and killed in October 1880. He was forty-five years old and had been with the Zoo for twenty-two years. He had cleaned the enclosure and was leaving when the stag attacked him. As he was an experienced keeper and this was the daily routine, the council could not work out exactly what had happened. Either Thomas Flood had not bolted the gate properly or had not moved out of the inner enclosure quickly enough after finishing the cleaning. Whatever the cause, the stag attacked him, fracturing his skull, breaking seven ribs, and cutting his hands. Despite his injuries, Flood fought off the stag, pushed him back into the enclosure and shut the gate. When the superintendent Edward Snow and keeper George Bristow got to Thomas Flood, he was barely conscious; as they lifted him up, he said, 'I think I'll walk.' He died shortly afterwards.

Haughton said that if forty men had been there they could not have saved Thomas Flood. He praised Flood for finding the strength and courage to secure the animal despite his great injuries. He called for donations for the family of a man 'who met his death at his post in the discharge of his duty, and whose last act in life was to secure the lives of the visitors and workpeople then in the gardens'. Thomas Flood's son, Christopher, then aged twenty-two, was employed in the Zoo with the promise that he would not be put in charge of the red deer.[61]

Elephants: Rama and Sita

On 9 March 1882, two young elephants arrived from Burma via Liverpool and were landed at the North Wall at seven o'clock in the morning. They were walked along the quays 'attended by 400 to 500 boys and idlers'. The proposal to name them Rama and Sita, in honour of the incarnate god of Hindustan and his bride, was accepted, although Haughton noted that 'some ignorant member of the council proposed to call them Cyrus and Atossa for the purpose of showing off his Greek, but in utter forgetfulness of the fact that Persia is the land of horses, not of elephants'.[62] Edward Snow, the superintendent, trained the elephants to stand on their heads and to move their trunks on command. They were considered 'so gentle … that they will take from the hand of the tiniest child its little offering of cake or sweet meat without causing the infant the slightest alarm'.[63] A month after they arrived, they escaped from their house and, trumpeting loudly, broke through a number of barriers and destroyed the pigeon house. When they were finally locked up they were very agitated. That did not stop the council from allowing them out to mix with visitors. A contemporary report describes a typical scene:

> The elephants daily go forth drawing an immense van along the roads of the Phoenix Park in order to strengthen their muscles and supply them with a good appetite for dinner. Our children, of course, get many a ride on the docile beasts who, with equal equanimity, convey a bevy of giggling servant maids along the shaded walks and back to the starting point, stalking silent and dignified under all the giggling.[64]

Captain Harrington, an elephant trainer, was employed to train the animals and their keeper, James McNally. In 1890, Rama died suddenly and lay in his house where he had fallen for twenty-two hours. When Professor D. J. Cunningham went to retrieve the body to take it to Trinity College for a post mortem, rigor mortis had set in and the door of the elephant house was only just wide enough to fit the rigid animal through it. Fifty policemen came to assist and the decomposing animal was transferred to the city for the dissection. The post

James McNally (left) training the elephants, Rama (standing) and Sita, under the supervision of Captain Harrington.

Elephant keeper, James McNally (right) with Rama and Sita.

mortem took place next day and the continuing decomposition overnight had resulted in the elephant blowing up with putrefactive gas. Cunningham reported:

> When the first incision was made through the wall of the abdomen, a somewhat sensational result ensued. There was a loud and sudden report and a volcanic display which scattered the operators far and wide, and gave rise to the greatest dismay in those who had never experienced a shock of a similar kind before.

The post mortem indicated that the elephant had suffered from advanced pneumonia and in that weakened state, enteritis had killed him.[65]

Haughton and politics

Home Rule and land reform were the major political issues in Ireland at the time. Home Rule MP, Charles Stewart Parnell, had become leader of the Irish Parliamentary Party in Westminster in 1880, when William Gladstone was the Liberal Prime Minister. In October 1881, Parnell and other Irish MPs were arrested and imprisoned in Kilmainham Jail. The Land League was outlawed the same month. Haughton was an outspoken Home Ruler and often used meetings of the Zoological Society to declare his politics. In October 1881, during a breakfast at the Zoo given to visitors from the Social Science Congress he said:

> Before England gives up Gibraltar, why not try the experiment nearer home and give up Ireland. I am a bit of a home ruler and would consent to the giving up of Ireland before Gibraltar. When England tries that experiment and likes it, she may then take into consideration the giving up of Gibraltar and Malta and Canada, and even South Africa (much laughter).[66]

In April 1882, he told a long story, which was related in the third person in a newspaper as follows:

> Some years ago, having given some very moderate evidence before the Royal Commissioners on Vivisection, he was warned by Professor Huxley that the time would come when philanthropists and the strong-minded women of the country, two dangerous classes (laughter), would interfere with his zoological gardens and

ask whether some of his practices were not cruel. He replied to Professor Huxley, 'I am not a law abiding Englishman – God forbid (loud laughter) – but I am an Irishman – a Dublin man, with sufficient influence to get up a riot if such an absurd thing took place.'

Professor Flower was almost tortured to death by the proceedings of the Secretary of the Society for the Prevention of Cruelty to Animals and, being a very nervous man, he had in six weeks lost 14lb in weight fretting under this persecution. Many of them would be surprised to hear that he (Professor Haughton) had been in the position of Professor Flower for the last fortnight. But so far from losing, he had gained weight by it.

The object of the sentimental nonsensical interest … was the Irish wolf dog, and the complainant in the case was an English lady who had twenty-five minutes' experience in the garden to set off against his twenty-five years. But, being an Englishwoman, and having command of the 'resources of civilisation' (laughter and some hisses) she, of course, knew a great deal more about the Irish wolf dog than he did. If there were any Englishmen or women present, he hoped they would excuse him saying that their common, vulgar, cockney notion of Ireland, that all Ireland consisted of a wolf dog sitting on his hunkers on a bunch of shamrocks (laughter) with a harp and a round tower behind him, was not Ireland at all. Ireland was harder to manage than that.

He took this opportunity of warning any gentleman who might come as an inspector for the Society for the Prevention of Cruelty to Animals in Dublin that he, Dr Haughton, had given positive instructions that when the inspector arrived and produced his tape and proceeded to measure a cage, the keepers were to souse him on the pond, or at a last resource they were to let out on him the object of his ill-timed benevolence (loud laughter) …

If he were walking in the Zoological gardens and a keeper rushed up to him and said, 'Good God, Dr Haughton, one of the wild beasts has got out of his cage.'

'Which of them, which of them?'

'The Bengal tiger.'

'God be praised,' he, Dr Haughton would say, 'that it is not the Irish wolf dog.' With the Bengal tiger a person could open his umbrella and the tiger would retreat, but the Irish wolf dog knew the ropes, and went straight for the calves of one's legs. (laughter)

The lady who wanted to bring the resources of civilisation to bear on him had written to the secretary for the Prevention of Cruelty to Animals. 'The creature,' she said, 'seemed to me very far from dangerous …' She then went on to say that it was probably the last specimen of its race and she added that all the other animals appeared to be in much too small cages.

The close of the lady's letter contained the pith of it. 'If your inspector has not visited the gardens lately, perhaps you would send him and let him see what can be done.' That is the inspector of the Society for the Prevention of Cruelty to Animals was directed by this lady or her friends to bring up Dr Haughton before the police magistrate like a drunken cabman who had over flogged his horse.

Cartoon from the Dublin Zoo newspaper archive, 1880s.

The police had hunted him (laughter). He believed there were at one time four detectives watching him in the College Hall, but an Irishman was so accustomed to police surveillance that he did not mind it.

In dismissing this part of the subject he had only to express a hope that what was thought to be close at hand would happen, namely, that Parnell and Dillon and the other suspects would be released but in the name of God that the Irish wolf dog should be left in his care (loud laughter).[67]

In May 1882, Parnell was released under the terms of the Kilmainham Treaty. Four days later, Cavendish and Burke were murdered in the Phoenix Park by a previously unknown group called the Invincibles. On 13 May 1882, a rare political statement was recorded in the minutes of the council meeting: 'Resolved. That the president and council of the Royal Zoological Society of Ireland desire to place on record their feelings of horror and indignation at the numerous murders that have recently occurred through Ireland culminating in the assassination of Lord Frederick Cavendish and Mr Thomas Burke [life member of their society] and beg to tender their heartfelt sympathy to the families of the victims.'[68]

Financial problems

Throughout this period, the poor state of the Zoo's finances dominated the work of the council meetings. In the late 1860s, a loan was raised from amongst the council members, causing several to resign in protest at the poor economy of the Zoo. Visitor numbers had been between 147,000 and 167,000 in the early 1870s but had fallen to between 105,000 and 125,000 by the early 1880s. To boost interest, Haughton investigated the possibility of

Old refreshment room, from a photograph reproduced in the annual report in 1906.

having a six-day licence to sell beer and porter in the gardens but, on consideration, decided to make no change for the present in this regard. He also sold the plesiosaurus fossil to the Natural History Museum in 1877 for £200, causing outrage among older members of the council who believed it should have been donated rather than sold.[69] In October 1878, Haughton invited Frederick Cavill and three of his children to perform swimming and aquatic feats as an entertainment in the Zoo. The children, two boys and a girl, all under fourteen, were dressed in tight, scarlet, India rubber waterproofs and, for two hours, 'remained in the pond, sometimes racing, sometimes resting, lying motionless as logs of timber, sometimes playing a kind of leap frog, in which each member of the group was submerged in pretty quick succession by all the others . . .' A newspaper reported that:

> A considerable number of respectable people surveyed the performances from a
> gratuitous stand-point outside the enclosure … Perhaps they thought that Mr Cavill

was an amateur who was devoting himself and his family to their amusement merely for the honour of the thing, or through an eccentric desire to instruct and benefit the public. Perhaps they thought that the Zoological Gardens have a large private estate to draw on to enable them to provide amusement and instruction for the public or perhaps they have been led to the conclusion that a man of Dr Haughton's inventive powers can always extract money whether from Irish country gentlemen or from British menagerie owners, or from a Bank Parlour ...[70]

In 1883, he organised the first of four annual dog shows. The shows were held under Kennel Club rules; only the first two shows generated a profit and the idea was abandoned. In 1884, Sunday opening hours were extended and the Zoo opened at midday rather than at two o'clock in the afternoon. This allowed shop assistants and others, who went to work at 2 p.m., to visit the Zoo. Haughton noted that: 'Their object in not opening the gardens until two o'clock was not to interfere with the hours of divine worship in the city. However when the council considered that as the bodies with whom they were competing were not places of public worship but public houses which opened at 2. o'clock, they came to the conclusion it would be well if the gardens were opened earlier.'[71] Protestant members of staff who wanted to attend church on Sundays were allowed to do so.[72]

Strife

Although Haughton had a reputation for pursuing ways of making money for the Zoo, it was not enough to maintain high standards of animal accommodation. Yet it was difficult to challenge him publicly because of his skilled oratory and renowned wit. He often addressed members who abused privileges at the annual meetings. In 1880, for example, he said,

In some cases they found that subscribers had curious ideas as to what constituted a family and in one case they found four gentlemen clubbing together to take a common name and become subscribers as one family and dividing the cost, which

was a very ingenious but scarcely honest kind of action. On another occasion a school of young ladies took a peculiar view of the domestic circle and family relations and the whole school, amounting to 37 passed in as the daughters of one well known member of the society. He did not quote these things as examples for imitation by the citizens but as examples to be avoided.[73]

Reports of Haughton's deliveries at the Zoo's meetings were often punctuated with references to 'laughter' or 'much laughter'. But, while Haughton's wit and obvious enjoyment of a skirmish created great entertainment for members and those reading the reports, it was irritating for those who wanted reform. Disgruntled members registered their growing displeasure with the council at the annual general meeting in January 1884. Dr Thornley Stoker and Dr Archibald Jacob, both life members, challenged the council on their management of the Zoo and its funds. On every issue, Haughton met their challenge, sometimes agreeing with them, sometimes disagreeing but always added a comment that made the audience laugh. The restrained row came to an end when Dr William Carte, a council member, said that in his opinion, 'the whole of this discussion was irregular'.[74]

In July 1884, a writer calling himself 'Gloomy decay' wrote a long letter to the *Daily Express*:

> It is most distressing to observe the steady and downward movement of these our once famous and national Zoological Gardens … It strikes me the root of the evil is not far to seek. The management is rotten, so to speak. Therefore, the whole concern is decaying. A zoological garden is not the place for scientific experiments and the pampering of the fancies of a few. It should be for the pleasure and instruction of the public … We do not want our Zoological Society to become a company of scientific experimentalists, a dog show committee, or yet purveyors of skating to the public, but we want it to be what it was intended to be, and what its grant from Government is for, a society to increase and cultivate in the public mind an interest in objects of natural history.
>
> Some time ago, an eminent naturalist, speaking to me of our society's gardens, said he had come to the conclusion that it was now but a place kept up to provide skins and skeletons for the Trinity College Natural History Museum … The fact is that the animals are not thriving but are rapidly diminishing, and what still remain in the gardens are not kept so as to interest or attract the public.[75]

Complaints appeared in the media now and then throughout the 1880s as visitor figures dropped to roughly 90,000 for several years in a row. In July 1890, Francis Guy was appointed superintendent to succeed Edward Snow. Guy was an experienced animal keeper, having owned a large private collection on a twenty-acre site at Raworth Park in Suffolk. When he arrived in Dublin, he identified the need for reform and believed that he was going to be given a free hand to modernise the Zoo. His immediate concern was to manage the staff and raise the standards of feeding and care. He told the *Evening Telegraph*:

> When I came to the gardens, I found that the loosest system prevailed as to the food. Sometimes the animals were overfed, and sometimes three parts starved. The food

was never the same either in quantity or quality, and there was scarcely a trough in the whole gardens in which food could be placed. It is absolutely necessary that we should have men who will treat the animals kindly, study their wants, and administer their food with care, otherwise the animals will become unhealthy and ill-looking.[76]

The council made it clear to Guy that he had no authority to hire or fire staff. The catalyst for conflict, however, lay in their instruction that he renovate and open the refreshment room immediately. The refreshment room was supposed to augment his modest salary but Guy found the rooms in such poor condition that it was not worth his while to open it; besides he had some private income and did not need the money. The council insisted, stating that it was part of his job and was in his contract. Guy objected, replying that 'unless attendance

Polar bear in the bath in the bear pit, originally built 1832. Undated photograph taken *c.* 1908.

considerably improved, it would be a losing game for him to open the refreshment room at present, Sundays excepted. Visitors do not average more than 40 a day.' At the annual general meeting, at the end of January 1891, Haughton praised Guy for the expertise he had brought to the Zoo, especially in relation to the monkeys' diet: 'So good was the dietary now that, should anything happen to him, he would prefer going to the monkey house rather than to the workhouse,' Haughton was reported as saying.

Patrick Supple with Hainan gibbon, mid 1890s.

Abraham Shackleton, a former member of council, was not amused and aired the dissension that had been simmering for some time. The *Daily Express* reported Shackleton as saying that:

> It seemed to him that the Gardens had passed through a period of depression ... He believed the reason was this, that the council had not been as efficient as it might have been ...
> Their principal duty appeared to be to eat a good breakfast at the gardens and, perhaps that was right for there were some members of it who were fit for little else ... He remarked further that the council, which was a self-elected body, was composed only of one class of society, and that the Catholics who happened to be members of it were those who were usually termed *Cawtholics*.[77]

When the election for new members of council was announced, Haughton said that 'Mr Shackleton had thought so well of them that he had proposed no alteration'. The status quo remained with Haughton's good friend, Sir Robert Ball as president, his brother, Valentine, secretary, and Jonathan Hogg, also a friend of Haughton, as treasurer. A few weeks later, Guy resigned out of frustration with the council. More condemnation appeared in the press. A Captain H. Church wrote:

> It is with a sad heart that I am bound to confess that the wholesale denunciations hurled at the defenceless head of the council of this Society are richly deserved.

Cape hunting dogs: image from the Dublin Zoo newspaper archive, 1890s. The Zoo was breeding the Cape hunting dog at this time.

It is painfully apparent to the most casual observer that a more deplorable state of things could scarcely exist, and I much fear that unless the people of Dublin wake up from their lethargy at once it will be too late to rescue our 'Zoo' from being numbered with the past.[78]

In February 1891, with visitor figures having dropped below 100,000 for several years in a row, there was a strongly worded report in the *Evening Telegraph*, entitled 'The Zoo controlled by opponents of reform.' It listed its findings:

Many of the animals were mangy.
Many of the birds were pitiable victims of disease.
The so-called aquarium was a laughable collection of minnows and a few larger, fresh water fish, such as a lad might keep for his amusement.
Several of the cages were entirely empty.

Many of the apartments were without labels naming the occupants.
There was an air of squalor and inattention suggestive of approaching bankruptcy.
That was the sad Zoological exhibition for which visitors paid 1s admission, which they quitted using unparliamentary language.[79]

At the end of February 1891, Thomas Hunt, a senior constable who had lived near the Zoo for twenty-five years, was appointed superintendent in the place of Francis Guy.

Death of Francis Wright

On Christmas Eve 1891, there was a tragic accident in which a seventeen-year-old man from Limerick died as a result of being mauled by a brown bear.
Francis Wright had been feeding sweets to the bear when he turned around to see where his six-year-old brother was. The bear grabbed his arm and pulled him over. Keeper Christopher Flood heard a shout and ran down to the bear pit where he found Francis Wright struggling with the bear. The superintendent and keepers were alerted and ran to his assistance. Thomas Hunt fetched the revolver and reported that, as he approached with the loaded weapon ready to shoot, Francis Wright was rescued. The young man was taken to Dr Steeven's Hospital by Hunt and Flood but died there shortly afterwards. His father called into the Zoo early in January to see the place where the accident had occurred and thanked the staff for what they had done in trying to save his son. Extra bars were placed in the bears' cage.

Cartoon from Dublin Zoo newspaper archive, 1890s.

The end of an era

In 1894, the agreement by which Dublin Zoo was granted 'permissive occupancy' of the site in Phoenix Park was drawn up. This gave the Zoo greater security on the site than before. An additional strip of land on the south side of the lake was also granted. The Zoo itself might have been in a poor state but it had consolidated its position with this agreement. At the last annual general meeting presided over by Samuel Haughton, he said that he had been:

brought into the Society by Robert Ball many many years ago . . . and [I] found that [at the time] it was the opinion of a great many, including Sir Philip Crampton and Sir Dominic Corrigan even, that the society could go on no longer. But Dr Ball said, 'The Society must not die; we must make another strenuous effort and another.' This went on and the Society was not allowed to die, but had gone on increasing and flourishing.'[80]

After that meeting, although he was an ex-president and therefore still an ex-officio member of council, Haughton virtually retired. In 1895, Valentine Ball died suddenly. Professor D. J. Cunningham was appointed secretary and immediately proposed a major programme of improvements. In 1897, the death of Samuel Haughton was announced. The council responded by opening a subscription and building Haughton House in his honour.

Cartoon from Dublin Zoo newspaper archive, 1890s.

Visitor numbers 1861–1895.

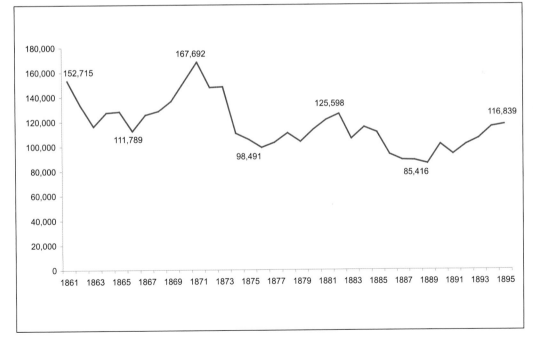

CHAPTER 3

EXPANSION AND WAR
1895–1922

Introduction

When Field Marshal Lord Roberts, commander-in-chief of the army in Ireland, was appointed president of the Royal Zoological Society of Ireland in 1898, Dublin Zoo entered a golden period with a stock of animals and visitor facilities that rivalled the best zoos in the world. Roberts was an unusual choice of president because he was unable to attend many meetings.[1] However, he encouraged Irish-born officers who were serving with the British imperial army around the world to send animals back to Dublin Zoo either as a donation or for transportation costs only. Consequently, for a period up to the commencement of the First World War, Dublin Zoo benefited directly from the colonialism that had supported so many other European zoos during the nineteenth century. Visitor numbers soared, reaching 260,000 during 1907 when the Dublin Exhibition was held in Herbert Park, and this allowed the Zoo to get new buildings, more animals, better facilities for visitors and generate a lively social atmosphere.[2]

Programme of improvements

Before the animals started arriving, a major programme of improvement and renovation was undertaken in which the aquarium was turned into a reptile house, an up-to-date rockery

Woman feeding
the elephant.

Camels and visitors
at Albert Tower.

for exotic goats was built on the west side of the lake, and a house for camels and llamas was constructed. The reptile exhibit had been especially embarrassing for a zoo with Dublin's status. At the time they shared the only high-temperature building in the Zoo with the chimpanzee, cheetah, Malayan bears and other animals that required constant warmth. Professor D. J. Cunningham, who succeeded Valentine Ball as Honorary Secretary, said that visiting naturalists were 'staggered at the *ominium gatherum* which they encounter in this room, at this association of reptile with the man-like ape.'[3] The display of animals by classification was

Donegal wild goats in the goat enclosure, which was completed in 1896. Photo taken 1910.

the most usual way for public zoos to display their animals in the nineteenth century and, to a large extent, Dublin Zoo complied: the lions, tigers and other big cats were kept in the lion house, birds were kept in the aviary and many of the primates were in the monkey house but sometimes lack of money meant that there was a mixture in one exhibition area. The attitude of the visiting naturalists was not helped by the fact that the chimpanzee was one of the more popular animals in the Zoo and the small room where this *ominium gatherum* was displayed probably became very hot and crowded on Sundays.

Renovating the old aquarium to house the reptiles was a good solution. An alligator pool was placed in the middle of the house, which allowed the animal to submerge the whole of its body under water for the first time in Dublin. A series of small, heated compartments with plate-glass fronts were installed for snakes and lizards, and a pool for 'diving birds', the cormorants and penguins, created at the other end. The decision was made at the time not to have venomous reptiles in the collection until the keeping staff became accustomed to handling snakes.

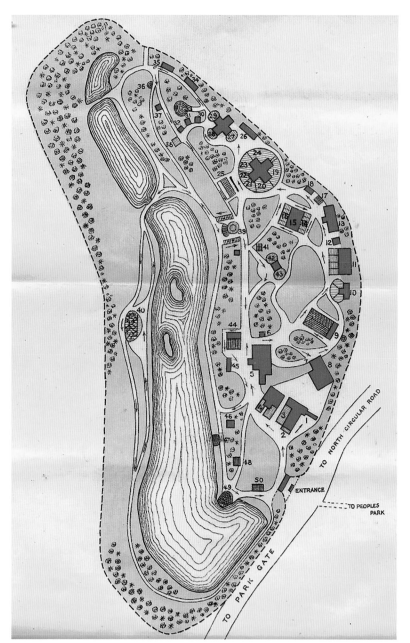

Map of the Zoo 1897. Arrows in the plan indicate the best route for visitors to take through the Gardens.

SELECTED KEY:

1–3	Kites, falcons, emus, ostrich and rheas
4	Superintendent's house and council rooms
5	Monkey house
6	Marten cage
7–8	Lion house
9	Open air aviary
10	Cattle paddocks
11	Herbivore house
12	Cape hunting dogs
13	Aquarium and reptile house
14	Capybaras, otter, etc
15	Nesbitt Aviary
16	Pheasant cages
17	Bear den
18	Wolves
19–24	Llamas and Bactrian camels
25	Polar bear
26	Eagles
27–29	Albert Tower (elephant and camels)
30	Burmese dog
31	Condor vulture
32	Hyenas
33	Elephant pond
34	Vultures and eagles
35	Bears
36	Kites
37	Rail and herons
38	Sloth bear
39	Bear pit
40	Goat rockery
41	Owls
42	Barbary sheep
43	Zebras
44	Proposed site for kangaroo house
45	Marmots, monkeys, coypus
46	Badgers
47	Herons
48	Wolves
49	Pelicans
50	Ravens

The goat enclosure, completed in 1896, was the first animal exhibit to be placed on the west side of the lake since it was annexed in 1864. It was also the first enclosure in the Zoo to incorporate the new, theatrical style of architecture that had been developed in Europe. Using blocks of undressed stone, a rockery was created for the ibex, angora and other foreign goats. It represented a naturalistic environment. Experiments with using dykes and moats to contain animals as alternatives to bars and fences were under way in Europe; the design of the goat rockery suggested that the Dublin staff were prepared to entertain such ideas.[4] The new goat enclosure in Dublin Zoo still had a fence around it but the open space and uneven surface was an improvement for the animals.[5]

The animal collection

The influence of Roberts' request to the army officers stationed around the world to assist Dublin Zoo began shortly after he took office in January 1898. In July, a Colonel Walters wrote from central India stating that he had heard from Lord Roberts that Dublin Zoo wanted animals and he promised to bring some with him when he was coming home. In September, a major in Hyderabad said he had received Roberts' communication and would endeavour to send some tiger cubs to Ireland. Over the coming years, up to eighty separate donations were made each year. Some donations were from traditional sources close to home, but others were sent from the British colonies and included meerkats, leopards, baboons, caracaras and pythons. Roberts also communicated with celebrated animal collectors such as Walter Rothschild, who presented several giant tortoises from the Galapagos during this period.

Meanwhile the Irish Lion Industry continued to produce cubs at a steady pace and, with their parents, provided plenty of interest for visitors in the lion house. Visitors could get a ride on Sita the elephant, feed the monkeys and take refreshments in the room run by Thomas Hunt, the superintendent. A new bicycle shed was erected by the entrance and the rule in which visitors needed permission to take photographs in the Zoo was dropped. In 1898, it was also possible to see specimens of the chough, a native Irish bird that was 'in the process of rapid extermination'. Nest robbing was blamed because the chough was considered 'the most engaging of pets'. Then, as the bird became rarer, there was an even greater demand for their eggs from collectors, who gambled on the bird becoming extinct. When the Zoo went to look for some choughs to include in the collection, a collector boasted that he had sold more than 300 eggs that season. The Society petitioned officials in several coastal counties to protect the chough.[6]

AN IRISH INDUSTRY.

According to Professor Cunningham, the average annual profit arising from the "industry" of lion-rearing in the Dublin Zoo for the past 45 years has been £110.

Clockwise from top left: Giant tortoise donated by Walter Rothschild, 1900; cartoon of the honorary secretary of the Royal Zoological Society, Professor D. J. Cunningham, in 1902, which reads, 'According to Professor Cunningham, the average annual profit arising from the "industry" of lion-rearing in the Dublin Zoo for the past 45 years has been £110'; Haughton House.

Opening of Haughton House

Lord Roberts attended the opening of Haughton House on 19 May 1899 and the Lord Lieutenant performed the official ceremony. The decision to construct a building that had cages for marsupials and monkeys on the ground floor and a restaurant and meeting room upstairs was an odd one. The council were desperate to attract new members and identified a need to provide exclusive facilities for them. The bulk of the Zoo's visitors came in on Sundays and during the evening when the entry was twopence for adults and a penny for children. Council members visited Zoos on the continent and discovered that, in some cases, splendid facilities were offered for the use of members only. Haughton House was Dublin's answer.[7] Combining it with much needed animal facilities – that later caused problems with smells drifting up to the tea rooms – was, presumably, a pragmatic decision.

Designed by Laurence McDonnell, the room upstairs had an ornamental fireplace, a small kitchen and pantry, and a balcony around three sides that provided splendid views over the Zoo. It was accessible via two external staircases, which led to the balconies on the west side of the building. The council discussed at length their guidelines for who might be allowed to use this building and under what conditions. On weekdays, the room was to be used as a tea room and place of rest, except on Wednesdays during the summer months when there might be a lecture or when a member of the society might want to give a garden party. A balcony might also be allocated to a member or Haughton fund subscriber who wished to give a garden party, provided they brought their 'own servants, refreshments, and appliances'. This was the beginning of many revised instructions as to who could use the upper floor and in what circumstances. However, regardless of the detail at any one time, the upper storey of Haughton House provided a facility for members and their guests.

Lord Roberts

While Lord Roberts was in Dublin in May 1899, he attended a meeting of the council and walked around the Zoo. On this walk he raised the crucial but hitherto unmentioned subject of public lavatories in the Zoo.[8] There were public conveniences of some sort because Roberts suggested that they be improved, but what they were, the records do not tell us. Certainly there was a lavatory in Society House, which was available to the council. There was also the 'Victorian toilet' outside the entrance to the Zoo. Haughton House provided more lavatories for visitors, although at busy times these were strictly available to members only. One wonders how the penny entrants coped!

IN THE ZOO. DUBLIN 6145. W.L

Towards the end of 1899, Lord Roberts' son, Lieutenant Frederick Hugh Roberts was killed in action during the Boer War. Roberts, now sixty-seven years old, immediately took up command and left for Africa, sending the council a note together with a picture of himself and information about the finalisation of the donation of two tiger cubs from His Highness the Nizam of Hyderabad. Overwhelmed, the council sent the following response:

that you should have written in your own hand to the council of the Royal Zoological Society at the present time and under present conditions we take as a very high honour. When we heard of the death of your gallant son we were filled

Scene from the west side of the lake in the Zoo in the early twentieth century.

Left: male tapir donated by Duke of Bedford (photograph *c.* 1909). Right: Field Marshal the Right Honourable Frederick Sleigh (Bobs) Roberts (1832–1914). He was awarded the Victoria Cross following action during the Indian Mutiny; served in Abyssinia and Afghanistan, was commander-in-chief of the British army in India 1885–1893, in Ireland 1895–1899 and in South Africa in 1900. He was president of the Royal Zoological Society of Ireland from 1989 to 1902.

with the deepest sympathy for Lady Roberts and yourself . . . and now while suffering from so heavy a bereavement, that you should have restored public confidence by taking the field yourself has filled us all with the greatest enthusiasm and admiration.[9]

In March 1900, the council sent him a telegram with 'warmest congratulations' in view of his 'recent brilliant victories in South Africa'.[10] He responded with a letter in which he approved of the annual report and checked on the progress of snow leopards, which he had arranged to be sent to Dublin. In this communication, he mentions 'that the letter was written as he was waiting to receive an answer to his summons for the surrender of Johannesburg'.

Keeper James Kenny was also in South Africa at the time. In May 1899, the council had been looking for a keeper to manage the new animal enclosures in Haughton House and had asked Lord Roberts to recommend a young retired soldier who was accustomed to handle horses. James Kenny had been a rough rider in the 8th Hussars and his job had been to break horses; it is likely that he was the man selected for the position. In January 1900, he re-enlisted and went to South Africa; the council guaranteed that his position would be available to him on his return. Thomas Hunt was asked to keep an eye on his wife and family during his absence and an allowance was given to Mrs Kenny.[11]

Roberts House

In 1900 Queen Victoria visited Ireland and agreed to accept an address in person from the Zoological Society of which she was patron. In 1895, she had donated a lion to the Zoo, which the council named Victor in her honour. The council had also written an address on the occasion of her diamond jubilee in 1897 in which they praised her enthusiastically: 'During your Majesty's reign the study of Natural History has been completely revolutionised by the genius and labours of Darwin and Wallace. It is a matter of pride to us that we are able to point to these distinguished Zoologists as subject of your majesty and as fellow country men of our own.' In January 1899, in response to the Royal Dublin Society's difficulties in placing a statue of the Queen in the Kildare Street property to celebrate her Diamond Jubilee, the council offered to build a house in her honour in the Zoo and call it 'Jubilee House'.[12]

On 18 April 1900, in the absence of Roberts, council members presented an address to the queen in which the Society 'expressed its loyalty to the Throne and its deep devotion to Her as their Sovereign'. Two days later, Victoria visited the gardens and was driven through the grounds to inspect the animals. The loyalty of the council was rewarded with a promise that she would donate more animals if they became available. The morning after Queen Victoria's visit to the Zoo, Society House was crowded with men of title and influence, who attended the council's breakfast. When Victoria died in January 1901, the council went into mourning, postponed the annual general meeting and trimmed the first pages of the annual report in black. Edward VII ascended the throne and, shortly afterwards, the council wrote to the home secretary to ask if the king would consent to be patron of the Society with the following message: 'Be assured sire, of our unswerving loyalty to the throne, and of our deep devotion to your person as our king.'[13] On 25 March 1901, the Privy Purse Office of Buckingham Palace wrote to inform honorary secretary D. J. Cunningham that the king had agreed to their request.

The council had already decided that a lion house should be built in their president's honour, 'because Lord Roberts restored the prestige of the British lion'.[14] Also designed by Laurence McDonnell, this was the finest of Dublin's Zoo's animal houses and the only one that emulated the elaborate houses that could be found in wealthy zoos around the world. The house was not complete when Lord Roberts visited Dublin Zoo in March 1902 so a single lioness, Hypatia, was transferred into one of the completed dens on St Patrick's Day 1902. Two weeks later, all the animals were moved and the house was officially opened by the Lord Lieutenant, the Earl of Cadogan, on 20 May 1902. The formal ceremony, with men in top hats and women in wide bonnets, was captured in a photograph by Lafayette.

Clockwise from top: photograph of guests at an event in Haughton House; interior of the Roberts House. The design of the high rail on the benches allowed people to stand on them to watch the lions being fed; guests on the balcony of Haughton House attending the formal opening of the Roberts House, 1902.

Top: exterior of the Roberts House.
Left: the Roberts House, with the old carnivore house on the left.

Hypatia, lioness, was transferred to the Roberts House on 12 March 1902 and was the first lion in the new lion house.

During the ceremony, the Lord Lieutenant opened the door of one of the outdoor dens 'and five young lions were turned out to gain their first experience of the open-air treatment and their first view of the beautiful gardens in which they reside'. After the opening ceremony 1,700 members, guests and military officers attended a garden party. Naval officers from the German fleet anchored off Dun Laoghaire added colour to the occasion, although Prince Henry of Prussia, a guest of the Lord Lieutenant, chose to play polo rather than accept the invitation of the Zoo council.

For the lions and other carnivores that were transferred to the new house, the accommodation was an improvement on their old lion house with much better light and better ventilation. The cages had curved bars overhead and glass in the roof of the building, allowing sunlight to filter in towards the animals. McDonnell had gathered information about carnivore houses in Europe and America and had used the design of the lion house in Zoologischer Garten in Berlin for some of the internal detail. There were ten indoor dens and one large and two smaller cages outside. McDonnell devised a system to ensure that the animals could move from one part of the house to another, from indoor cages to outdoor, and to safe zones so that the staff could clean the cages.

Scene in the Zoo, *c.* 1910: polar bear and visitors.

Successive councils had been nervous about changing the living conditions of the lions for fear that it would interfere with the success of the Irish Lion Industry. 'The old house, shabby and unsanitary as it is,' said Cunningham at the opening ceremony of the Roberts House, 'pervaded as it has been by an aroma which certainly cannot be said to be that or Araby, has a remarkable history . . . Within that house 217 lion cubs have been born.' He said the council had been warned that if they removed the lions from the 'stimulating atmosphere of the old house and place them in the pure air and well-lighted dens of the new house',[15] that the lion industry would come to an untimely end. But they need not have been concerned – three lion cubs were born in September 1902, six the following year and nine in 1904.

Acquisition of a giraffe

Dublin Zoo's good fortune continued with the acquisition of a giraffe, thanks once more to the influence of Lord Roberts. The giraffe was a major 'star' animal and therefore could attract many repeat visitors. Although giraffes had been popular in European zoos and had bred reasonably well, Dublin had not acquired any since the death of Albert during the Famine. There had been a disruption of the supply of giraffes to Europe in the late nineteenth century but this had been restored in 1899.[16] Butler Bey, an Irish officer stationed in El

Top and bottom left: arrival of the giraffe, 1902; Bottom right: giraffe and visitors.

Entrance to the Zoo,
early twentieth century.

Obeid, Sudan, acquired a giraffe and offered it to Dublin Zoo if the council would pay for
its transport. He also offered to send his Sudanese servant to accompany the giraffe to Dublin.

The council readily accepted the offer, insured the giraffe for £1,000, made arrangements
for its transport with Thomas Cook, and crossed its collective fingers. It was an expensive
undertaking and there were no guarantees that the animal would make it to Dublin. A head
collar and a broad strap were placed around its neck and long ropes attached to assist the
seven men to control the animal on the 280-mile walk from El Obeid to Omdurman. The
journey took thirteen days. In Dublin the Council were concerned for the men: 'A kick
from a giraffe is known to possess great elevating power; and further, the giraffe is troubled,
at times, with an exuberance of spirits which it is most difficult to cope with. When these
fits come on, it prances and jumps, and not infrequently throws itself on the ground, and
pretends to be dead.'[17]

Left: kangaroo and keeper, 1902. Right: sea lion feeding time, 1908.

Once in Omdurman, Stanley Flower, director of Giza Zoo, Cairo, took charge of Dublin's animal. He was in the region with thirteen attendants and a specially equipped train to transport animals, including four giraffes destined for London Zoo. At one stage, the train was to pass under six bridges; the Dublin giraffe was so tall that a special padded case with a sliding roof was constructed so that its head could be bent low enough to get under each bridge without incident. Eventually it arrived in Dublin and more than 9,000 people visited the Zoo the following Sunday. The Zoo achieved record crowds in the following years of 197,000 visitors in 1902 and 195,000 visitors in 1903. The giraffe was fed on dried clover, following information from London Zoo, but the following February, it died from pneumonia without ever becoming popularly known by a name. The carcase was sold for £30.

Shortly after the giraffe died a massive storm caused huge damage to buildings around the Zoo. The roof of the superintendent's house was blown off and Thomas Hunt spent 'an uneasy night' wondering which of the animals might have escaped. The carnivores and bears were secure but many of the birds escaped. The cost of repairing the buildings was crippling, and when Sir Reginald Wingate, the Sirdar of the Egyptian Army, offered to present two young giraffes and a lioness to the Zoo, the Society patched up the buildings and diverted all spare money to pay for the transport. The two giraffes arrived the following August and once more the exotic animals drew crowds. The female giraffe was subject to trembling fits but both seemed to settle in well. A special house was prepared to protect the animals from the cold. A glass screen was fitted and two radiators connected to a new boiler were placed inside the shelter to keep the temperature above 50 °F (10 °C) in winter. The animals were encouraged to go outdoors into their paddock in summer but remained in their house in winter.[18] The male died the following April of blood poisoning following an accident; the female lived on until 1909, growing taller and requiring the roof of her house to be raised so she could stand comfortably. She died suddenly when, it was believed, she had an attack of colic that caused her to throw herself violently about and fracture her jaw when she fell. In 1913, Lord Roberts offered to try and obtain another giraffe but without success. It was many years before Dublin received another giraffe.

The elephants

When the period covered by this chapter began, Dublin Zoo had one elephant, a female called Sita. James McNally had been a keeper in the Zoo since at least 1873 and had looked after Sita since the mid-1880s. In February 1897, while still considered 'perfectly tractable' and not showing any 'vicious tendencies' Sita had taken to butting down the wall of her house. The wall had been rebuilt with brick and cement and a further buttress was placed on the outside. The council decided that if she continued to butt the walls, they would have to put strong spikes in the walls to discourage her from doing this. There is no record to suggest that this was ever done. A few months later, on a Sunday in May, a large crowd had gathered around Sita and were offering her pennies to buy biscuits and buns. When she was passing the biscuit back to the man who had given her the penny, another person in the crowd offered her something. According to official report:

> In its anxiety to get this [other offering] the animal pushed its trunk out across McNally's chest and his feet slipped out from underneath him and he fell backwards . . . Unfortunately in the fall his head came in contact with the railing and it was somewhat severely cut. He never lost consciousness and was not on the ground for more than three or four seconds. He is convinced that the elephant made no attack on him when on the ground and that she did not kick him even accidentally. Of course the shouting of the people around somewhat excited the elephant but the keeper had no difficulty even though suffering from shock in obtaining command over her and putting her in her house.[19]

McNally's head was badly cut but he insisted that the elephant had not attacked him and therefore was no threat. No further action was taken and McNally and Sita continued as before – until a summer evening in 1903.

On 9 June 1903, McNally had ordered Sita to kneel down so he could dress her foot. She had an overgrown toenail and was probably suffering immense pain every time she put her foot down. McNally, under instruction from a vet, was administering lotion to her foot. The usual procedure was that she would kneel on command but this time, according to McNally's twenty-year-old son, John, who witnessed the event, Sita ignored James McNally's shouted instructions. Without warning, the elephant turned on him, knocked him onto his side with her trunk and crushed his head with her foot. John McNally and another keeper called to Sita to

ELEPHANT CRUSHES ITS KEEPER'S HEAD.
AWFUL DEATH IN THE DUBLIN ZOO. THE IRISH CHILDREN'S PET MURDERS ITS CUSTODIAN.

Depiction of the death of James McNally from the British periodical *The Illustrated Police Budget*. The caption reads: 'Elephant crushes its keeper's head: awful death in the Dublin Zoo. The Irish children's pet murders its custodian.'

fall back, which she did. The young man said the incident was over in about two seconds. The coroner ruled that James McNally's death was instantaneous and an accident. A subscription was opened for his widow and John McNally received a permanent job as an assistant keeper.

When closing the case, the coroner stated, 'the animal had met the fate usually meted out to animals guilty of deeds of this character. It had been destroyed that morning.' It was common practice in zoos at that time to destroy any animal involved in a fatal incident for fear that further human lives might be sacrificed if anyone entered its space. In this case, a large, female elephant, over twenty years old, in a small pen in a zoo without her regular keeper, was particularly dangerous and, the council recorded, it was a 'painful duty to order the creature's destruction'. They tried to poison her with cyanide of potassium concealed in an apple but Sita spat it out immediately. Colonel Sir Neville Chamberlain, of the Royal Irish Constabulary, offered to shoot the elephant if an elephant rifle could be procured.

Clockwise from top left: The elephant Padmahati, c. 1904; Roma, the elephant, helping to dig a ditch outside Haughton House, 1912. James Kenny, Roma's keeper, is beside her; Elephant House, 1910, with the metal arch that is now near the Education Centre.

Clockwise from top: James Kenny with Roma, 1912; Orang-utan, purchased by council member Dr Scharff in 1911, called 'Bella'; 'British Association Breakfast "waitresses" 1908'. guests at a function at Dublin Zoo.

Keepers on an elephant, possibly Roma.

Staff photo, early twentieth century. Identifiable staff members include front row, seated, 3rd from left, Patrick Supple; 5th from left, Christopher Flood; far right, James Kenny. Middle row, 4th from left, Jack Supple. The men in cloth caps were possibly grounds staff, the men in bowler hats were possibly gate and office staff and the man sitting in the front, centre, may be Captain Arbuthnot, superintendent from 1908 to 1911. The rest of the staff in the picture were probably keepers.

The council sent to London for such a weapon and it arrived several days later. Chamberlain shot two bullets between her eye and ear and had five of the best shots in the Royal Irish Constabulary on hand to shoot at her shoulders if the head shots were not sufficient to kill her. The elephant rifle in Chamberlain's hands was adequate and Sita died instantaneously. Forty RIC men with three tug-of-war ropes took an hour and a half to pull the dead elephant into an outer enclosure where she could be dissected. The foot of the elephant was presented to the RIC in thanks for the work they had done for the Zoo.[20]

Shortly before James McNally's death and Sita's execution, the Duke and Duchess of Connaught had presented a young elephant called Padmahati and a young panther to the Zoo as a gift. Padmahati was placed close to the elephant house in a derelict den. She was ten years old and it was hoped she would accept a saddle fairly soon so that she could provide rides. James Kenny went to Portsmouth to collect the elephant from the Duke and, on their return, took charge of her. An elephant trainer was engaged for a few weeks to train Padmahati to carry a saddle. In May 1904, she was ready to give rides and James Kenny was given a commission on the takings.

In 1907 Padmahati died from intestinal inflammation. Elephants were hired for the summer months each year for the next few years. Lord Roberts also arranged for several elephants to be donated to the Zoo but problems arose with each one. In 1912, the council purchased a new elephant from Hagenbeck in Hamburg. The mahout accompanying the elephant, which was named Roma, was not impressed with Ireland's weather saying that it was too wet for the animal. Roma, however, according to reports 'is very docile and takes kindly to biscuits, sugar and other dainties'.[21] Then another elephant arrived as the Maharajah of Mysore honoured his gift promised to Lord Roberts by sending a three-year-old female, Sandari, who had been trained in the Maharajah's private gardens and already carried children. The council tried to sell Roma back to Hagenbeck but the elephant had grown considerably in the year she had been in the Zoo and was too large for Hagenbeck to sell on. Roma remained in the Zoo and on the market.

August 1913

In August 1913, Patrick Supple, who had worked in the Zoo since his father's death in 1867, died; he was seventy-two years old. In a mark of respect for their 'faithful and devoted keeper of the monkey house', a wreath and carriage were provided by the council for his funeral. His son, Jack Supple, who succeeded him as keeper of the monkey house, said in later years, that his father had been employed as a boy in the Zoo to carry water for 2s 6d a week. He also recalled in the 1960s, that 'he remembered his father saying that he took a half day off work to get married'.[22]

The Dublin Lockout also occurred in August 1913, when William Martin Murphy (a long-term member of the Zoological Society) dismissed members of the Irish Transport and General Workers Union from the Dublin Tramway Company and Independent Newspapers. In response to the industrial unrest in the city, the council thought about looking into the question of staff wages. There was no indication of unrest in the Zoo at the time although working conditions for the staff had changed very little since the 1830s. All staff worked seventy to eighty hours per week, seven days a week and were given leave on request; the night watchman was the only exception – he worked ninety-eight hours per week. There were no fixed closing times and, in summer, the Zoo might be open until 9.00 p.m. The Society regularly paid bonuses for success with breeding animals or organising events or undertaking extra tasks. The elephant keeper was allowed to keep any money he raised through selling buns for the elephant; it is also likely that other staff were allowed to keep tips and other

Clockwise from top left: visitors at the sea lions, August 1913; 'Mr McCann and W. E. Peebles in February 1912.' Peebles was a keen ice skater and president of the Society in 1916; 'Rebuilding of the old lion house, 1909.' The new lion house, which was attached to the Roberts House, was designed by Batchelor and Hicks, architects, and opened in September 1909.

Clockwise from top left: Patrick Supple with orang-utan, 'Bella'; Chimpanzee 'Kitty' with an unidentified member of staff; Patrick Supple in the monkey house.

small payments made to them by visitors. The superintendent was no longer responsible for running the refreshment room since Haughton House opened but compensation was incorporated into his salary. The Society paid small pensions to staff or their wives who left after many years of service or who were ill.

Every year, in spring, the council undertook a wage review and raised the wages of a few staff each time. In 1913 the most senior keeper was on 26 shillings a week. In September, the council discussed staff wages again but, in the end, decided to leave it until their usual May review. They did, however, give an allowance to each member of staff to cover their liability to contribute under the Insurance Act.

Towards the end of August 1913, Michael Coyne, the eighty-year-old gatekeeper, was assaulted during an incident at the gate. He was sitting by the table where members signed their names on arrival. Two men came to the gate, paid their entrance fee and then, apparently for a joke, took the ink bottle from the table. As Coyne tried to get the bottle back the ink spilt over the visitors who walked off. Later they returned to the entrance lodge, where one of them hit Michael Coyne, knocked him back into the small gate lodge, hit him again and left the elderly man on the ground with two broken ribs and other injuries. The aggressor was jailed for the assault and Michael Coyne retired after thirty-three years service. In March 1914, the case for compensation for Michael Coyne arose and the Zoological Society were the nominal defendants. In the climate of the time, the council was concerned that it looked as if they were refusing to compensate their former employee. They issued a press release to state that they did not contest Coyne's claim but employers 'have now obligations to their servants, against which they take the precaution of insuring.' They pointed out that it was the insurance company that had challenged Coyne's claim and that they had paid him his standard pension of half his wages pending the court case, and would continue to do so after the compensation ran out.[23]

The Great War

In June 1914, sixty-four people sat down at tables in the refreshment room in Haughton House for the Ladies' Breakfast. Sir Charles Ball, the president and third son of the early honorary secretary Robert Ball, sat at the top of the long, central table, which was decorated with sweet pea, yellow daisies and other floral decorations. The menu included salmon, tomatoes, crumbed sausages, bacon, eggs, cold ham, mayonnaise, home-made jams and the speciality rolls for which Haughton House had become famous, followed by strawberries and cream. After breakfast, the guests wandered around the different houses and visited the three-weeks-old lion cubs. The issues dominating the council meetings at the time were the problem of curtailing the growing rat population,[24] deciding whether to create a small dark room where visitors could change plates on their cameras for a fee, and making plans to use a picture of the chimp called George on the advertising hoarding, which was to be hung by the railway companies in their various stations around the country.

Leopard in the moveable, connecting cage in the new lion house. The cage is visible above the exit doorway of the extension to the Roberts House.

In August, Britain declared war on Germany and the impact in Ireland was immediate. British soldiers left for the continent, food prices soared, the Horse Show in the Royal Dublin Society was cancelled and tourist travel was restricted. The council responded quickly by writing to London Zoo and asking what arrangements they were making for the admission of the wives and children of men on active service. As a result the wives and children of Irish serving soldiers were to be admitted free on weekdays on production of a certificate that identified their relationship to a serviceman. In September, the council made special arrangements with the manageress of Haughton House to welcome convalescing soldiers. In the same month, L. Doyle, a staff member signed up. His job was kept open and his wife was to be paid during his absence. In October 1914 the council sent a letter to Joseph Nugent Lentaigne, a long-time member of council, with their condolences on the death of his nephew, Lieutenant Victor Lentaigne.

The shortage in tourists during their busiest time of year, particularly those from the Isle of Man who were notable for visiting Dublin Zoo in great number, caused a significant drop in income. The sharp increase in food prices and the loss of income from animal sales added to the council's financial woes but, in their annual report for 1914 they said, 'in the present terrible state of many European countries, we may be thankful that our chief trouble is a temporary shortage of money . . . Antwerp Zoo had to kill all of their larger carnivora for

the sake of safety during recent bombardment of their city.' Dublin Zoo promised to help Antwerp restock their zoo on 'the return of happier conditions'.[25]

At the outbreak of the war, Dublin Zoo had a good stock of animals to attract visitors. Besides having two elephants, one of which was giving rides to children, they had a young gorilla named Empress and a young male chimp named Charlie. The two animals had been imported together and seemed to get on well. Jack Supple was now looking after the precious apes and was credited with keeping these animals alive and in good health. Sandy, the orang-utan, who had been in the gardens for over a year, was also in good health. These were joined in the monkey house in 1914 by a male hoolock gibbon, which had been a pet of the officers of a battalion of the Gordon Highlanders who had now gone to the continent. The Society claimed that, as far as they knew, the four types of anthropoids: gorilla, chimpanzee, orang-utan and gibbon, had never been exhibited together before in any zoo.[26]

The lions were also a great attraction and were producing cubs regularly. Two well-known lions called Red Hugh and Fiona had cubs in the height of the summer of 1914; they were all male, a 'remarkable and unusual preponderance of one sex', the council observed. There were five tigers in the carnivore house including two cubs, which had been a gift of Dr G.

Photograph of the gorilla Empress by Professor A. Francis Dixon, School of Physic, Trinity College Dublin and a member of council (from 1904 until his death in 1936). In October 1917, he gave a lecture in the RDS about the gorilla.

Combes, principal medical officer for the Cochin States, South India.[27] Several popular animals died during 1914, including two American black bears, two sea lions, and a pair of snow leopards. Very few animals would be replaced before the end of the war. Lord Roberts died in northern France while on a visit to the British Expeditionary Force but his imperial officers had not forgotten Dublin Zoo. In March 1915, the council received a financial donation from a Captain Corsellis who was stationed in Cameroon with the British forces. In the accompanying letter he wrote, 'Our column has been operating in some parts here in which big game abounds. About six weeks ago a company was out reconnoitring and came in touch with the enemy and were preparing for the offensive when two elephants charged in among first our troops and then those of the Germans with the result that hostilities had to be postponed ... A small patrol close to where we were camped encountered and shot an elephant with quite good ivory a couple of weeks ago.'[28]

As the war continued, managing the Zoo became more difficult. In April 1915 Dr Benjamin Ferrar the superintendent since 1911, accepted a temporary commission

Dr Benjamin Ferrar, superintendent, with chimpanzee Kitty at Haughton House.

in Royal Army Medical Corps and was on daily duty in the Dublin barracks of military hospitals. He continued to live in the Zoo and gave what spare time he had to his job as superintendent. There was no question of replacing him, although it was agreed that if he were sent out of Dublin on service, his wife, Mrs Ferrar, would take on some of his duties.[29] The ladies' breakfasts were cancelled but lectures were held and a golf putting competition was organised, which was well attended. Donations of vegetables, leftover greens from the markets and seeds were willingly accepted as the cost of food for the animals increased. Fuel to heat the animal houses was also proving difficult to acquire but somehow they managed to get enough for the present.

Soldiers were frequent visitors at the Zoo. Men in uniform were allowed in for half price but those with wounds, convalescing or invalided soldiers were admitted with greater reductions or free of charge. Tickets stamped 'complimentary invalid soldiers' were given to council members to give to wounded soldiers personally known to them. Bands were specially organised to entertain the wounded men. In May 1915, the following announcement appeared in the *Freeman's Journal*:

By special request of some of the wounded soldiers who have returned from the battles around Ypres, the descriptive piece called the Battle of Ypres ... will be repeated at the band promenade at the Zoological Gardens ... This piece, which brings in many stirring trumpet calls, mingled with a wonderful representation of big guns and rifle fire and a splendidly effective rendering of the national airs of the allies, has been received with much applause whenever it has been played and we learn that on Wednesday the friends of the different hospitals are arranging to commandeer all the motors they can get to bring the wounded soldiers to the Zoo. These band afternoons are becoming more popular every week.[30]

In September the condolences of the council were sent to Dr O'Carroll, a member of council, on the death of his son who had been killed in the Dardenelles. Mrs Barrington, the manageress of Haughton House, was sent condolences on the death of her husband.

The Easter Rising, 1916

In April 1916, the Zoo was preparing for a busy Easter. The hay bill was causing concern but the half-price entry for the entire Easter weekend held the promise of a solid boost to the funds. On Monday 24 April, Benjamin Ferrar had gone to the Royal Barracks as usual. The Zoo was busy in the morning but, as word filtered out about the troubles in the city, most people left. A family from Dalkey could not get home and returned to the Zoo to be lodged in Haughton House for the night. The restaurant in Haughton House was fortunately well stocked. The family and several of the keepers, as well as some of the animals which could share the food of humans, were catered for. The family left the next day but keepers Jack Supple, J. Flood and Tommy Kelly stayed in the Zoo for the next week or so to help Mrs Ferrar, who took charge in the absence of her husband. As bitter fighting continued, other keepers risked their lives to call into the Zoo to help Mrs Ferrar and the three men. Benjamin Ferrar was able to reach the Zoo on three occasions by way of Islandbridge or Chapelizod. He brought in some urgently required supplies but left again each time.

There was heavy firing around Phibsborough on Tuesday 25 April, which was audible at the Zoo. On Thursday 26 April rifle bullets passed over the gardens but there were no injuries, nor were there reports of animals being injured through fright or otherwise. On Monday 1 May, the fighting in the city came to an end and the military authorities who had restricted access to Phoenix Park allowed horse meat to be delivered. It arrived just in time to avoid disaster. Wild rumours about the Zoo having to shoot the lions and tigers were untrue: an old pony, a donkey, a goat and a few dingoes were killed to feed the carnivores but supplies arrived before any more drastic action was required.

The superintendent's house, which was pebble-dashed in 1911.

Strangely, a gift of monkeys arrived at the Zoo in the week after the Rising even though access to Phoenix Park was still restricted.[31] A few visitors who had permission to enter Phoenix Park visited the Zoo during that week. On Saturday 6 May, nearly two weeks after Easter, six members of council assembled for their meeting at nine o'clock but there was no breakfast owing to the shortage of coal and the absence of gas. On 13 May, the Park was re-opened to the public. Normal activities resumed at the Zoo and nineteen members and three guests attended breakfast followed by the council meeting. For the war years

The northwest corner of the Zoo, 1911. The Ice House, now in the Amur tiger exhibit, is visible at the right of the picture.

Chimpanzee with
Professor J. Alfred
Scott, a council
member from 1907
until his death in
1926. 'His scientific
attainments and
profound knowledge
of animals and their
ways, and his
enthusiasm for their
welfare and their
happiness, were an
inspiration to his
colleagues.' (Annual
Report, 1926)

this was an unusually high number and was a clear statement that the council members were
ready to carry on. Mrs Ferrar was thanked for her courage in looking after the Zoo in such
difficult circumstances: by way of thanks, they gave her an engraved silver potato dish.

In July 1916 General Sir John Maxwell, the military governor appointed when martial
law was imposed in Ireland after the Rising, visited the gardens. George the chimp was let out
on the lawn to entertain him by washing dishes that had been left ready in a bucket near
the water tap outside the monkey house. On 3 August 1916, Roger Casement was hanged
in Pentonville Prison, having been found guilty of high treason for his role in attempting
to import guns from Germany for use in the Easter Rising. Casement was a former corresponding member of the Society and had donated numerous South American animals when
he had been with the British Colonial Service in Rio de Janerio. Corresponding members
were elected by the council after due consideration and Sir Roger Casement, as he was
known then, had fitted the profile for membership of this select category.

The Great War continues

Following the Rising, the work of the council focused on keeping the Zoo going in increasingly difficult circumstances. The quality of hay was very poor and hard to get, as were most supplies. In 1917 the Board of Works granted the Society permission to grow potatoes in the Zoo so long as the land was returned to its present state within a year after the end of the war. Stockpiling coke and coal was suggested, as prices in 1917 increased rapidly and there was a danger stocks would run out. The aquarium had been closed up by now because there was insufficient fuel to heat the house: the donation of a pair of pythons had to be refused. London Zoo was rearing pigs and the Dublin council thought of doing the same thing, but by the time they got sufficient information on that enterprise, the war had ended.[32]

Meanwhile every effort was made to encourage wounded, convalescent and invalided soldiers to visit. Handbills were sent to barracks and camps advising soldiers and sailors that they could be admitted to the Zoo on weekdays for threepence. Wives and children of men on active service were still being admitted free. Books of tickets were sent to large city and nearby hospitals.[33] Pensioners in the Royal Hospital[34] were admitted free. The Royal College of Surgeons entertained 400 soldiers for tea in the Zoo and no admission charge was made. The matron in the Children's Hospital in Harcourt Street where soldiers were also being treated, was sent a book of tickets when she wrote to ask for them.[35]

In June 1917 the council announced that 'Blue uniform men', or wounded soldiers, were to be admitted free on any day except Sundays, bank holidays or public holidays. The financial condition of the Zoo was disastrous, with visitor numbers dropping to between 130,000 and 140,000 for the years 1916 to 1918. The numbers coming through

Above: Potato dish presented to Mrs B. B. Ferrar to thank her for managing the Zoo when it was closed following the Easter Rising in 1916. The inscription reads, 'To Mrs Ferrar from the Council of the Royal Zoological Society Ireland in remembrance of her brave help in the Gardens during the Rebellion of Easter week 1916'; Left: Visitors at the open air carnivore dens, opened 1906.

the gates had not been as low as this since the 1890s and many of the visitors now were coming in free or at a reduced price. Subscribers resigned and new life and annual subscribers were limited in number. The president of the Society, Sir Frederick Moore, used his own money to pay for a man to clean the gardens periodically, and also to defray the cost of planting the potatoes. Two weeks of skating in February 1917 helped matters: the entrance fee was increased and the gates were closed to the general public except soldiers and sailors in uniform. In 1918 foreign soldiers who paid half price boosted gate receipts slightly. Australian soldiers were said to prefer Dublin to London when they were on leave and many visited the Zoo to see the famous lions: Dublin's lions were well known in Melbourne Zoo and Taronga Zoo in Sydney.

Few animals were added during the war and many died. In August 1916 some stock arrived from the Toronto Gardens, including a Canadian black bear, two beavers and four tree porcupines. In 1917 the Society agreed to look after two black bear cub mascots belonging to a Canadian Battalion until the end of the war. The bison, which had been a gift of the Canadian government, were breeding well in the Zoo, although a Canadian official visiting the Zoo in 1918 was not impressed with the small amount of space given to these animals and suggested that the Zoo should ask the Board of Works for more land. The council duly did this but were told that the Commissioner of Public Works would not make a decision on such matters until after the war ended.

In November 1916 a letter of condolence was sent to the Society's vice-president, Sir R. H. Woods, whose son had died in action. And in September 1918, just before the end of the war, a similar letter was sent to Cecil Pim, a council member, whose son had also died in action.

End of the war

Dublin Zoo went through a boom period after the war ended and in 1919 visitor figures soared to 223,000, a number exceeded only in 1907 during the Dublin Exhibition in Herbert Park. The number of wounded or invalided soldiers who were still being let in at half price, dropped to about 5,000 (from almost 7,000 the previous year). Demobilised men organised by the Department of Labour, undertook considerable work in cleaning and tidying the grounds. A program of reconstruction and renovation on the existing houses most in need of repair was also undertaken. After four years during which only the cheapest of maintenance work could be carried out, many of the houses were in very poor repair with rotting woodwork, collapsing roofs, unsafe doors, and cages that were 'useless . . . objectionable . . . ugly

Eagle cage,
completed 1910.

. . .and unsightly.'[36] Materials were still difficult to get and labour was expensive but a legacy
from the late W. Edward Peebles, a former president, was used to fund the most urgent works.

Many of the lions had survived the war and were still producing litters of cubs. After five
cubs were sold or exchanged in 1919, there were seven males and seven females in the collection. Tigers, bears, an elephant, many monkeys and parrots had also survived the war.
Empress the gorilla died in May 1917 of a digestive disorder, having lived for three years and

four months in the Zoo. The Society claimed that the gorilla's longevity in the Zoo was exceeded only by a gorilla in Breslau which had lived for seven years in captivity.[37] The hoolock gibbon, which was never named, died in October 1918, while Charlie and George, the chimpanzees, lived on until 1920 when both died from colon inflammation and resultant peritonitis.

Zoos around the world were beginning to stock up again. On 16 November 1918, five days after Armistice Day, the animal dealership Hamlyn contacted the Zoo and asked if it had any young lions for sale or exchange. Monkeys, cockatoos, a Brazilian tortoise, a wolf, a chimp and other animals were purchased; parakeets, a macaw, an antelope and other animals were donated. And Dublin honoured its pledge to Antwerp Zoo by presenting Nuala, a Dublin-born three-year-old lion and agreeing to sell the six-year old lion, Seamus, a son of Red Hugh.[38] An attempt was made to take advantage of the presence of Irish officers abroad to get some interesting animals before the army was disbanded. Officers serving in Egypt were asked for camels and giraffes. However the costs had escalated and, on hearing that a camel, which had been £16 before the war, was now £50 or £60, the council had to drop that idea for the time being. The Zoo was offered some war trophies including a German mobile pigeon loft that had been captured in France, but transport difficulties made it impossible to get this gift to Ireland. In 1920, a complete German submarine periscope was received and erected in the loft over the elephant house.[39]

The council decided to have a five-day-long fete in June 1919. They were nervous about it, wondering if it was wise to put their limited funds into such an enterprise. There was no hint yet in the Society's records that the War of Independence, which had begun in January 1919 in Tipperary, was having any impact on the Zoo. Mrs Barrington applied for an occasional bar licence for Haughton House because she did not think it would be possible to run dinners satisfactorily during the fete without the licence.[40] The fete raised over £4,000 through such entertainments as 'the Gipsy encampment' by Mrs Reginald Peacocke, a white elephant stall by Lady Headfort, a basket stall by Lady Moore, a dance organised by Mrs O'Carroll, antique stall, stationery stall, dolls' house, Paradise tea gardens, bean bags and other stalls, games, activities and amusements to entertain Dubliners. The goodwill generated by the fete encouraged new life and annual members.

In April 1920, the volunteer stallholders and helpers – 450 people in all – were invited to the Zoo for a garden party to show them the results of their fundraising. Another fete was organised when it became apparent that there would not be enough money to reconstruct the bear enclosure. This was the beginning of a new trend in which fundraising and social

Clockwise from top left: (L–r): Lady Moore, Miss Percy and Mrs Panter at the Zoo Fete, 1920; Women on slide at the Zoo fete; (L–r): Sir Hamar Greenwood, Lady Beatty, Sir Andrew Beatty, Lady Greenwood and Mrs McMahon at garden party in the Zoo, June 1920; Sir Frederick Moore, president of the Zoological Society, at the Zoo fete.

events organised by the Ladies' Committee became an increasingly dominant feature of Dublin Zoo in the mid-twentieth century.[41]

The impact of the War of Independence was finally noticed in January 1920 just as the Black and Tans were being recruited. Coke and coal were still difficult to get and the Council had just sourced two tons but Ferrar advised against asking the military to assist in bring the supply up to the Zoo.[42] Seed potatoes were sown once more but, apart from that, there were few indications of the war that was escalating outside the Zoo. During the year, the entrance fee was raised twice to meet the increasing costs in maintaining the Zoo.

Nevertheless a fete was held once more in June with a military band entertaining the guests. General Sir Nevil Macready, the commander-in-chief of forces in Ireland, Sir Hamar Greenwood, Chief Secretary for Ireland, and nine government officials from Dublin Castle became members of the Zoological Society. In November 1920, three weeks before Bloody Sunday, the council decided to postpone the dance it was planning in the Royal College of

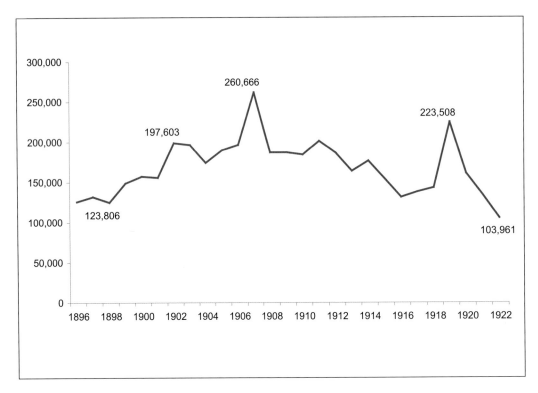

Visitor numbers 1896-1922.

Surgeons, saying, 'after careful consideration the council feel that under existing circumstances, the holding of a dance by the Society might be misunderstood.'[43] On 25 November, when ten of the British officers murdered on Bloody Sunday were carried through the streets of Dublin to the North Wall to be brought back to England for burial, the Zoo remained closed until one o'clock for the 'Officers' funeral'.[44]

When the Government of Ireland Act in December 1920 set up the six-county parliament and administration in the North, and a similar provision for the South (which was ignored), the council became concerned about where it was going to get its annual government grant, which was still £500. On investigation they were assured that until the Southern Irish Parliament came into existence, its grant would be made 'by the imperial parliament or by the crown colony government which may come into existence for the south of Ireland'.[45] At the annual general meeting the council thanked their staff for their loyalty over the past few years. Then they returned to the matters of buying and selling animals and chasing up exotic donations. They also took note for future reference that the group called the Order of Buffaloes, who entertained 564 poor children in the gardens in September 1921, had 'without permission . . . brought in large quantities of stout, whiskey and other stimulants. As a result very little assistance was given in looking after the large number of rather disorderly children.'[46]

In January 1922, the Provisional Government took over from Dublin Castle and in March 1922, the council received a letter from Constable Major Fitzgerald of the Royal Irish Constabulary saying,

The foot of Sita the elephant: 'Presented to the Royal Zoological Society of Ireland by the members of the Sergeants Mess of the R.I.C. Depot Phoenix Park on the disbandment as a token of recognition of past favours to the members of the force April 1922'.

> The RIC sergeants' mess desired to present to the Society the foot of the elephant 'Sita' which was shot in the gardens by a party of RIC on 11th June 1903 after it killed its keeper. The foot had been dressed, mounted and presented by Colonel Sir N. Chamberlain to the sergeants' mess. In view of disbandment, a general meeting of the mess resolved that the foot should be presented to the Royal Zoological Society of Ireland in recognition of past favours towards members of the mess.[47]

CHAPTER 4

PEACEFUL RESORT
1922–1950

Introduction

The period covered in this chapter was a peculiar one for Dublin Zoo. It should have been an unsettled time with the new political environment in Ireland in the 1920s, the Great Depression in the 1930s and the Second World War. Yet the records, the newspaper reports, visitor memories and the loyalty of the staff all suggest that the Zoo was a place of 'peaceful resort'[1] that grew steadily from attracting 173,000 visitors in 1923 to attracting 320,000 visitors in 1949. Few 'star' animals were purchased during this period but the lions kept breeding, the bison had a few calves, tigers and leopards shared the steamy atmosphere of the Roberts House, the chimps entertained, the children's corner was created and Sarah the elephant arrived. A dominant feature of this period was the social activity for members and their friends: parties, dances, dinners, fetes and bridge tournaments were so popular that one wit suggested that the Zoo should sell their own tickets on the black market to raise extra funds. While the parties kept the Society afloat, the bulk of the visitors went to the Zoo when the entry was cheapest.

The relationship with the new government

If the Society's close association with the British government in Ireland since 1830 was

Bison and calf in Dublin Zoo, 1920s.

cause for concern among council members after Independence in 1922, there was no hint of it in the official records. They noticed that an 'alarming' number of members were resigning from the Society, many of whom said they were leaving the country.[2] New members joined, including Ernest Blythe, the Minister for Finance, and Patrick Hogan, the Minister for Agriculture.[3] The government approved the continuance of the grant of £500 in April 1923 and raised it to £750 in 1925. Even in these difficult times, the Zoo proved to be politically neutral, a common characteristic of zoos around the world. At Easter 1923, the *Mail* contained the following report on a visit to the Zoo:

> Since 1916 Easter Monday has been a day of public uneasiness. But that is passing away. Never were such crowds seen in the Park as on yesterday afternoon. Paterfamilias had prepared himself for a thoroughly peaceable holiday. The Zoo elephant was working overtime. Everything in the Gardens was lovely. Perspiring humanity struggled bravely for moving space in the lion house. There were more empty cages than usual. Several lions were missing. Nobody knew why.

The monkey house was easily first in favour. It was besieged by everybody, old and young. The only dissatisfied visitor was a venerable lady who remarked in a polite whisper, as she endeavoured to force her way to the exit door: 'A little of this goes a long way'. The Zoo was the scene of our only rebellion yesterday. It began when the announcement went for the umpteenth Easter Monday in Dublin's history that the wonderful institution would have to close its doors.[4]

At the time there were fourteen lions, three tigers, leopards, a puma, wolves, dingoes, a polar bear and several brown bears in the collection. Sandari was the resident elephant and she was giving rides under the supervision of James Kenny (senior). Rodger was the surviving chimp; Sam, the other chimp, had died of TB earlier in the year. During the summer, large crowds visited the Zoo and on the first Sunday in August, over 8,000 visitors were recorded. Later that year, Rodger also died of TB.

The council invited Timothy Healy, the first Governor-General of the Irish Free State, to breakfast. Healy, who had been a member of the Society since 1898, accepted the invitation in June 1923. In a friendly address, Sir Robert Woods, the president, congratulated Healy on his appointment and pointed out that the Zoo was 'maintained as a resort where useful and inspiring knowledge may be acquired amidst delightful surroundings'. Woods wished happiness to the Governor-General and his family during his term of office. In his response, the Governor-General praised the Society for its work in 'creating an interest in natural history and a love of living creatures'. He mentioned the success with breeding lions and quoted a comment made by a keeper on St Patrick's Day 1900, who said to him, 'them forest lions, sir, are nothing to ours!'[5]

The one noticeable development in the Society's minutes during this period was a new

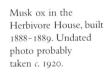

Musk ox in the Herbivore House, built 1888–1889. Undated photo probably taken c. 1920.

interest in encouraging people from Belfast to visit the Zoo. Prior to this, Belfast, or indeed any Irish city other than Dublin, had seldom been mentioned in the council minutes. In 1923, the council contacted the Belfast Naturalists' Field Club to attract membership and for several years took the unusual decision to support the Club journal through advertising and donation. It also advertised on handbills and posters produced by the Belfast YMCA in connection with their tours to Dublin, and offered half price on production of a return railway ticket to Belfast. The council had always been conservative about advertising because of cost and had tended to focus on public transport by putting posters at tram and railway stops. Of course, reductions in the entrance fee were given on request to school and charitable groups, organisations that wanted to hold large parties in the Zoo negotiated a reduced rate each time depending on numbers. The arrangements that were being made for the people of Belfast were exceptional.[6]

Building the collection through the 1920s and 1930s

Throughout the 1920s and 1930s, the Zoo's friends from abroad sent many animals to Phoenix Park. Sir Geoffrey Archer, governor of Uganda, sent a young lion in December 1923, which was called Selim Bey. A poem, written by Charles Green, was published in the Annual Report. The first of the five stanzas read:

> Do those wide eyes watch the shadows
> Move in Ruwenzori's meadows,
> Far away-
> See the shy Okapi flick its
> Ears in Semiliki thickets,
> Selim Bey?[7]

In 1927 Selim Bey sired one litter with Deirdre, and died shortly after their birth.

Mrs J. F. Kenny-Dillon, wife of a bank official in Tanganyika, brought with her several smaller cats and some deer from Africa when she was visiting Ireland in 1925. The same year Mr Shirley V. Cooke, District Commissioner, Kwali, in Kenya, arranged for several batches of animals to be sent to the Zoo. He put an advertisement in the local paper in Nairobi asking Irish men to try and secure animals for Dublin Zoo. He was unsuccessful in getting permission from the local authorities to send a hippo and a rhino to Dublin but he did send lions and other cats. He also sent a pair of elands in 1923 but, owing to concern about foot-and-mouth-disease in Britain, they remained in quarantine in London for nearly two years. Eventually the animals were allowed to enter Ireland but the female died shortly afterwards from gastritis. Cooke sent the next batch of animals to Ireland via Antwerp. In 1928 and 1930, Dr A. B. Monks of the Health Department in Sierra Leone sent chimpanzees, monkeys, a baboon, a crocodile, a pelican and a python. In 1929, Captain A. T. A. Ritchie, a game warden in Nairobi, sent baboons, a civet cat, bat-eared foxes, mongooses, a vulture and other stock. During the 1930s, Cooke continued to send animals to Dublin Zoo from Africa and again after the end of the Second World War. In one of his letters, Cooke commented, 'it is a great thing that the council has such a fine institution that Irish-men of every shade of politics and religion can wholeheartedly support.'[8]

Selim Bey, lion cub presented by the Governor of Uganda.

Canada and the United States became a new and important source of animals for Dublin Zoo in the 1920s. Lord O'Shaughnessy, president of the Canadian Pacific Railway, arranged a donation of animals to Dublin Zoo. Rocky Mountain goats and sheep, Canadian black bears, porcupines, and a pair of wapiti arrived in February 1924.[9] The wapiti stag had been in captivity for six weeks and was confined to a wooden crate on the trip across the Atlantic. He looked feeble and shaky when he was let out of the crate but, suddenly, with a surge of energy, he jumped the fence of his enclosure and escaped into Phoenix Park where he ran for many miles until he

stopped by a small pond near the Castleknock gates. The keepers watched him for a while and decided to leave him there for the night. Next morning, they approached but he ran, jumping over the barbed wire fence surrounding the Magazine Fort and down the hill. He collapsed and a soldier from the Fort stayed with him until the keepers arrived. They tied his legs and brought him back to the Zoo. The animal died later that day. The female wapiti, which came with him, lived on.[10]

The success of Dublin Zoo in attracting international support for its collection was noticed by *The Irish Times*, which published an article entitled 'The Free State "Zoo"' in October 1923:

> The formal debut of the Irish Free State, first at Geneva as a member of the League of Nations, and later at the Imperial Conference as a member of the commonwealth of British Nations, is bound to have many desirable results. One

Undated photo of bears in the bear enclosure, which is now the location of the waldrapp ibis cliff.

of the first Irish institutions to benefit from the new order of things ought to be the Dublin Zoological Gardens. Hitherto that institution has suffered not merely from a lack of funds, but almost more from a lack of distinguished donors of live-stock ... Now a small but highly desirable gift of alligators and tortoises has been received from the New York Gardens. These are but an indication of what may be done if President Cosgrave and his colleagues will remember to put in an occasional word for the Dublin "Zoo" when they are conferring with the representatives of foreign states.[11]

The article was on page four of the newspaper in the news column and there was nothing to indicate that it was anything other than a serious suggestion. In November *Dublin Opinion* picked it up and produced a satirical piece entitled 'Big game' by Lucius Flood. It included several tableaux, one of which was as follows (with the original spellings):

Tableau IV

Scene: a tent on the Circassian border, in which is met the army staff of the little State of Colaps. Desmond Fitzgerald enters wrapped in a military greatcoat.

D. Fitzgerald: Gentlemen, I regret to say that I cannot promise you Ireland's support in the League of Nations Debate on your boundary dispute with Bulgaria. That is my final decision.

General Debilite: At the risk of seeming irrelevant, I may mention that I have at present a couple of Afghan hounds and an ant-eater which I intend despatching either at once, or to the Dublin Zoological Gardens.

D. Fitzgerald (wavering): My decision is final.

Major Rubitin: And I have a couple of choice blue litmuses, which I am more or less at a loose end with.

D. Fitzgerald: Say no more . . . Deliver them immediately and I will try to do the same for your country.

Young animals

The Irish Lion Industry continued to flourish in the hands of keeper Christopher Flood and his son, Charles. In 1932, the council invited the popular Lord Mayor, Alfie Byrne, to name five cubs in the first ceremony of its kind. In the tradition of giving Irish names to Irish-born lions, the male cubs were named Baedan, Bricrui, Breas and Branach, and the female cub, Blanaid.[12] The council was now building up its tiger and leopard collection in the hope of establishing breeding groups of these animals. In 1932, there were four tigers and eight leopards in the collection, as well as sixteen lions. Most of these animals would have been housed in the Roberts House and would have been very expensive to feed. But still, only the lions bred.

Christopher Flood, the head lion keeper who had been with the Zoo since his father's

Christopher Flood with lion Jerry in 1907. The famous lion keeper died in 1933 after fifty-three years working in the Zoo.

tragic death in 1880, died in the Lion House in July 1933. He had been showing visitors around when he collapsed. His death was noted in the newspapers: 'the passing of Mr C. M. Flood, keeper of the Lion House at the Dublin Zoo, will be regretted by thousands all over the world,' said the *Sunday Independent*. 'Everyone who visited our Zoological Gardens and took an intelligent interest in its inmates knew Mr Flood. Two points in his character struck every visitors, his intense love for his charges and his pride in telling the visitor about them.' The report of his funeral included a long list of mourners.[13]

Scenes from the swimming gala in the Zoo lake in the 1920s.

The Zoo as an international swimming venue

In September 1923, Dublin Zoo hosted a major event when the Army swimming champ-ionships were held in the lake. A swimming gala had been held in the Zoo during the fete in 1919 but the events of the mid-1920s took on a new level of professionalism. In 1924, the Aonach Tailteann Games were held in the Zoo with athletes from Scotland, Wales, England and Australia as well as Ireland. The Zoo was closed for the duration of the games to all except Society members and those who paid in to see the swimming. The Tailteann Games committee paid a sum to cover the losses from normal gate revenue during what would be one of the Zoo's busiest weeks in the year.[14]

Later that year, and for the remainder of the 1920s, the Zoo was used frequently for swimming galas. The Army Athletic Association and the Gardaí held swimming practice, galas, diving competitions and water polo games there. The Leinster Amateur Swimming Association also used it for competitions. The Tailteann Games organisation's request to the council to maintain the diving platform and to play an active role in organising the swimming events was refused. The platform continued to be used for many years afterwards for pike fishing competitions and fly-fishing casting competitions.[15]

The parties

The success of the fetes of 1919 and 1920 inspired the council and the Ladies' Committee to continue the practice of having social events in the Zoo to raise much needed funds for animal accommodation and visitor facilities. The range and frequency of the parties increased and the breakfasts, garden parties and dances became fashionable events, which were reported in the media. In the 1930s, the garden parties were attracting more than 400 people, the dances about 800, while several hundred people attended the bridge tournaments and dinners. In 1932, the council decided to elect members of the diplomatic corps in Dublin as honorary, temporary members. Representatives from the United States, France, Germany, Argentina, Belgium, Canada, Italy and Great Britain were elected, as was the Papal Nuncio. The presence of foreign representatives at Zoo parties added a social layer to the events, which usually took place in and around marquees erected on the lawn outside Haughton House. Of course, the Zoo was still a venue for large and small events held by external individuals and organ-isations. In 1932, the Lord Mayor arranged a party in the Zoo for 4,500 children from schools all over the city. Bands, dancing and a gymnastic display by boys from the Artane school provided entertainment.

The Elephants

Sandari, the elephant that had been giving rides to children, died in 1930. An elephant had been acquired from Singapore in 1927 but died the same year. Dangiri Amma and Chanchal Perry, both females, were purchased in 1929 and 1932 respectively. In 1936 the Governor of Madras presented another elephant, a young female called Saraswathi, who became known to generations of children as Sarah. Soon after she arrived, Sarah damaged her house, broke down the doors and pulled down brickwork. Nevertheless, she turned into a most docile animal that could be relied on to give rides safely and patiently to children.[16]

The Zoo now had two spare elephants, at least one of which had a reputation for being temperamental. In 1938, Benjamin Ferrar, who had retired as superintendent earlier that year, brought some friends into the elephant house to see the animals. One of the elephants

James Kenny, *c.* 1936.

Dr Benjamin Ferrar, superintendent from 1911 to 1938, with a chimpanzee.

crushed him against the wall when she was turning around and broke several of his ribs.[17] The council barred anyone other than staff from entering the elephant house after that. James Kenny (senior) said that it would be very difficult to train anyone else to manage Dangiri Amma because of the risk of accident. The council were concerned about how the elephant could be managed in James Kenny's absence and in November 1939 decided to destroy her.

Making arrangements to shoot Dangiri took several months as the council and the army officer who was assisting could not agree on where she should be destroyed. The council wanted her shot in her house; the army officer wanted her to walk down to the lake to be shot where the high bank would be a safe background. A compromise was reached and sand bags were brought into the Zoo to create a background near the rabbit rockery. Cedric Flood, appointed superintendent in 1938, recommended that the second elephant be destroyed

1932 photograph of the staff. Front row (l–r): Jack Supple, Christopher Flood, James Kenny. Back row (l–r): Charles Flood, Joseph Rice, Tommy Kelly, Christopher Caffrey and Ernest Newsome.

at the same time. Word about the impending 'execution' of the animals leaked out. It was presumed that the decision had been made to get rid of two of the elephants because of the cost of feeding three of them. A Mr Dickson of Belfast Coalfields offered to take at least one of the elephants but suitable transport could not be arranged.[18] A letter-writer to *The Irish Times* encouraged the public to support Dangiri Amma with donations: 'she is not a very good tempered animal but yet on account of her clever tricks she is a great favourite'.[19] Another wrote, 'It is indeed tragic to see this gentle creature blissfully accepting pennies for plates of potatoes from her young admirers, whilst a few yards away the post is ready for her, complete with shooting platform and sandbags.'[20] It was also reported that a woman in Mount Merrion wanted to turn one of the elephants out to graze on half an acre of land at the back of her house, and a little boy in Stillorgan wanted to keep one as a pet.[21] In July 1940, both elephants were shot and no public statement was made. However a report in *The Irish Times* said:

> Dangiri Amma is dead! The news, in that form, may not convey anything to anybody, but in simpler terms it means that the large elephant at the Dublin Zoo, that majestic exile who for many a year has been the awe-inspiring joy of every youngster and has caused even the grown-ups to pause and brood on such immensity, is no longer with us . . . the death of an elephant is no ordinary event. It is like the removal of an imposing landmark, and the Dublin Zoo will not seem quite the same without Dangiri Amma . . . Her smile at a bag of buns was almost notorious![22]

James Kenny retired in 1940 and Jimmy Kenny, his son, succeeded him as the elephant keeper. Mr Kenny, as he was known to many young visitors, established a partnership with Sarah that was to surprise, delight and provide lasting memories to many Zoo visitors in the mid-twentieth century.

The superintendents

Dr Benjamin Ferrar retired in 1938. In 1925, he had been asked to act as secretary to the council and attend meetings.[23] This was an important development in terms of the management of the Zoo: the council was still making all of the decisions, great and small, about the running of the Zoo but now their senior manager was privy to their deliberations. Ferrar

Left: chimpanzee with Cedric Flood, superintendent from 1938 to 1952. Right: chimpanzee with Jack Supple and Cedric Flood.

was replaced briefly by Lieutenant Colonel A. G. Doherty who commenced in March 1938. Shortly afterwards he was given leave to travel to West Africa with the British Colonial Office on a project. Cedric Flood, who had also applied for the position when Ferrar retired, was asked to act as superintendent. The following year, in March 1939, Doherty resigned and Flood officially became superintendent.

Cedric Flood was an engineer who had spent many years managing tea plantations in Assam and Ceylon (now known as Sri Lanka). His dignified and well-dressed appearance, and his genial manner, made him a 'good mixer'. He encouraged casual visitors to become members, and provided the press with photo opportunities and stories about the animals. During his fourteen years as superintendent,

> A whole generation of Dublin children grew up, and Mr Flood was known and loved by many of them, even by those to whom the small charge for admission was a barrier, and who were forced to make unauthorised entry over the boundary railings. Mr Flood's kind heart would not allow him to take too strong action against the trespassers, who, provided they behaved themselves, were often allowed to remain in the grounds . . . Mr Flood could be seen walking with a chimpanzee by the hand as often as with a child, and when he entered the lion

house the lions would come to the fronts of their cages and rub their flanks against the bars so that Mr Flood could reach across and stroke them.[24]

Cedric Flood became the face of Dublin Zoo and, during this time, many stories appeared in the newspapers from the Zoo. Sometimes he was photographed with an animal; sometimes his assistant, Terry Murphy, who began working in the Zoo in 1944, featured in the photographs.

Staff relations

The continued popularity of the Zoo during the 1930s ensured that staff employment was not affected by the Great Depression. Visitor numbers remained fairly constant around the 150,000–170,000 mark, although this slipped to 126,000 in 1935. Yet the staff's working conditions had barely changed since the nineteenth century, despite the gesture made in 1913 to consider their conditions. In 1938, Cedric Flood informed the council that some employees had joined a trade union. They responded by ordering an investigation into staff wages, holidays and time. Within months, wages were increased, all keepers were given a half-day's leave each week and all employees allowed paid annual leave. Random bonus payments continued for busy weeks and successful breeding; in addition, the elephant-keeping staff were allowed to keep the money generated by the sale of buns and other food to the public for the elephant. In 1940, no pay increase was given but an emergency bonus was paid to help with the rising cost of living owing to the war.[25]

The start of the war

The Second World War affected Dublin Zoo immediately by cutting off access to new stock, and making food and fuel difficult to acquire. Stories from other zoos about having to destroy dangerous animals, and the destruction of zoos by warfare were noted in Dublin. The council hoped to use Ireland's neutrality to build up a fine collection of healthy animals so that they could help to restock overseas zoos at the end of the war. In the months after the declaration of war, several British zoos contacted Dublin to see if it would take some of their animals. In most cases, they wanted Dublin Zoo to pay for transport costs, which was not possible. The council was also concerned about the potential cost of feeding some of the larger animals and declined most of them.

Children's Corner

In 1940, Cedric Flood suggested that the camel house should be turned into a pet's corner where tame animals could be housed and children would 'be able to make friends, going amongst them without danger'. Children's Corner, sometimes called Pets' Corner, opened the following spring and remained open until autumn. The Children's Corner quickly established itself as a place where young children could interact with tame or domestic animals. Over the coming years, it became steadily more popular, despite the fact that there was a separate entrance fee to enter it. The stock changed each season, depending on what was available. Lambs, kid goats, rabbits, puppies, tortoises, and pigs were often there. Young raccoons that could not mix with the existing group were in Children's Corner one summer,[26] as were lion cubs when they were still small enough to be played with safely. Cedric Flood's daughter, Yvonne Ward, and Yvonne's half-sister, Peggy Shannon, managed the Children's Corner. The women were given Zoo overalls and permission to wear slacks. A teenage boy helped to keep houses, cages and enclosures clean and tidy.

Arrivals

As the war progressed, Irish people turned to the Zoo in the hope that they could leave their own pets with the Zoo staff to be cared for. Many budgerigars and parrots were donated or deposited in the Zoo as bird feed became very difficult to get. In 1941, one person donated twenty-six budgies; another donated twenty-four budgies and another fifteen. Many people donated pairs of budgies; the republican and statesman, Seán McBride, was amongst those who donated a single budgie. Tortoises, rabbits, goats, geese, badgers, and occasionally lizards, a chameleon, deer, lion cubs and monkeys were also donated. A most unusual donation was brought in by the tenor, Pat McCormac, in 1942. He arrived with a lion cub called Flame on a lead. The story was that Flame had been born on a stage in Leeds during an air raid and its mother had been killed. McCormac had rescued the tiny cub and fed it on Cow & Gate baby formula. When Flame was eight months old, McCormac brought her to Ireland, keeping her on the plane with him, then walking around Dublin city with her on a lead. Flame became a well-known lioness and bred her own young in October 1945.[27]

Bringing two lions together to mate was always problematic. The two animals to be mated would be put into adjoining cages in the lion house. If they were deemed compatible, they were put into the same cage and staff would stand by with a high-pressure fire hose to separate them if they started to fight. Terry Murphy described a typical scene:

Pat McCormac (left) with Flame, and Cedric Flood.

During mating, the male tends to grasp the female by the neck, holding her with his mouth. Afterwards, she jumps back and snarls at the male. If she has been roughly treated her response may be quite aggressive. The male runs off and the female will perhaps pounce a short distance after him and then give up. In the confined space of a cage the male has no retreat and a fight could break out – hence the hoses.[28]

In 1952, Flame died from dislocation of the neck, injuries received from lion Albert when she was introduced to him.[29]

The Lion Arena

During the early years of the war, Dublin Zoo was supported by government in terms of grants under unemployment schemes to renovate and build enclosures in the Zoo. Work undertaken included an open-air bear enclosure for the smaller bears, a seal pond (for which there were no seals yet), and an open-air, bar-less lion enclosure called the Lion Arena. So grateful was the council for the support of the government authorities that they considered naming a lion or tiger after Hugo Flynn, the parliamentary secretary, who was sympathetic to the needs of the Zoo. The parliamentary secretary responded by saying that he did not think it advisable to do that.[30]

The Lion Arena was a significant new development in terms of location, size and style. It was situated on the west side of the lake and was the first major bar-less exhibit in Dublin Zoo. The concept of using a moat to contain dangerous animals was developed in Germany in the late nineteenth century and had gradually spread around the world.[31] In 1939, the lion keeper Charles Flood had gone to see the lion enclosure in Edinburgh and returned with ideas for Dublin. The high wall at the back and sides of the exhibit was made from concrete and granite. A water-filled moat separated the lions' 'stage' from the wall behind which the visitors stood. Granite was used to hold up the retaining walls and renowned botanist, Robert Lloyd Praeger, a member of council and later president, planted the surrounds with shrubs.[32]

In August 1941, a pair of lions, Brennus and Noreen, were transferred to the Lion Arena.

Lions Laurie and Noreen in the new Lion Arena in 1941. Brennus, who was moved in with Noreen when the Lion Arena opened, drowned in the moat.

Brennus had been presented by Bristol Zoo in 1936 and Noreen had arrived from Chester Zoo in 1937. Both had lived in cages in the Roberts House since then. When they moved to the new exhibit, they were 'terrified on finding no obstacle between them and the public, or between them and the open sky'. Brennus was startled by a jackdaw and he jumped into the moat and drowned. Imitation railings were placed in the enclosure to help other lions adjust to their new environment.[33] The railings were gradually removed and the lions settled down. Caibre and Noreen mated and, in December 1941, Noreen had a female cub. The lions had proved once more that the change in venue within the Zoo did not interrupt their breeding.[34]

The bomb

On 31 May 1941, early in the morning, German bombs were dropped in Dublin, mostly on the North Wall, and thirty-seven people were killed. A bomb fell close to the Dog Pond in the Phoenix Park, 150 yards from the boundary. Michael Ward, who was living with his grandfather, Cedric Flood, in Society House in the Zoo, remembers the night vividly:

> I woke up when I heard the plane and shouted, 'that's a German plane'. I had lived in Heathfield in the South of England, which was known as 'Bomb Alley', before I was evacuated and I could easily identify a German plane. I went to wake my aunt, Peggy Shannon, in another bedroom and was standing beside her bed when the bomb exploded. Every pane of glass was blown out but all of the shutters were closed and they took the glass. No one was injured. The family were up like a shot and ushered down under the stairs. My grandfather took a gun and went outside with Peggy who was holding the torch. He was only worried about the wolves because they're scavengers and would vanish quickly. Lions and leopards would make for the open. But all was in good order. Not a pane of glass was broken in the Lion House.
>
> Next day, my grandfather noticed that the bison had charged the railings but not broken through. And Sarah [the elephant] had opened her door, gone down to the lake, and then returned to her house. We found her footprints and noticed that her door was open.[35]

In August, 1941, the council gave the Department of Defence an undertaking that all dangerous animals would be destroyed in case of emergency and cartridges for the rifle were made available.

Clockwise from top left: Michael Ward, older grandson of Cedric Flood; Patrick Ward, younger grandson of Cedric Flood; Peggy Shannon, aunt of Michael Ward, and co-manager of the original Children's Corner; Yvonne Ward, daughter of Cedric Flood, co-manager of original Children's Corner.

Clockwise from top: The tuatara from New Zealand, which lived in the Zoo 'for thirty years at the cost of two worms per week' died in 1941. It was stuffed and mounted and is currently in the director's office. Even then the tuatara was extremely rare in the wild and the council did not anticipate receiving another. Yet in 1963, the New Zealand Department of External Affairs presented a tuatara, which died in 1970; Queuing to get in, 1940s; Ice skating at the Zoo, 1940.

The war continues

Advertisements were put in the newspapers asking for donations of broccoli leaves, old cabbages, small apples and greens, to which many people responded. Gifts of condensed milk, tinned meat, pears, honey, peas, leeks, cheese, birdseed, white maize and acorns were also donated. Sources of hay fluctuated, as did the price. The supply of wheat stopped in 1941 and, later in the war, bread was strictly rationed. Licences were required for other supplies but the Department of Agriculture said that the Zoo could purchase barley and oats for use of animals without a licence.[36] Apple trees were planted in the Zoo to provide fruit for the animals and for use in tea rooms.

Meat for the carnivores was a constant problem and, in summer 1941, the council announced that they would have to destroy some of their animals if they could not get a supply of horseflesh. Shortly afterwards, the Zoo received permission to shoot a herd of wild goats at the Scalp outside Dublin and the Department of Lands sent carcases of deer to the Zoo. Donations of donkey, pony, horse and deer meat were received from private donors, and several property owners, including Kathleen Lawless of Newcastle, County Dublin, and Miss Tottenham of Ashford, County Wicklow, allowed the Zoo to kill deer on their properties.

More parties

The strange twist that characterised Dublin Zoo's experience of the Second World War was the huge increase in the number of people attending the breakfasts, dances, dinners, bridge parties and any other social event the council and the Ladies' Committee could find an excuse to organise. Haughton House provided some of the catering for the parties but outside caterers – often the Dolphin Hotel[37] – had to be used for major events. In 1940, 1,800 people attended the functions during fete week and 350 attending the members' breakfasts. The lake froze in January 1940 and the ice was measured at 3.5 inches deep. Ice skating for members was free of charge; their family and friends were charged two shillings and sixpence, and the general public were charged five shillings. Skating continued for five days and until 11.00 p.m. each evening with oil flares lighting up the lake. The refreshment room remained open for these hours also. The staff looked after the ice and provided refreshments and safety equipment.

Thousands of people attended the summer fetes, breakfasts, dances, dinners and other events. Many of the guests used taxis, cabs and horse-driven vehicles to get to the Zoo but for those who arrived on bicycles changing facilities were provided: the men were given a tent while the women could

Compilation of scenes of ice skating from *The Irish Times*, 23 January 1940.

change in Haughton House. Morning dress for council members at the garden parties was abandoned in 1941 but the women's fashions still attracted attention. In 1942, *The Irish Times* report about the garden party said,

> Fashions were mainly of the practical, tailored type. Many of the smartest women wore tailored suits of flannel or lightweight pastel-coloured tweed. Navy blue and white was a popular colour combination, many attractive ensembles in these shades being accompanied by little navy or white toques trimmed with veiling.[38]

Demand for tickets for all social events was such that, by 1944, tickets for the dance were issued to members of the Society only.

The numbers of ordinary visitors who came to look at the animals, ride on the ponies or the elephant and have tea in Haughton House also increased dramatically during the war years as fuel restrictions limited the number of recreational activities available to Dubliners. In 1943, more than 250,000 people visited the Zoo and the annual number has never dropped below that since then. The increased numbers put great strain on the catering services in Haughton House and it was often full to capacity. Fortunately the entire building was now devoted to catering; in 1938, a blind kangaroo, which had been kept in the cage on the ground floor of Haughton House, died and the cages were dismantled. The Veranda Cafe opened there in 1939.

In January 1942, Haughton House provided a 'delicious tea for 1s 6d [which] included hot scones, home-made jams, and assorted pastries, and was served in pleasant proximity to the new log burning fireplace, where a huge fire roared defiance at the iciness outside'.[39] Four-course lunches were also available, which was a considerable feat on the part of the manageress, Ella Murphy, who ran the restaurant from 1940 until 1943. In February 1942, a notice was put up in the members' room that, owing to gas rationing, the gas fire would not be lit but tables near the fire in the large tea room would be reserved for them. In 1943 she informed the council that it would be impossible to cater for large parties, such as a special tea for the Engineering and Scientific Association. Parties of more than fifteen now had to get special permission from the council.

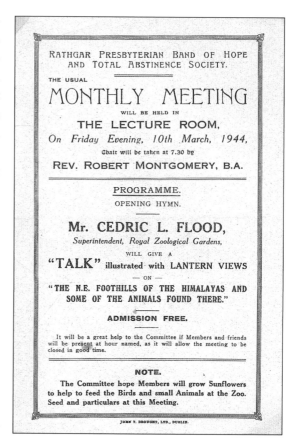

RATHGAR PRESBYTERIAN BAND OF HOPE AND TOTAL ABSTINENCE SOCIETY.

THE USUAL

MONTHLY MEETING

WILL BE HELD IN

THE LECTURE ROOM,

On Friday Evening, 10th March, 1944,

Chair will be taken at 7.30 by

REV. ROBERT MONTGOMERY, B.A.

PROGRAMME.

OPENING HYMN.

Mr. CEDRIC L. FLOOD,

Superintendent, Royal Zoological Gardens,

WILL GIVE A

"TALK" illustrated with LANTERN VIEWS

— ON —

"THE N.E. FOOTHILLS OF THE HIMALAYAS AND SOME OF THE ANIMALS FOUND THERE."

ADMISSION FREE.

It will be a great help to the Committee if Members and friends will be present at hour named, as it will allow the meeting to be closed in good time.

NOTE.

The Committee hope Members will grow Sunflowers to help to feed the Birds and small Animals at the Zoo. Seed and particulars at this Meeting.

JOHN T. DROUGHT, LTD., DUBLIN.

Notice of a lecture by Cedric Flood. He was a keen photographer and a large collection of his glass slides remains in the Dublin Zoo archive.

Breakfast with the council

In February 1942, a journalist from the *Evening Herald* attended a council breakfast and left wondering how he could become a member of the group. There was a blazing fire in the council room as the men stood and ate 'a bowl of as nicely-cooked porridge as ever I tasted'. The reporter had made the mistake of sitting down to eat his porridge but his host 'murmured in an undertone that it was the custom of the council to take their porridge standing and, slightly embarrassed, I corrected my gaffe'. The porridge was followed by eggs, bacon, sausage and thinly sliced black pudding. At the end of breakfast he withdrew and sat by a fire in another room while the council got on with business.[40] If it was not possible to cook breakfast for a council meeting because of gas restrictions, a cold meal was served instead.

Elephant Sarah, 1945.

Sarah the elephant

Sarah was the star of the Zoo during the war. Under the control of Jimmy Kenny, she gave rides, ate buns, knelt, raised her trunk, lifted her leg, played a mouth organ and stood by patiently as visitors had their photograph taken beside her. In 1941, Sarah developed severe problems with her feet and rides had to be discontinued until she recovered. She received a regular pedicure from Jimmy Kenny and grooves were put in the concrete floor of the elephant house in the hope of easing the pressure on her feet but it was not enough. A set of boots was made for her by Wilson of Capel Street with leather uppers and iron soles. According to *The Irish Times*, her boots 'make a noise like that of a weary labourer in hob-nailers crossing a cobbled street'.[41]

However, the boots were expensive, costing £14 a set, and they were rapidly frayed on the hard path near the elephant house where she walked up and down with children on the howdah on her back. In 1942, Cedric Flood managed to get five tons of turf mould, which was spread to a depth of several inches along 200 yards of path directly beside the lake. The elephant rides remained by the lakeside until they officially ended in the late 1950s.

At Zoological Garden Party

Jimmy Kenny with Sarah.

Post-war

A huge party was held in the Zoo to celebrate the end of the war and, according to Michael Ward, it went on all night. All staff were given an extra day's pay in anticipation of the crowds expected on 29 June 1945 on the day of National Thanksgiving. In May 1945, an acknowledgement was sent to Dr Hempel, formerly German Minister to Ireland, who resigned his honorary membership because his mission had been terminated. In November 1945, the council deferred their discussion as to whether to admit the Czechoslovak consul as an honorary temporary member of the Society until some research had been carried out.[42] In 1946, the Czech consul was among the 1,200 guests at the June garden party. The dance was hugely popular; Hugh Brett, a *Sunday Independent* reporter, managed to get tickets for the dance in 1946 and described the scene:

> Any husband who wanted to convey bright news to his wife last week had only to tell her that he had two of the coveted tickets. I met a bookmaker who told me he had offered a pony[43] for four tickets, but there were no takers. If the Zoo people had decided to black market the tickets themselves, he hated to think of the extra monkeys they might have collected. We had a whale of a time. I enjoyed particularly the two speciality dances, the camel dance, Humps-a-daisy and the Llamabeth [sic] walk . . . It was novel going round the houses in the Gardens at night-time. 'Any water?' said the parrot. 'Any whiskey?' riposted a sarcastic bystander.[44]

The problems with supplies for the restaurant and the animals continued for some time after the war. Eleanor French, who was now manageress of Haughton House, was having severe difficulty providing the level of service that was being demanded of the restaurant. In April 1946, she told the council that the lack of cold storage was creating waste meat and ice cream; it was impossible to know how much of either was required and, without cold storage, either some would go to waste or there would not be enough on the day. She said that the ice cream wafers were being lost through contamination by mice, that the Zoo's sweet and biscuit rations were too small to be of any use, and that she had no time or transport to get to the market for fruit. Gas restrictions were hampering her use of ovens so the hot scones were only available in quantity at tea time and even then, it took twenty minutes to make forty scones provided the turf was dry and the wind was blowing in the right direction. This made an average of 140 teas a day but often there was a demand for 300 teas. She said that

she was getting less sugar in 1946 than in 1940: advertisements for members' breakfasts in the Zoo had been carrying the message 'No sugar will be supplied' since 1945. She wrote to the council:

> Everything depends on sugar. Without it we cannot hope to make money or keep our popularity. Far too much time is taken up in never ending search for butter, margarine (last season we were getting up to 20 lbs, this season nil), sugar and other essential foods which we are denied owing to lack of custom prior to 1940.[45]

Her level of frustration was evident when she completed her list of requirements with the message, 'some of these need immediate attention; but as things are at present, it is not always easy to obtain from the members of the committee the necessary advice on the action to be taken'. The council responded by refusing a request for a children's party with twenty guests, then turned their attention to the need for more attendants at the garden party and additional mirrors for the ladies' changing room. Eleanor French soldiered on, making do with limited supplies.[46]

In 1947, the council announced,

> In view of the critical position of the country with regard to food and fuel the council felt that they would lay the Society open to charges of irresponsibility if the Annual Fete was held under such circumstances, and it was with great regret that they decided not to hold a fete in 1947.[47]

The lack of fuel threatened the health of the valuable animals.[48] The council was forced to apply to the Office of Public Works for permission to chop down trees to provide fuel. Lloyd Praeger identified forty-seven trees that could be felled. They still had to pay the Office of Public Works for the fuel as if it had been purchased from an outside source. Even with that number of trees, there was still not enough fuel for winter and a further twenty-two trees were marked for felling but a month later, November 1947, the council got permission to buy some coal.

In 1947 the pressure of making ends meet prompted the council to increase the adults' entrance fee, which had not changed since 1872, from one shilling to one shilling and sixpence. Children remained at sixpence but all half-price days were abolished.[49] A great tradition had ended but the visitors continued to pour into the Zoo as the numbers consistently passed the 300,000 mark. The following year, the council was able to distribute electricity to the animal houses.

The fete, dance and other parties returned again in 1948 and were more popular than ever. By now tickets were rationed to members and causing some anxiety. The Ladies' Committee and the council received a large allowance each and this may have been what prompted a Society member to write to the council in July 1948 protesting about the allocation of dance tickets and tendering her resignation. A few months later, another member sent in his subscription but said that he was joining only on condition that he would receive dance tickets for the annual dance.[50]

Post-war: restocking the Zoo

During the years following the end of the war, zoos around the world were attracting greater numbers of visitors than ever before and major expeditions were organised to capture wild

animals to restock these zoos. Dublin received many offers of animals from abroad but, owing to lack of transport, quarantine restrictions and, of course, the usual lack of money, it could purchase only a few animals. The hope that Dublin might become a source of stock after the war was not realised and even the stock of lion cubs was low. In 1947, the first consignment of animals to arrive to Dublin Zoo by air flew into Shannon from New York and included two chimps; the council noted that it was an expensive way to transport animals but that they had arrived in perfect condition. Sea lions also arrived by air and a new sea lion pool was created at the upper end of the lake, transforming this previously neglected part of the Zoo. The old sea lion enclosure was adapted for beavers and otters.

In winter 1947, fifty-six birds were poisoned by bread soaked in strychnine over a two-week period. The poisoned bread had been scattered along the margin of the lower lake where it had been accessible from the public road. Wildfowl had also been poisoned in the nearby People's Garden. Shortly afterwards, poison from coal stored in an area of the Phoenix Park some distance from the Zoo drained into the lakes after some heavy rain. The lake began to change colour to a rich brownish red and there was no hope of improving this situation until the coal was removed from the Park. The sea lion pond was affected and they stopped eating. They were moved to a small enclosure but it was too late and two of them died. The third did not eat for fifty-four days but began to recover once it started eating again. There was no question of returning it to the sea lion pond until the contamination had ceased or until a by-pass around the pond was constructed to control the water inflow. The surviving sea lion was sent to Chester Zoo.[51]

Tuberculosis

Even as animals were arriving from abroad, a major problem arose with an outbreak of tuberculosis in the Roberts House and the monkey house. Several primates had died of the

Left: Paddy O'Brien, 1947. 'On my first day at work, the superintendent told me to feed the sealions. I was scared – I had never seen a sea lion in my life before!' Right: Sarah being 'interviewed' in January 1948.

Miss Manders, a
member and regular
visitor, with
chimpanzees in the
monkey house.

infectious disease in 1923 and again in 1940. At the time, all the cages in the monkey house
were disinfected and feeding utensils were sterilised. In 1943, a tiger, which the Zoo had
received from the Bertram Mills Circus, died of TB and a lion died of advanced TB the
following year. Any animal in the lion house showing any sign of 'wasting without apparent
cause' was to be destroyed.[52]

The chimpanzees and monkeys were, of course, among the most popular of the animals
and any danger to their health was serious. The *Carlow Nationalist* described a typical scene
in its 'Dublin Diary':

> Saturday afternoon finds us at the Zoo paying our respects to the tenants of the
> monkey-house. . . . The citizens gathered around Charlie's apartment wear the
> unmistakeable aspect of persons waiting for something to happen. What precisely
> they are waiting for is not quite clear. At the moment Charlie does not seem to
> be doing anything besides squatting on the floor of his cage, huge and gross and

jolly, like a mediaeval baron recovering from a seven-day binge. Then someone, a small character in a seedy waterproof says, 'Give him a cigarette . . . We light a cigarette and heave it into the cage. It drops at the feet of Charlie who betrays only the faintest flicker of interest. The small character in the seedy waterproof emphasises the cigarette by poling at it with a stick. His attention thus engaged, Charlie allows a monstrous finger to fall athwart the cigarette which he rolls back and forth until the glowing cinder is barely visible.[53]

In November 1946, the keepers began to suspect that both Charlie and Susie, the other popular chimp who had been 'taught by the children of Dublin to spit',[54] might be suffering from TB. A glass screen was put outside their cages to protect them from germs. A disinfectant was sprayed, the cages were scrubbed out with boiling water and washing soap to dissolve grease, then sprayed with hot Lysol or Dettol. Where possible, a blowtorch was turned on bars, doors and all other ironwork in the cages. Isolation houses were provided away from the public and steps were taken to check whether, firstly, the type of TB was human or bovine, and then to test each monkey in the monkey house. Arrangements were also made for employees to have their chests x-rayed.

In the case of Charlie and Susie, these measures were to no avail. Charlie died and Susie was destroyed. When the Siamang gibbon showed signs of the same illness, the monkey house was closed to the public. None of the Society's official reports or the media mentioned the dreaded tuberculosis but referred to it as an 'outbreak of sickness' caused by poor diet over many years, lack of sunshine during the past summer and the impossibility of maintaining a suitable temperature in the house in the late autumn. By coincidence, in the same month, a new, comprehensive tuberculosis scheme was announced by the Minister for Local Government and Public Health. In January 1947, two more monkeys were destroyed and the council considered destroying the remaining animals in the monkey house. A report in *The Irish Times* said that because of,

an overdose of the wrong type of food, provided by thoughtless visitors, the monkeys in the Dublin Zoo . . . are at present languishing in loneliness behind closed doors. Most of the animals have been sick recently, and in no mood to perform their normal antics. During their enforced solitude an opportunity is being taken to extend their enclosure and provide them with more space for fun and frolics when they have recovered from their illness.[55]

In the end, the green monkey was destroyed and the sooty mangabey, who was about twenty years old and 'on being offered food, turns a somersault,[56] died after the TB test. They considered vaccinating the remaining monkeys with the BCG. More monkeys died and those monkeys that showed no sign of TB in a test were removed before any new monkeys were brought into the monkey house.[57] TB then appeared in the Roberts House where a leopard died of the disease. A gibbon and two more monkeys died but the worst of it was over for the present. A big collection of animals was received in spring 1948 and all the monkeys were given a clean bill of health.

Stories from the Zoo

During the post-war period, Dublin Zoo became a regular source of material for Brian O'Nolan, who wrote the 'Cruiskeen Lawn' column in *The Irish Times* under the name Myles Na gCopaleen. 'Irishman's Diary', written under the name Quidnunc, also featured the Zoo periodically. In April 1946, Quidnunc was visiting the Zoo with a party including Sybil le Brocquy and her son, the artist, Louis. A visiting English writer called William Corp and an American journalist for *Harper's Bazaar* called Helen Strudwick were also in the group. While Louis le Brocquy and William Corp, 'in holiday mood, are speaking of existentialism', Quidnunc was talking to Helen Strudwick:

> I tell Miss Strudwick that this particular lion is stuffed. The live ones are inside in the den and only come out when the crowds have gone. Miss Strudwick says: 'But look, he's breathing.' I tell her that the effect is achieved by an internal bellows, worked by electricity. I am becoming a little light-headed, what with the heat and the holiday mood . . . We pass by the pond in which Slinky, the seal, once used to leap and play. There is a notice on the railings, a photograph of Slinky and the words: 'Slinky is dead, killed by a . . .' and there, stuck on the notice, is a small, actual nut. Mrs le Brocquy says to Miss Strudwick: 'that is the nut that Slinky swallowed. They recovered it afterwards.' Miss Strudwick accepts this so patiently that I begin to wonder whether she believed the bit about the lion with the internal bellows.[58]

The le Brocquy family were long-term members of the Zoo. In her biography of Louis le Brocquy, Anne Madden relates a startling tale about Sybil le Brocquy's father, Peter Maurice

ZOOLOGICAL GARDENS, PHŒNIX PARK, DUBLIN .
Guide to Grounds

Main Lake

Entrance

New features :

Waders' Pool at North
end of main lake near
bridge (24)

Night Heron Enclosure
near Sea-lion pond (21)

de Lacy Staunton, who died in 1946. In his old age, Staunton visited the Zoo where he
engaged in one of the traditional activities of feeding penny buns to the elephant with the
assistance of the keeper.[59] The routine was that the visitor would place the penny on a bar
from which the elephant could lift it with its trunk, and pass it to the keeper. However,
when the keeper left the enclosure to get some more buns, Peter Staunton put the penny
on a difficult corner of the crossbar to test Sarah's intelligence:

> Annoyed and frustrated, the huge animal backed his bulk towards 'Pop', who in
> turn backed into the corner of the cage, terrified, pressing himself into it, mak-
> ing himself as inaccessible as he could while the elephant swayed back and forth,
> one, two, three, boom-si-day with apparent nonchalance but in fact with the
> intention of crushing him. The corner of the cage being narrower than the great
> backside, 'Pop' Staunton was barely saved before the keeper's return pacified the
> infuriated mammoth.[60]

A 1949 map of
the Zoo.

Fingers and the primates

Michael Clarke began working in the Zoo in 1949, first as a member of the ground staff, and then as a keeper in the monkey house. He remembers a woman who sat outside the Zoo entrance with a sign saying, 'Peanuts for the monkey'; children bought nuts and, once inside the Zoo, pushed them through the chain-link fence at the monkeys with their fingers. Small fingers, however, were at risk from the sharp teeth of the animals. In 1943, a young girl lost the first joint of her finger, which had to be amputated after Susy the chimp bit it. In 1948, an eight-year-old girl had her second finger badly bitten by a rhesus monkey. In 1949, a three-year-old crawled under the barrier rail in the monkey house to feed the capuchins

Mary, 1940,
'52 years at the gate'.

and the top of the child's finger was bitten off, and that same month a Glasgow visitor had his index finger lacerated when he was petting the white-handed gibbon. A few months earlier, an eleven-year-old girl had the top of her index finger bitten off by a rhesus monkey when she tried to burn its nose with a cigarette. Each case was referred to the insurance company and railings were raised a little higher or extra chain-link fence installed.[61]

Royal Zoological Society

On Easter Monday 1949, the Republic of Ireland was formally inaugurated by the Taoiseach, John A. Costello, and was no longer part of the Commonwealth. In December, Frank Aiken, a senior member of the Fianna Fáil party (then in opposition) asked the Taoiseach whether organisations using the word 'royal' would be asked to drop that word from their titles before the estimates for the coming financial year were completed. Costello replied that he

Clockwise from top:
Entrance gate, late
1940s; 'Grandad's day
out', late 1940s. In
the monkey house;
another view of the
monkey house,
later 1940s. It was
transformed into the
South America House
in 1990–91.

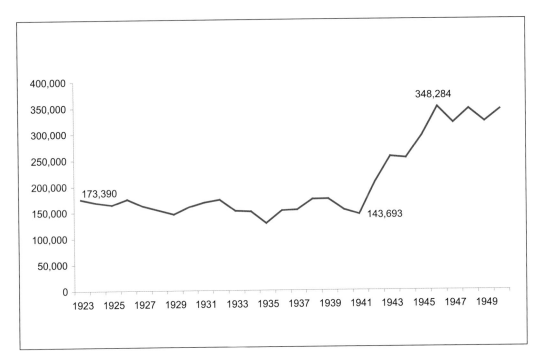

400,000

350,000

300,000

250,000

200,000   173,390

150,000

100,000

50,000

0

348,284

143,693

1923 1925 1927 1929 1931 1933 1935 1937 1939 1941 1943 1945 1947 1949

Visitor numbers
1923-1949.

would not be putting any of them under pressure to do so. At this stage the Royal Zoological Society of Ireland was receiving an annual grant of £1,000. Frank Aiken was not satisfied with Costello's response and he asked,

> Is the Taoiseach aware that there is a certain resentment in the country that organisations drawing monies from the public purse should continue to use these descriptions? Even *The Irish Times* has dropped from the Court and Personal column the Royal Coat of Arms, and what is good enough for them should be good enough for the Taoiseach.[62]

TD Con Lehane of Clann na Poblachta joined in:

> Is the Taoiseach aware that the retention of this objectionable anachronism is motivated by a desire on the part of these organisations to parade their hostility to the aspirations of the majority of the people and will the Taoiseach at least make

it plain that they will not be permitted to cock a snook at the people while at the same time accepting a subsidy from them?

To which Costello replied:

> The view I take of this word 'royal' is that it is a historical evolution of our own country . . . I regard this word 'royal' as a matter of no significance or importance, and not worth wasting time over.

And that was the end of that matter, as far as Dublin Zoo was concerned, for another forty-five years.

CHAPTER 5

GROWTH AND DECLINE 1950–1980

Introduction

This was a period of redefinition and change in the international zoo world but in Dublin the constant need to raise funds made implementation of new ideas very difficult. Arising out of the need to rebuild so many zoos and the demand for wildlife in the post-war years, zoo professionals developed international networks to cooperate rather than compete with each other.[1] They explored the rationale for having zoos and identified four objectives: education, animal conservation, research and recreation. The extent to which individual international zoos explored innovative ways of developing these objectives depended on their management and resources but Dublin Zoo's resources were extremely limited and it was slow to respond to these changes. However, visitor numbers and membership climbed steadily during this period and even the economic hardship in Ireland in the 1950s and 1970s did not halt this growth. New, exotic animals were acquired and there were numerous opportunities to interact with animals. Similarly the number of parties, dances, breakfasts, bridge parties and other events for members and their friends increased. The council worked hard to meet the needs of both the ordinary visitors and the visitors who were attending social events. This left little time to address the challenges set by the global zoo community and, as a result, modernising to international standards did not become a prominent part of the council's agenda during this period.

Aerial photo of the Zoo from the south, 1950.

The day out

Membership rose steadily throughout the 1950s from 1,713 members including life members to 3,302 in 1960. This was despite a falling national population owing to widespread un-employment and mass emigration.[2] Some of the new members would have been attracted by access to dance tickets but there was a growing number of members who wanted family access to the Zoo all year around.[3] In 1955, the 'Irishman's Diary' in *The Irish Times* stated:

> It was good to hear that membership of the Society has risen sharply in the last few months. None of the Council members knew why, but it seems most likely that the advantages of membership, especially to family men, provide the answer. Like the fine for pulling a railway communication cord, membership of the Zoological Society offers extremely good value at pre-war prices.[4]

For £1 as a joining fee and £2 per annum, members, their families and 'domestic servants' were entitled to free admission all year around except on special occasions, such as when

Clockwise from top left: Bubbles (left) and unidentified pony with, from left, Sheila, Patricia and Olwyn Lanigan in the Zoo in 1961. The Lanigans were family members from 1955; Tiny the pony, carrying Michael de Courcy in 1956 with his father, Sean de Courcy, family members from 1955, and an unidentified 'pony boy'. Tiny was a gentle, docile pony while Little Ginger, the pony walking away from the picture, was more contrary and better suited to older children. The boiler suits worn by the pony boys were changed for jackets in late 1950s; Group picture of the ponies and the 'pony boys', c. 1960. Most of the pony boys lived locally and came in at weekends to help out. Ponies (l–r): Fanny, Betsy, Blackberry, May Blossom, Dot, Tiny and Bubbles. Identifiable staff members include Seamus Stone (back row, right), head stable man Paddy Mahon (standing, left), Charlie Stone, Gerry Creighton (senior), Frank Burke and Derek Murphy (fourth, fifth, sixth and seventh from left, front row); Fanny the pony with Lonan McDowell, family member from 1962.

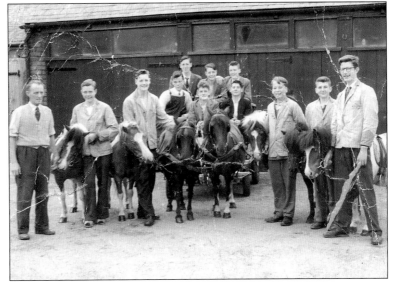

ice skating was possible. Each member was given free vouchers for elephant rides, the children's corner, and pony or carriage rides. Members could also buy books of tickets for their friends at a generous discount and could hold parties in the members' area of Haughton House.[5] By now, the Zoo had become a very popular place for birthday parties or for First Holy Communion celebrations. Of course, the tradition of children finding their own way into the Zoo without being noticed continued and enthusiastic youngsters managed to find a way over the fence, slip through the turnstile or attach themselves to members' families. Martyn Linnie, now Chief Technical Officer and Curator of the Zoological Museum in Trinity College used to make his own way to the Zoo from Walkinstown:

> I was passionate about animals as a little boy and my favourite way to get into the Zoo at the time was to go under the stile when people were paying their money.

I was only ten or eleven at the time and I would walk or cycle to the Zoo. I sometimes went in through a gap in the fence. The lads in the Zoo would seal it up and then I would have to find another gap. Mostly I would go on my own; sometimes I went with other kids. Once I went through a gap, through the shrubbery and then over another fence and found myself in with the cheetahs! If I couldn't get in, I'd walk around the outside of the Zoo and look at the animals from there.

Tommy the croc was one of my favourite animals. He was enormous. And he ended up here [in the Zoological Museum, Trinity College Dublin]. We put him in a Hiace van and drove him down the quays. He was so large and rigid that his tail stuck out the back.[6]

Cheetah with visitor and keeper William Brophy.

Terry Murphy

Terry Murphy was appointed superintendent in December 1956, succeeding Cecil Webb who had held the position since 1952. Murphy had been employed in the Zoo since 1944. In 1956 he travelled with council members to the Netherlands, Belgium and Denmark to develop contacts and look at exhibits. He also managed to get the rat problem in the Zoo under control and he had written the *Official Guide to the Dublin Zoo*.[7] He continued the easy relationship that Cedric Flood had built up with the media and, when RTÉ television began to broadcast in 1962, Terry Murphy pursued ways of using it to promote wildlife and the animals in the Zoo. His great love of animals and the enthusiasm with which he spoke about them brought the Zoo and the animals to a national audience.

Brown bears in the bear pit, with the Pelican bridge visible in the background.

In 1960 Terry Murphy went to Africa with two members of the council where they covered 6,000 miles and made contact with game wardens with a view to purchasing larger animals. They made a film of the trip called *Not Ours To Keep*, which was shown in the Rupert Guinness Hall in St James' Gate nearby. Demand for tickets was so great that copies of the film were made for distribution to schools and other public bodies. In 1964, he appeared on television several times to talk about wildlife and the animals in the Zoo. This was the first of many television appearances by Murphy. Any fear that film and television would reduce the interest in zoos proved false as visitor numbers surged after each broadcast.

Parties for adults

The social events for adults of the early 1950s continued the trend set in the previous decade. The members' breakfasts were held in the summer months and the annual fete included a garden party, a dance, a dinner and a bridge tournament with at least sixty tables. Tickets for the dance were allocated at two to a member and only journalists from the magazine *Social and Personal* were invited. In 1954, for example, nearly 3,000 people attended functions during Fete Week in June.[8] Everything was organised by the Ladies' Committee, which was composed mainly of wives of council members. Sweets, cigarettes and food for the animals were sold and raffles held. It made a profit of nearly £1,000, matching the government grant. Events were held in the marquee and a portable dance floor, owned by the Society, was laid down.[9]

Each year, the Ladies' Committee met in spring to organise the forthcoming social season. Refinements for the smooth running of the events were arranged, tasks such as the floral arrangements allocated, catering facilities discussed and prizes for the raffles organised. In 1959, for example, prizes included dinner for two, a bottle of whiskey or a quarter ton of coal. In 1957, fork suppers for members and their guests on summer evenings were added to the list of functions. In 1958, the council considered holding a second dance to cater for demand but decided not to do so for the time being, for fear that it might undermine the prestige of the dance. No such fear got in the way in the following years as the number of dances held each year escalated.

Dublin Zoo's social events were an organisational success with few, if any, complaints. Perhaps because of the success of the parties, the Zoo became known as a place for private and business parties. One of the largest of these parties was held in 1958 when 5,000 women from many countries attended the Mothers'

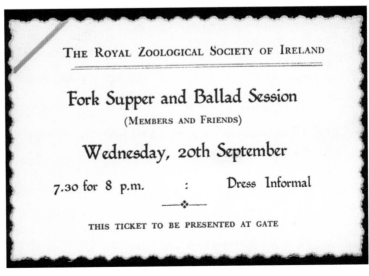

Ticket for one of the many social functions in the mid-twentieth century.

THE ROYAL ZOOLOGICAL SOCIETY OF IRELAND

Fork Supper and Ballad Session
(MEMBERS AND FRIENDS)

Wednesday, 20th September

7.30 for 8 p.m.   :   Dress Informal

THIS TICKET TO BE PRESENTED AT GATE

Clockwise from top left: Free-range Canada goose and young visitor; Sarah the elephant with Rose McGrath and son Conor, mother Mrs Howard (centre) and aunt Mrs Fotterall. Tom McGrath, electrician, plumber and general maintenance man from 1953 until he retired in 2001, said, 'Jimmy Kenny would say to Sarah "up Sarah up", and as Sarah held her pose for two to three minutes, the visitors would stand close to her for the photo. It was a real treat and only done on special occasions.'; Members and friends ice skating, 1963.

Union Garden Party; the scale of the event put the Zoo under great pressure, particularly with regard to toilet facilities. Tom McGrath, an electrician who maintained the Zoo's facilities for many decades, said there were very few toilets in the Zoo at the time:

> There was one at the gate, one at the restaurant, one at the back of Pets' Corner and one near the elephant house. I was a member of An Óige and, on my suggestion, we put up a marquee with a trench and plywood with holes.[10]

In March 1955, there had been the suggestion of making the members' toilets for ladies in Haughton House available to the general public and in 1956, Bord Fáilte financed new toilet facilities in the Zoo. However, by 1964 at the annual general meeting, a question was raised about the condition of the toilets in Haughton House 'which appear to be used by non-members'.[11] The shortage of adequate facilities for the large visitor population remained unresolved for some years.

Being unable to provide non-members with alcohol was causing constant frustration to the council as they repeatedly attempted to get a full bar licence. The Zoo had a club licence, which allowed alcohol to be served to members and their guests; they also had a dozen bar extension licences a year, which had to be allocated carefully to ensure that the Zoo's own social functions could continue late into the night. But they could not get a full bar licence because the population in the licensing area had not increased enough for an additional one to be granted and they lost numerous functions as a result.[12]

Chimpanzee tea parties

In 1950, the council introduced the chimpanzee tea parties. The four young chimpanzees selected for the performance:

> proved to be delightful and intelligent little creatures, and soon adapted themselves to the 'tea party'. Watching them during this performance one is struck by the fact that they appear to enjoy the 'party' as much as the thousands of children that have delighted in the chimpanzee's antics every day during the summer season.'[13]

The chimpanzees were managed by Jack Supple. Prior to this, he had often wandered around with young chimpanzees and mingled with visitors. The tea parties were a more formal

Clockwise from top: Chimpanzee tea party; Chimpanzee tea party with cross bars at the base to prevent the chairs from toppling over; Jack Supple and Johnny the chimpanzee.

occasion and were held at a pre-arranged time on the lawn near the monkey house. Michael Clarke, a keeper who worked with Jack Supple, said that the table and chairs were set up and the chimpanzees were taken out of the house and over to the table:

> At first, the 'party' took place behind a wire fence but then it moved to the lawn and the crowds would sit in a wide circle around the table. The chimps would

pick at the fruit and play with the mugs. They were never hungry so it was impossible to get them to eat. After a while, the keepers would take the chimpanzees around and allow the children to touch them or have their photograph taken with them. If they were frisky, a collar and chain would be put on them and they would be hooked to a chair; they often hopped down and dragged the chair along.[14]

The chimpanzees were sometimes dressed in bonnets, frilly dresses or dungarees and T-shirts and large nappies, and children watched in delight as they tipped the cups upside down, played with their food, threw things at each other and generally behaved in a way that children were not supposed to. Some adults were not comfortable with this performance. 'There were complaints with some people suggesting it was a form of abuse,' said Michael Clarke, 'but the chimps looked forward to it, they wanted to get out.'[15] The routine was so successful that Chipperfield, the British animal dealership, offered to rent the chimpanzees and their tea party for six weeks; the council refused. As visitor figures climbed and interest in the tea party increased, semi-permanent barriers and chairs were provided on the lawn for warm days.[16]

The difficulty with the chimpanzee tea parties was that the animals could only be used for these events when they were young and safe to have around children. As soon as they grew too big, they were confined to their enclosure. Nevertheless the council decided that, rather than breed chimpanzees, they would maintain a stock of young chimpanzees for the

Left: Chimpanzee playing with a tricycle; Right: chimpanzee exhibit, which was formerly the bear pit, with Haughton House visible behind it.

Frank Burke and Bill Thompson killing the weeds on the lawn in front of the entrance, 1960.

tea parties and put them on the market when they could no longer be used for that purpose.[17] Two young chimpanzees were brought over to Dublin on trial from the Netherlands but 'did not appear to have the disposition suitable for the 'Tea Party', and it was decided to return them.[18]

Superintendent Terry Murphy suggested that an outdoor exhibit should be created for the chimpanzees, because it would be healthier for them and they might breed. In 1965, the chimpanzees were transferred to the former polar bear pit on the slope between Haughton House and the lake. It had been used more recently for the rhesus monkeys. When the pit was remodelled for the chimpanzees, the wall on the lakeside was removed and a moat was used to contain them. Roses were planted around the top and front of the chimpanzee enclosure and an electric fence was installed.[19]

By the time a young chimpanzee was born in 1974 the tea parties had come to a halt.[20] In 1973 the council had considered re-establishing them but decided against it because there was no longer a market for animals that were too old to be used for this purpose. In 1983, when the council was struggling desperately to find ways of raising funds, the idea of a chimpanzee tea party was suggested once more but quickly dropped as running contrary to present sensitivity of animal exploitation.[21]

Giraffes

Three giraffes arrived in 1951. They had been held up in London for eighteen months because the Irish Department of Agriculture was concerned about the possibility of the hoofed animals bringing in foot-and-mouth disease. A young giraffe was born in 1954. It died soon afterwards but the staff gained valuable birthing experience. The next birth, on 12 August 1955, required staff intervention. The following account was recorded in the council's minutes:

> Front legs appeared about 10.45 a.m. Mr Cosgrove [veterinary surgeon] was sent for. At 11.45 (approx.) no progress had been made and it was decided to assist by attaching ropes to feet. After some delay ropes were successfully applied and after long and strenuous pulling the head appeared. As the result of four men pulling their hardest calf eventually came away at 12.45 p.m. 'Bashful' not affected by birth and immediately mothered the newly-born calf.[22]

She was named Happy in a ceremony involving the unveiling of a plaque on her cage. Another calf, named Dopey, was born in 1957, and two more calves were born in 1959. One

Left: Giraffes, Bashful (left) and Doc, and visitors. Right: Staff, July 1964. Front row (l–r): Paddy Whelan, Joe Smart, Bob O'Neill. Middle row (l–r): John O'Connor (senior), Tommy Kelly, Michael Clarke, Tommy Conlon, Danny Gannon, Head keeper Martin Reid. Back row (l–r): Gerry Creighton (senior), Tommy O'Halloran, Matt Wilson, Charlie Stone.

Bashful (left) and Happy. Photograph by Douglas Duggan: 'I spent three days waiting to get a good photo of Happy and just as I was about to take the shot, a small girl walked into the picture.'

died and the other was exchanged for two young Bactrian camels. When Doc, one of the giraffes which arrived in 1951, died in 1960, he had sired nine calves in his nine years in the Zoo.[23]

Hippopotami

In 1953, Dublin Zoo decided to purchase a hippo or a rhinoceros and in 1957, following the sale of a young giraffe, they had enough money to buy a hippo. Named Gilbert, he arrived in April 1958 and, despite the poor weather, attracted great crowds. On Easter Monday, 8,000 people visited the Zoo.

[Of] particular interest was the hippopotamus and it was found necessary to arrange a queuing system for visitors to view the animal . . . Noted that in the

Hippopotamus Gilbert
and Matt Wilson.

gardens generally there was a very orderly crowd and only one incident worth mentioning occurred and this was a case of pickpocketing.

Gilbert continued to attract crowds and in the annual report, the council reported, 'he has been a great favourite and has played up marvellously to the public'.[24] Four years later, in accordance with the council's determination

Hippopotami
Gilbert and Hilda
with Jimmy Kenny.

to breed the animals if possible, a female was purchased from Rotterdam Zoo. Named Hilda, the eight-year-old was considered wild and on several occasions she was seen to stand on her hind legs in her stall and reach up to the ceiling 12 feet up and bite chunks out of the wooden beams. Eventually she settled down and was slowly introduced to Gilbert. Hints that she might be pregnant in 1968 came to nothing.

The tiger cubs

Many other species in the Zoo were breeding. In 1958, for example, the newborn animals in the Zoo included two Himalayan bears, a Bennett's wallaby, eight lion cubs, a zebra, a penguin, lots of birds and four tiger cubs. The tiger cubs were special because breeding them had long been the desire of the staff and the council. In 1952, two tiger cubs had been born but did not survive. Another four were born, three died immediately and the fourth died a few weeks later. In 1958, Arja gave birth to four cubs. She rejected them but Terry Murphy and his wife, Kay, hand-reared them successfully. Two collie dogs called Flossie and Dolly, who were nursing their own puppies, were brought in to nurse the tiger cubs.

> The collie puppies and the little tigers got along famously and Flossie and Dolly didn't seem to find anything unusual or odd about nursing a couple of tiger cubs among their own offspring. The experiment went very well, even though our kitchen was overflowing with baby animals.[25]

When it was time to transfer the tiger cubs to their own enclosure, the media were invited to see them. The cubs were so used to human contact that Murphy allowed the journalists to handle them. However, it was believed that one of the journalists had a cat that was suffering from feline enteritis and the infection was passed on to the tiger cubs. Within forty-eight hours, all four were dead. 'It was one of the saddest moments of my life,' said Terry Murphy in his memoir.[26] A year later, Arja gave birth to three cubs and rejected them again. One died and the other two were retrieved by Terry Murphy and hand-reared. They called the male Buster and the female Not-So-Good, as she was very weak and sickly. But both grew strong and the pair became celebrated animals in the Zoo.

Tiger cubs Buster and Not-So-Good in Terry Murphy's kitchen.

Rhinoceros Laura and
calf Ringo.

Rhinoceros

In 1960, a young African black rhinoceros arrived from East Africa and was called Congo.
It was still very young and was being fed with a bottle by the keepers. It died of the cold
in 1962, even though it was in heated quarters. That same year a female black rhinoceros
was purchased from Rotterdam Zoo and a year later a male was purchased from Bristol Zoo.
Both animals were zoo-bred. A new enclosure was built for them on the west side of the
lake near the entrance. In summer 1969, a young black rhinoceros was born. In anticipation
of the birth, a special maternity stall had been constructed to allow the mother complete
seclusion. Staff monitored the birth through closed-circuit TV. The calf was born on 9 July.
He gained strength quickly and, within a few hours, suckled on his mother. However, soon
afterwards the staff noticed the mother becoming agitated and could see no sign of the calf.
On investigation, it emerged that the newborn rhinoceros had squeezed through the bars

of the maternity stall gate and wandered down the service passage towards the father 'who was attempting to savage the calf through the bars of his stall'. The calf was carried back to maternity quarters and the mother 'misinterpreting our good intentions became more aggressive and charged the stall gate. Eventually the baby was pushed into her stall and she immediately quietened down.'[27]

Ringo, as the calf was named, was sold two years later to a British zoo. In 1976, the Zoo switched to the white rhinoceros species.[28]

Lion cub in the arms of Mary Neville in the 1950s; Mary was part of the group that completed the first Zoo volunteer programme in 1987.

Bim, the elephant seal

Some animals were memorable in their own right and an elephant seal was one of these. In 1965 Dublin Zoo acquired a southern elephant seal. When the large marine mammal arrived, he was reluctant to eat. Gerry Creighton (senior) looked after him but said, 'It was six weeks before he would take a fish.' From then on, the elephant seal ate 75-80 lb of herrings a day and it cost roughly £1,400 a year to feed him.[29] Fortunately Bord Iascaigh Mhara, the national fisheries agency, agreed to sponsor him and the elephant seal was given the name Bim.

Bim escaped from his enclosure twice. He had a habit of flopping his head and shoulders on top of his 4-foot iron railings but the staff did not think he would have the energy or initiative to get over the top. Then one day, he was seen waddling along one of the side roads in the gardens; it was late in the day and there were few visitors around. The keepers got a tarpaulin, lured him on to it by offering him some fish, and dragged him back to his enclosure.[30] He was still quite young then. 'He was very popular because of his giant size,' said Gerry Creighton (senior). 'I would walk past and he'd respond to me and kids would yell, "Hey mister, he knows you."' In 1966, Bim escaped again. By now he was a 15-foot, 2-ton animal. The keepers succeeded in enticing him into the nearby giraffe enclosure where they manoeuvred him into his original crate with the help of a dump truck. A mobile crane lifted

Bim the elephant seal being fed by Zoo electrician and maintenance man Tom McGrath, in a picture specially posed for *The Irish Times*. Gerry Creighton (senior), Bim's regular keeper, used to go into the enclosure with Bim to hand-feed him but as the elephant seal grew and sexually matured, there was a danger that he would lunge at the keeper. A platform was built, from which he was fed. Bim also lunged at the concrete wall and cracked it, causing the pool to leak. The chain-link fence bolted into the wall to prevent Bim from reaching the wall is visible in the photograph.

the crate, with Bim inside it, back into the enclosure. An additional fence was placed on top to prevent further escapes.[31] Bim died in 1969; this surprised the council as elephant seals were known to live up to the age of forty years in captivity. The post mortem revealed he had a disease causing atrophy of his heart muscles, which developed into a fibrosis.

'Here comes the boss and he wants his chair!' 1955 cartoon by Micheál Ó Nuailláin (he signed his drawings Michael O'Nolan). The 'boss' is Cecil Webb, superintendent from 1952 to 1956, who bred hares, a difficult feat.

Funding the Zoo

Judging by the lists of guests in the social columns, the Zoo functions at this time were attracting well-connected captains of industry. The government grant was limited to £1,000 and there were no indications that the council was making any great attempt to have this increased.[32] Through sponsorship and animal adoption, companies and wealthy businessmen were able to help out. Esso adopted a tiger, which related to its contemporary 'Tiger in your tank' campaign. Guinness adopted several animals including the toco toucan and the sea lion, both of which featured in its colourful advertising campaigns. Council member Kenneth Besson, who owned the Royal Hibernian Hotel and the Russell Hotel, adopted the lion Herbert and the giraffe Doc. Merville Dairy, which was owned by the Craigie family, adopted the rhesus monkey enclosure. Victor Craigie was honorary secretary to the council from 1954 until 1977 when he became president for four years; he was a close confidant of Terry Murphy during the latter's term as superintendent. His sister, Florence, was a member of the Ladies' Committee, and his other sister, Irene, ran the Children's Corner. The Nesbitts of Arnotts department store were also long-time supporters of the Zoo: Mrs Nesbitt was known for her spectacular hats and legend had it that she turned up to garden parties with a spare hat or two in the boot of her car; if another woman chanced to be wearing the same hat, she sent her chauffeur to the car to retrieve her spare.[33] The adoption and sponsorship schemes and the social functions contributed modest amounts of money but they raised considerable goodwill, publicity and enthusiasm and contributed to the increase in membership during this period.

Memories

The artist Micheál Ó Nualláin won first prize in an RDS art competition in the early 1950s when he was a student in the National College of Art and Design. He had created a series of lifelike drawings based on animals in the Natural History Museum and was given a pass to go to the Zoo to draw whenever he felt like it:

> I felt so important then, I could go there any time. The open sky and open space were wonderful after the claustrophobia of the NCAD. I visited the lion house a lot. They all looked half asleep and didn't move when I went in. After a few weeks, I noticed that they would all stand up when I walked in; maybe they recognised my footsteps and thought I was a keeper. I would spend most of my day at the Zoo and, because Ashton Freeman's drawings were in the *Evening Press*, I approached *The Irish Times* to see if they would be interested in my drawings. They were and they let me draw anything I liked. I remember the polar bears at the far side of the lake. They were very playful. The penguins were great to watch. The birds were wonderful. In fact all of the animals were favourites. At the time several hotels were sponsors of the Zoo and I sold some of my drawings to them. One day I had enough money to buy lunch in Haughton House and I can't remember what it was but I do remember that it was simply awful. It was a wonderful time and that pass made it all possible.[34]
>
> Once, a lady was introduced to my brother, Brian O'Nolan, who wrote the 'Cruiskeen Lawn' column in *The Irish Times* under the name Myles na gCopaleen and was very well known. She asked him if he was related to the artist Michael O'Nolan. I wasn't known at all at the time and he used to tell this story as a joke against himself.

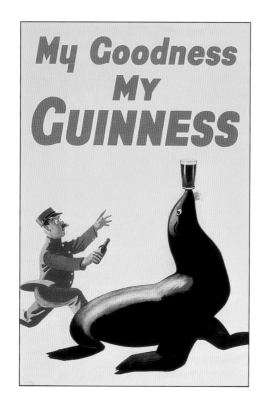

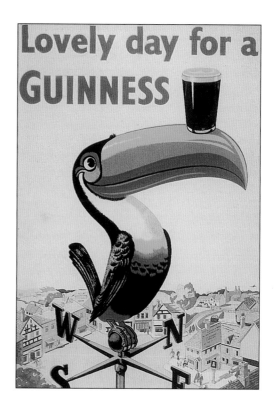

Guinness beer was a sponsor of numerous animals in the Zoo, including the sea lion and the toco toucan.

The actor Jim Bartley was also a regular visitor to the Zoo.

> I remember riding on the elephant, sitting on the side-car and going down by the lake. It was a swinging walk. And the little pony trolley, I loved that. I was seven or eight. And I loved the lion house. They used to walk up and down in their cages and I'd walk up and down beside them, keeping pace. Then they'd get mad and growl and I'd run out of the place. My favourite of all were the penguins. One would come out of a gap in the wall and then turn around and stand staring at the wall. Another would come out and stand beside it and look at the wall, and another might join them. I gave them all names – boys' names like Hughie, Vinnie and Ollie – and then make up an imaginary conversation about them looking at the wall: 'Hey, Hughie, come and look at this wall.' 'That's a great wall, Ollie.' 'Look at the crack, Hughie,' and so on. There would be other kids around and they would love this.[35]

Drawings by artist,
Micheál Ó Nualláin

Elephant rides in the 1950s

Of the scheduled events in the 1950s, a ride on Sarah the elephant was unquestionably the most memorable experience. Olwyn Lanigan's father was a life member in the 1950s. He brought his family, together with another family from Fermanagh, on regular visits to the Zoo. Olwyn rode on Sarah down by the lake:

> I remember the crude howdah; it had a seat on either side and a metal chain across the seat where three children sat. The child at either end could hold onto a metal bar on the arm of the seat but the child in the middle only had the chain to hold on to and I remember it was loose enough and I was small enough to slide under-neath it. The steady walk down the lake was fine with the elephant swaying but the turnaround was quite terrifying. During the turn there seemed to be a shift in the balance and as a small child I felt that if the angle was any greater, I could slip under the chain. I held on to the metal bars hard.

Margaret Sinanan, now a member of council, remembers the terror of being given the back seat on the howdah: 'You were on your own, facing out behind the elephant.'

Jimmy Kenny was very well known by visitors of all ages to the Zoo and had a knack of creating moments that provided lasting memories. 'If it was your birthday or some other important event, Mr Kenny would allow you to sit up front with him on the neck of the elephant; it gave me a great sense of being special,' said Mary de Courcy.

Jimmy Kenny and
visitors on Sarah.

Ann Murphy remembers,

Jimmy Kenny made it feel that the ride on the elephant was a fun thing to do
and I had no fear; he was great, a lovable sort of man who knew how to talk to
children. The elephant was the pinnacle of the visit; once you'd had your ride, it
didn't matter whether you got on the train or the pony and trap after that.

Paddy Halpin remembers her daughter, Mary Pat, running straight to the elephant house
when they arrived at the Zoo in the late 1950s. Her daughter, aged four or five, called out to
Mr Kenny who recognised her. Paddy Halpin remembers seeing Mary Pat taking a shortcut
under the elephant to get to a plate of bread in the elephant house. 'It happened in such a
flash that I didn't have time to be concerned,' she said, 'but I can still visualise it to this day.'
Dorothy Kilroy, now a council member, remembers visits to the Zoo in the 1950s:

Clockwise from top left: Boarding Sarah by the lakeside; Jimmy Kenny and young visitors coming up the steps from the elephant walk down by the lake; Elephant Sarah with Dorothy Kilroy; Sarah, Komali, Jimmy Kenny, Dinnen Gilmore, president of the Royal Zoological Society of Ireland (right), and guests watching Lt Col. J. H. Williams cut the ribbon at the opening of the new elephant house in February 1957. Williams was known as Elephant Bill following publication of his autobiography about working with elephants in Burma before and during the Second World War.

I came here frequently as a child and all I wanted to do was go down to the elephants and feed them bits of potato from battered tins. I used to hang around at the time when the elephant was going down to do the rides in the afternoon. Mr Kenny would select a few kids and put them on Sarah, who knelt down so we could get on. Then she stood up. Sitting up front by myself was scary and exciting. I remember the sensations, the rocking from side to side, and going down steps, it was highly dangerous.[36]

Paul Kenny described the popularity of his father:

It used to take us at least forty-five minutes to get down Grafton Street with my father. Everyone knew him, from high court judges to kids. If anyone said 'hello', he'd stop for a chat. Many of the people who came to the Zoo were regulars and he'd remember them all. If they had a camera, he would pose them beside Sarah and Komali and take their photograph.

Bob Mooney was Jimmy Kenny's assistant. Paul Kenny said:

Sarah played with Bob. She would walk down by the lake in the usual way with

Bob and the children on her back. When it came to turn at the lake, she would start backing into the lake. Bob worked out that she was doing it deliberately, and also knew that she would continue to do it regardless of what he said. So he would tease the kids and, when it came to turning around, he would say, 'now, Sarah, back into the lake!'[37]

In July 1958, Sarah fell while carrying a full load of children on her back, officially ending the elephant rides in the Zoo. Sarah had been having trouble with her feet for some time and, in June 1958, it was believed that she had tripped over a protruding stone on the elephant walk, fallen onto her front knees, and then over on to her side. The children remained in their seats, secured by the chain. When the chain was removed, they ran away 'a little frightened but nothing further than one girl complained of pain in her back'.[38] There had already been discussions about the safety of giving elephant rides; a letter from London Zoo was received saying 'all zoos are considerably worried about the attendant risk and are seriously considering giving up these rides'.[39] Despite her fall and continuing problems with her feet, Sarah continued to give rides until 1961. She was put down in 1962 after all attempts to cure her foot failed.

Sarah washing Komali.

Komali the elephant

The other elephant, Komali (pronounced 'Cummalee'), had arrived as a two-year-old from Ceylon in 1950, having been found abandoned and brought to Ceylon Zoo in the back of a car. She was a lively animal and a month after she arrived, a ten-year-old child had her arm broken when she was trying to feed her. Jimmy Kenny soon got control over Komali and she became very popular with visitors who were allowed to feed her with carrots or bread on a tin plate.[40] In 1958, after Sarah's fall, she was not ready to give rides with a howdah on her back yet. Nevertheless Jimmy Kenny often allowed children to sit on her back and go for a very short ride.

Clockwise from top left: Sarah and Komali with keeper Willie Brophy and Brian Flood; Paul Kenny on Komali: 'I was nervous during this photo because the bears were in the enclosure right behind me!'; Connie Kenny, wife of Jimmy Kenny, with son Pat and daughter, Anne Marie; Visitors feeding Komali.

Opposite page: Komali with The Life Boys.

189

He would get Komali to sit on the ground, put a grey blanket on her back, sit the child up close to her head and then command Komali to stand up slowly and walk forward a few steps. Olwyn Lanigan remembers a ride on Komali: 'Mr Kenny told me he had to be careful how he put the grey blanket on her back to avoid ruffling her hair because that would be uncomfortable for her; she was a very peaceful, very intelligent animal.'[41]

Although Jimmy Kenny was renowned for having total control over Komali, the council was concerned that other keepers might not be able to manage her. Alterations were made to the elephant compound to stop visitors from having contact with her and they explained this in the annual report, pointing out that 'One assistant keeper received cuts and bruises as a result of her temper, and on another occasion she over-turned the Zoo tractor.'[42] This was a reference to an incident in May 1963 when Komali had gone 'wild' while Jimmy Kenny was on sick leave. Terry Murphy described the scene:

> She became agitated and the assistant keeper found he could not control her by his voice alone and, using sheer force, she managed to break away from him and out into the grounds. Close by, a group of school children were enjoying a visit to the Zoo. They were being led by a nun. As they turned at the sound of Komali's trumpeting, the nun rushed forward to stand in front of the children. Komali moved past them at some speed, nudging the nun as she went by and knocking the poor lady to the ground. She was not hurt but, understandably, rather shaken.

Jimmy Kenny was sent for and, as they waited for his arrival, Komali spotted a tractor on a construction site and rushed over, stopping in front of it. The driver was petrified as Komali approached his vehicle, lowered her massive head and proceeded to turn the tractor over with one strong nudge from her forehead. The driver was unhurt. Jimmy Kenny arrived shortly afterwards and, after she 'performed a few playful charges away from him and a couple of trumpets of frustration', he lead her calmly back to her stall.[43]

Lion cub Patrick, with Mark Duggan in the Children's Corner, 1964, with Rabbit Ville in the background.

Later that year, when Jimmy Kenny was again on leave, John O'Connor (senior) had been giving her a bucket of water to drink from when she reached out her trunk and pulled him towards the railings of the stall. His arm went in between the bars and Komali butted his arm against the wall with her head. Slowly but surely the elephant house was altered to restrict public access to both Komali and Jill, the elephant that had arrived in 1964. The public still tried to feed them, and at least one elephant fell into the dyke around their enclosure as a result. Over the next twenty years, numerous Asian elephants and a few African elephants were purchased or borrowed; some died, some were sold on or given in exchange but without the opportunity to ride them or feed them. None became as well known as Sarah or Komali, who was put down in 1966. Jimmy Kenny retired in 1976 after forty-three years of service. In a most unusual gesture, he was invited to the meeting of council so they could thank him for giving so much pleasure to the visitors in the gardens.[44]

In 1967, the actor Tony Tormey was on one of his periodic visits to the Zoo with his parents at the same time as a television crew were recording Ireland's Eurovision entrant Sean Dunphy singing 'If I Could Choose' on the back of Jill, now the only elephant in the collection. Tony recalls:

The crew saw me and put me up on the elephant with Sean Dunphy – possibly because I had white-blond hair. I was about four. Then Sean Dunphy, who was sitting behind me, started singing that love song in my ear and I bawled my eyes out, it was all so strange. I had always wanted to touch an elephant and I can clearly remember the grey blanket on his back and the feel of the elephant's skin, it was not as tough as I thought it would be.[45]

The lion house

The smell in the lion house was one of those powerful memories from Dublin Zoo in the mid-twentieth century. However well designed for its time, however clean the keepers kept it, the cramped quarters for big cats made it a particularly strong-smelling place. In December 1952, as part of an attempt to reduce the smell, an 'Aerovap' dispenser that released a perfume was installed in the lion house but the alternative smell had its own potency and one member of council complained that the house 'now smells like a perfumery'.[46] The idea was dropped and another generation was allowed to experience the smell of the lion house.

Feeding Sarah and Komali.

The Guinness Festival Clock, which was displayed periodically during the summer months in the Zoo.

Watching the lions being fed was a major event for visitors that continued for many years. Gerry Creighton (junior) described the scene:

The smell of urine in the Lion House first thing in the morning was so strong, it would make your eyes weep. When I was a young lad, I would help my father [Gerry Creighton (senior)] during feeding time by pushing the meat cart for him. The lions would pace: they were so in tune with the keepers that they would react as soon as they sensed them coming; they would rub up against the glass and make a lot of noise. With the cats, the noise, the smell and so many people, it was a very intense atmosphere. The cats were in such a confined, sterile space that they would look at one another through the bars and their sense of competition for the meat would prompt them to stalk while they were waiting for the meat and when they got to the meat, they would demolish it in no time. Their close proximity to each other was one of the reasons they bred so well.[47]

Royal pythons, Terry
Murphy, Tommy Kelly
and a young visitor.

Snakes

There were several other potential close encounters that made a day in the Zoo memorable for children. The mynah bird talking to a visitor from behind the glass in its small space in the Parrot House was one such moment. Being allowed to hold a snake in the reptile house was another. This was the domain of Tommy Kelly, another legendary keeper of the 1950s and 1960s. Margaret Sinanan said:

> I remember the wonderful and scary feeling of having a snake around my neck several times. Once I had a boa constrictor around my neck. It was enormous, or at least it seemed enormous, I was about eight at the time. Tommy Kelly got talking

Boy on the giant tortoise, 1964.

to someone at the other end of the reptile house and left me with the boa on my shoulders. I could feel it tighten and began to get very uncomfortable. It was difficult walking with the snake around my neck to ask him to remove it. He didn't bat an eyelid. Then, years later, when I was on the council, I used to do 'Behind the scenes' in the reptile house with [council member] Elizabeth Lamb and we put the snakes around children's necks so they could feel them.'[48]

Education

'Behind the scenes' was one of several educational programmes organised and delivered by council members. Around the world, formal educational programmes were being developed within zoos as the zoo community explored innovative ways to use the animal collections to spread knowledge and an interest in wildlife. Dublin Zoo had, for many years, hosted large numbers of school children, particularly in spring and early summer. In a deal with CIÉ, the state transport company, busloads of school children were brought from all over the country on what was ostensibly an educational visit to the Zoo. Many of them were fed in Haughton House and, by 1960, the council had to set a limit of 200 children at lunchtime, and the same number for afternoon tea and 'high tea'. Concerns about the lack of discipline

Interior of the monkey house in 1966 after it was refurbished. It is now the South America House.

of the children on these trips was raised but nothing was done about it.[49] The volume of children included on these tours can be gauged when, in 1963, there was a bus strike that lasted five weeks and the number of children visiting that year was reduced from 26,000 to 17,000.

In the late 1950s, the council organised their own highly successful tours for members' children, although it was on a very small scale. In March 1959, members of council conducted a children's tour of the gardens and then quizzed them about what they had learnt. On 30 and 31 December 1959, a series of tours was held for children and teenagers. A total of 321 children, and some adults went on the tours with one of six council members acting as a tour guide. These popular tours were repeated on occasion during the 1960s.[50]

Car badge issued by the Society.

Memory of a young visitor in the 1970s

Ireland went through more tough economic times in the 1970s. Visitors numbers reached half a million in 1970 and 1971, then dropped to a low point in 1974 when there was a bus strike and bomb explosions in Dublin. The figures rose again and reached a record high of 671,381 in 1980. Still, the youths of Dublin managed to find their way in without paying. Brian O'Reilly used to visit the Zoo once a year with his family:

> We would buy nuts from the dealer outside the gate with the intention of feeding them to the monkeys, and the elephants and the hippos. By the time we left the monkeys all of the nuts were gone. It was very exciting because we came here for the entire day once a year and loved it. Then, when I was older, maybe thirteen or fourteen, I'd come here with a friend to see the animals; we would have no money so as we got closer to the gate and I would start tapping my pockets as if I was looking for money. Then I'd turn back with tears in my eyes and say I'd lost the fiver. The woman at the gate would always let us in. It worked a few times! We'd stay all day looking at the animals. Winter was best because you could stay and watch them without having to move on because there were no crowds.[51]

Social Events

The social events shifted to a new level in the early 1960s. When the Ladies' Committee analysed the enormous success of the 1962 fete, at which 1,700 people attended the garden party alone, they decided that a catering company should be hired. Until now, they had been doing all the work themselves. Other refinements that year included moving the Garda Band away from the main lawn at the garden party in order to spread the crowd out. They decided to have dinner available upstairs in Haughton House for the council members and friends to a maximum of 120 people on the evening of the dance, and have the self-service restaurant open during the dance. Donal Nugent's band, which had played at events before, was employed once more and a steel band was also hired to play for a short period. As usual, the diplomatic corps was invited to the garden party. In the course of their analysis of the 1964 social events, the Ladies' Committee asked the council and the diplomatic visit-ors to mingle more with the crowd and not to cut themselves off.[52]

The number of events escalated and no detail was too small for the Ladies' Committee. The sound system, the number of toilets, the availability of easy access to a bar by older bridge players, how to handle lost tickets, the location of the band, the floral arrangements and, of course, the food, were analysed in great detail and improvements made each year. New events were added and, by 1963, members' dinner dances were being held monthly in the off-season, and a dance for the sons and daughters of members and their friends was held before Christmas.

In 1963 an additional event was held in September to raise funds for the construction of a new reptile house. The existing one had been built in 1868[53]; besides being out-of-date, it

Left: bridge party; Right: Jenny the donkey with Anne May (right), now a Zoo volunteer, and her siblings, Michael, Bernadette and Margaret, in the Children's Corner c. 1972.

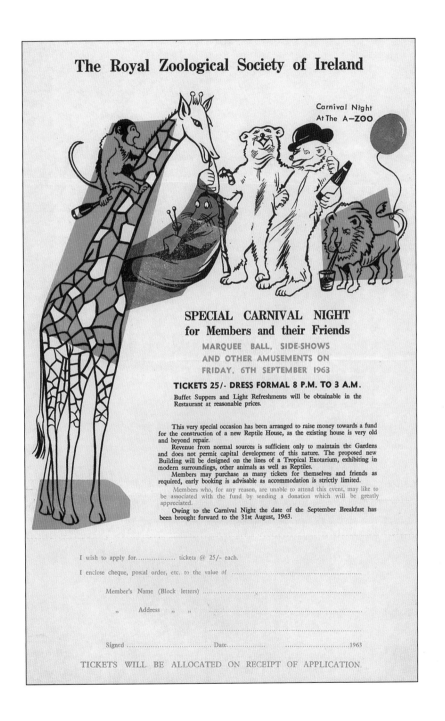

Left: Dorothy Kilroy, now a council member, on the pony and trap, being driven by Tommy Conlon. Right: Brian O'Reilly in Pets' Corner in the early 1970s.

was potentially dangerous because the roof was collapsing. Terry Murphy visited zoos in Germany and Belgium and came back with a plan for a new reptile house, which was to be located on the west side of the lake near the polar bears and would cost £30,000. A carnival night with Caribbean dancing, a marquee ball, a tombola stall and other sideshows, and a raffle was held; 1,500 people attended and it raised £3,640. The following year, another carnival ball was held for the same cause and raised £2,172. With only £5,812, the council had no option but to repair the old reptile house. The enclosures were transformed by using artificial rockwork and tropical plants; the old hard-fuel boiler was replaced by an oil-fired boiler, the roof was reconstructed and the skylights repaired.[54]

Through the 1960s and into the early 1970s, the dances, bridge parties, garden parties, fashion shows and fork suppers in the Zoo were frequent occurrences. Dances now occurred at Shrovetide, March, April, the summer fete, September, Halloween, November, Christmas and New Year's Eve. The society columns reported many of the events, listing the names of

Clockwise from top left: The Ladies' Committee raising funds; a ticket for the 1963 Dinner Dance; the renovated reptile house, 1965; Jill, an Asian elephant who arrived in the Zoo in 1964, with Maeve and Robert McDonald in April 1966. Robert, aged eight, had just come out of hospital after three and a half years; the children were given a week off school to celebrate and the visit to the Zoo was a highlight. Hearing the story, Jimmy Kenny brought Jill out to the lawn for this photograph. Komali, who is visible in the background, was euthanised some months later.

Princess Grace and Prince Rainier of Monaco attending a Red Cross garden party for children in the Zoo on 12 June 1961. The Zoo was open only to members and their guests on the day. Later that year, Prince Rainier donated a leopard to the Zoo.

some guests and what the women were wearing. Margaret Sinanan went to several of the dances in the 1960s:

> They were a major social event, and very Protestant! Major business people used to go to them. I went to a few. There was a big marquee. I remember walking into one of the houses; it might have been the reptile house. There were cockroaches running across the tiled floor and up the sides of the windows. I was in a long dress and high heels and I could hear the clacking sound as they ran across the floor. I backed out quickly.[55]

In 1969, the dance during fete week was very successful with 1,420 people attending. Events in 1970 included two dinner dances in February, one in March, one in April, a fork supper in May, breakfasts in May, July and September, as well as the fete week in June with a dance, a garden party (attended by 1,440 people) and a bridge tournament (with ninety-one tables). There were also dances in October, November and three in December as well as a fork supper in October.[56]

The decline in interest in Zoo's social activity began in the early 1970s and got rapidly worse. Dance tickets were becoming difficult to sell and intensive advertising about the charm, romantic setting and facilities for eating at the events was required. One by one the dances were dropped. In 1976, it was noted that the fete week was 'socially a great success' but the dance only attracted 800 guests and all the other events had reduced numbers also. The dances in March, April and November were abandoned that year.[57] In 1979, the fete week was cancelled due to the postal strike. The Halloween dance was cancelled in 1982 due to a poor response and the formality of the New Year's Eve dance put some people off although the dances continued for several more years. Discussions at different times during the 1970s about how to attract the younger generation suggests that the enthusiasm for going to parties in the Zoo was confined to a generation that was now ageing and less inclined to take part in these events. Children's entertainments with Santa, however, remained and to this day are still booked out every year.

Developing International Relations

In 1966 the title of superintendent of Dublin Zoo was changed to 'director', a more popular term for the senior management position in zoos around the world. Later that year, Terry Murphy attended the inaugural meeting of the Federation of Zoological Gardens of Great Britain and Ireland. The Federation was formed 'with the object of encouraging proper care of wild animals in captivity, also for the benefit of all Zoos in promoting [the] interchange of information, new ideas in Zoo practice, and adherence to certain recognised standards.'[58] Until now, zoos had built collections to suit themselves and their resources: quantity, diversity and appeal had governed the development of many collections. Breeding success, acquiring

Above: Cedric Flood's badge from the 1951 meeting of the International Union of Directors of Zoological Gardens, which held its first meeting in 1946. Left: Haughton House with extensions in the 1960s. Right: one of several art exhibitions held in Haughton House and organised by the Ladies' Committee.

the first of a rare species and keeping animals alive longer than any other zoo had also been sources of competition. But the massive growth in collections in the 1950s and 1960s was putting a strain on stocks of animals in the wild and was creating a need for inter-national cooperation. Even a relatively poor zoo like Dublin experienced expansion in its collection during this time. In 1956, Dublin Zoo had a total of 442 animals; by 1968, it had 1,057 animals in the collection. Some of the increase was as a result of Dublin's successful breeding and improved animal husbandry practices, but some animals were still being purchased from the wild. Pam McDonough, a secretary in the Zoo from 1959 to 1968, said that dealers' lists of animals came into the Zoo every day: 'Huge numbers of animals were being caught and offered to zoos; it was very tempting but of course we did not have the money for them.'[59]

International associations for different groups of zoo staff were being created as forums for exchange of information and ideas. In 1950, Cedric Flood had represented the Zoo at an annual meeting of the International Union of Directors of Zoological Gardens.[60] The objective of the Union was to improve their animal collections and institutions, and by the mid-1960s, it had become an influential force in the evolution of modern zoos. Over the

Pam McDonough, staff member, and her husband, Maurice in the Zoo trap on their wedding day in 1965. Pam said, 'We came out of Haughton House after the wedding breakfast and saw the pony and trap decorated with flowers. It was a wonderful surprise.' Frank Burke is driving the trap.

following decades, a complex network of local and international organisations was to emerge and establish controls over the acquisition and breeding of animals in zoos. Dublin Zoo willingly participated in the conferences and other discussion groups but, in practical terms, the impact of the controls did not begin to register until the late 1970s.

In 1967 the International Union of Zoo Directors made an agreement prohibiting members from participating in any form of trade in orang-utans, Galapagos tortoises and several other highly endangered species. The purpose was to prevent trafficking in these animals and to make it clear that the Union planned to have a real impact in the fight to save endangered species. From now on, these animals would be allocated to zoos depending on their facilities and the possibility that they might breed. Of course, a zoo could purchase an animal from a dealer and continue to breed without reference to the central studbook, but it would undermine the status of the zoo in the international community and no good zoo would be interested in purchasing its young animals.

Just as the International Union was making this arrangement, Dublin Zoo received two young orang-utans, courtesy of the Minister of Law and Development in Singapore and the Orang-Utan Recovery Service in Malaya.[61] The Zoo already had Adam, who had arrived in 1958 and they hoped that the young female from Singapore, called Eve, would breed with Adam. A new enclosure was built on the west side of the lake so that they could be taken

Left: new entrance, 1968. Bottom: the Entrance Lodge in the 1970s.

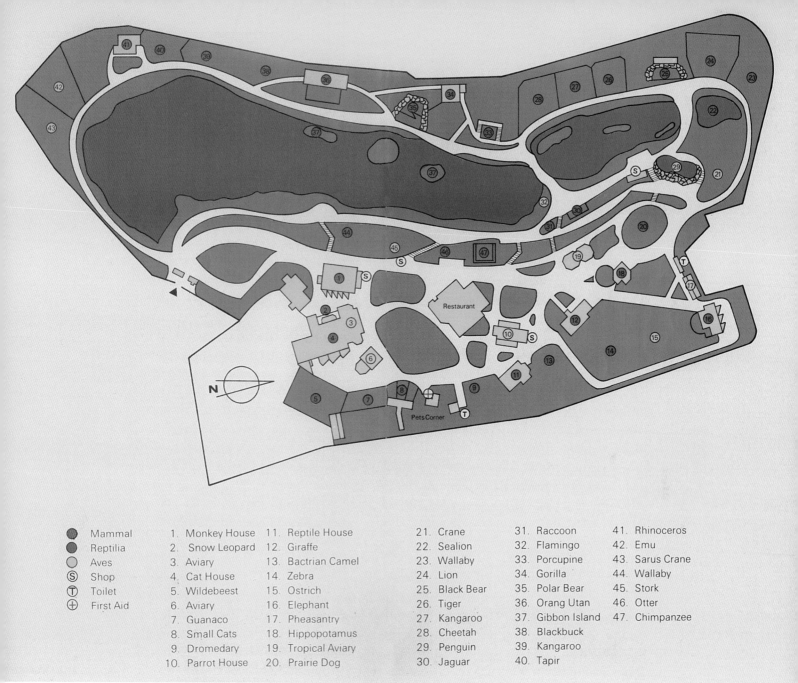

● Mammal	1. Monkey House	11. Reptile House	21. Crane	31. Raccoon	41. Rhinoceros
● Reptilia	2. Snow Leopard	12. Giraffe	22. Sealion	32. Flamingo	42. Emu
○ Aves	3. Aviary	13. Bactrian Camel	23. Wallaby	33. Porcupine	43. Sarus Crane
Ⓢ Shop	4. Cat House	14. Zebra	24. Lion	34. Gorilla	44. Wallaby
Ⓣ Toilet	5. Wildebeest	15. Ostrich	25. Black Bear	35. Polar Bear	45. Stork
⊕ First Aid	6. Aviary	16. Elephant	26. Tiger	36. Orang Utan	46. Otter
	7. Guanaco	17. Pheasantry	27. Kangaroo	37. Gibbon Island	47. Chimpanzee
	8. Small Cats	18. Hippopotamus	28. Cheetah	38. Blackbuck	
	9. Dromedary	19. Tropical Aviary	29. Penguin	39. Kangaroo	
	10. Parrot House	20. Prairie Dog	30. Jaguar	40. Tapir	

Undated map of Dublin Zoo in the 1970s.

out of the monkey house. The ape house, as it was called, was designed also to keep gorillas.[62] The orang-utans were transferred there in 1971. A dry moat was used to contain them, and to protect them from the peanuts and other food still being given to the apes by the public. The house was officially opened at the strawberry breakfast in July 1972.

Funding

Undoubtedly the council members put an enormous amount of effort into making ends meet at the Zoo but little had changed in its style of management since the 1830s. The minute details of running the Zoo were discussed at each weekly meeting. Great effort was put into raising small amounts of money while the wages, food, and other bills grew rapidly. Between 1961 and 1966, the annual wage bill alone doubled from £20,000 to £40,000. Yet the proceedings of the council and the Society maintained the character of a nineteenth-century club. Every year the president, secretaries, treasurer and three ordinary members were elected to council. There was seldom any competition – at the election stage at least – for these positions. The rule that three members would resign still existed and this allowed for some new blood. However, it is likely that even the new blood was drawn from the small section of Irish society from which the majority of council members had come since 1831. Many of them had close contacts with Trinity College Dublin, which was predominantly a Protestant university.[63] There were few Catholics on the council and when the Catholic Church invited a representative of the Society to a ceremonial mass – which they did quite often – Dr Sheridan, Mr P. E. Dunn and Mr J. Meenan were the only three council members who attended over a twenty-year period and often no one was nominated to attend.

150th anniversary celebrations

In 1980, celebrations to mark the 150th anniversary of the Zoological Society were approached with great enthusiasm. A week of celebration and parties was held, starting on 10 May, the date of the first meeting in the Rotunda in 1830. President Hillery attended breakfast, following which he presented the Zoo with an elephant, which had been a gift from the President of Tanzania. He also unveiled a bronze statue of a squirrel by sculptor Colm Brennan. Indifference to Zoo dances was shelved for the occasion as 1,400 people attended the carnival ball. Sideshows were provided as additional amusement. The garden party was cancelled due to lack of interest but the Children's Day attracted over 1,000 adults and children to be

ROYAL ZOOLOGICAL SOCIETY OF IRELAND
150th ANNIVERSARY

PROMENADE
AND DINNER

Monday, 12th May, 1980

7.00 p.m.
(Dinner at 8.30 p.m.)
Tickets : £7.00

Period Dress (any era of
the 19th century) or
Black Tie.

Top left: picture of guests at the 150th anniversary promenade and (top right) ticket for the event. Below: Terry Murphy with an African grey parrot.

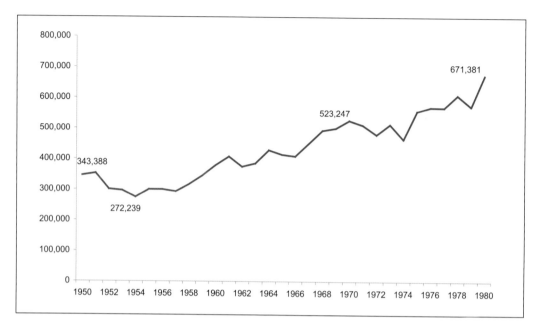

entertained by Eugene Lambert and O'Brien, his well-known puppet, and the Lower
Crumlin Majorettes. Perhaps the greatest symbol of the 150 years of Zoological Society history was the Promenade Night as a century and a half of fund-raising parties, dances and
dinners were celebrated by a party at which guests wore colourful costumes modelled on
nineteenth-century clothes design.

It was described as follows in the annual report for 1980:

> Our lady member of Council, Mrs Lamb, with her friends, organised the
> Promenade Night on Monday, 12th May. It was a night to be remembered.
> Vintage cars and carriages moved quietly around the Gardens while the guests,
> dressed in the fashion of the last century, promenaded on the lawns and paths to
> the music of the No. 1 Army Band before dining in Haughton House. A young
> 'match-boy' and children in period costume offering for sale violets and fruit of
> many descriptions, added to the charm of this colourful and unusual event.[64]

While the party was a celebration of 150 years of achievement, it also marked the end of an
era. Dublin Zoo in 1980 was an anachronism. The space was too small for the size of its

collection and many of the animals were being kept in enclosures that had not kept pace with the best international design standards. Staff and visitors were also beginning to express disquiet at conditions for the animals in Dublin Zoo. The four objectives of the modern zoo – conservation, education, research and recreation – were seldom mentioned by the council. Dublin Zoo was in danger of losing respect at a local and an international level and the forthcoming period was going to test it to the limit.

CHAPTER 6

RADICAL CHANGE
1980–2000

Introduction

This was the most difficult period in the Zoo's history. Having survived the Famine years, world wars, civil war and economic depression, Dublin Zoo had fallen so far behind modern zoo development by the 1980s that it was in danger of being closed down. Indeed, in December 1989 at a special meeting, the council agreed to consult its legal advisers 'about the best procedure for conducting an orderly winding up'.[1] Dublin Zoo was not the only nineteenth-century institution under threat of closure at the time; anti-zoo sentiment and the public demand that zoos modernise or close nearly brought London Zoo to an end in 1992.[2] Public support for Dublin Zoo was still very strong in the 1980s and early 1990s and membership increased while visitor numbers stayed reasonably strong. However, this was unlikely to continue unless a significant improvement in animal accommodation could be achieved. For informed zoo critics, Dublin Zoo also needed to integrate the guiding objectives of education, conservation and research in all its operations. But without the resources, the future of the Zoo seemed as bleak as the Irish economy at the time. Yet, once more, it not only survived but was transformed. As staff, management and council struggled to deal with the issues and challenges facing them, they brought the activities of the Zoo under a national microscope. Public debate on animal welfare in the

Above: members of council, May 1980.
Back row (l–r): R. J. Dennis, P. Wilson,
L. B. O'Moore, D. W. Jeffrey, A. Brady, A. Ganly,
J. McCullough, M. Russell, P. N. Meenan,
D. McConnell, B. Blennerhassett. Front row
(l–r): E. J. Clarke, M. Maguire, M. Taylor,
A. E. J. Went, E. Lamb, N. J. Hogan, J. Bigger,
J. Carroll, J. S. East, V. Craigie (President),
A. G. Mason, P. Ó Nualláin, J. Adam, G. Burrows,
E. D. Weavers. Left: young girl walking
through the floral display, 1980. Colourful
floral displays were a feature of Dublin Zoo
in the twentieth century.

Clockwise from top left: Bactrian camels and giraffe in exhibits on the east side of the Zoo, early 1980s; peafowl were – and still are – a common sight around the Zoo; sea lion pond; orang-utan house in 1980. It was built on the west side of the lake in 1971 and set into the hillside so it would be relatively inconspicuous from Phoenix Park.

Zoo was followed by a groundswell of public support and the powerful intervention of senior government minister, and later Taoiseach, Bertie Ahern, who was a lifelong supporter of the Zoo. By 2000, after a stressful and difficult time, Dublin Zoo had doubled in size and had everything it needed to evolve into a truly 21st-century zoo.

The day out

The Zoo was having great success with its breeding programmes and this undoubtedly contributed to visitor numbers of well over half a million between 1980 and 1982. In 1980, newborn animals included a chimp, a flamingo, lemurs, a gibbon and a giraffe. The following year, the Siberian tiger, the lion, jaguar, leopard and clouded leopard all bred. And in 1982, three American black bears, two giraffes, a Bactrian camel and a zebra were born. In 1980, the Zoo received two polar bear cubs from Canada, named Spunky and Ootec. They were purchased from Winnipeg Zoo after they had been caught on a rubbish dump in Churchill, Manitoba. Many wild polar bears congregate in autumn in this area waiting for the ice to form along the coast of Hudson Bay so they can disperse across the ice in search of seals and other prey. The people of Churchill managed this wild and potentially dangerous population by chasing some off or catching and relocating others. Those who returned to the rubbish dumps frequently were considered 'problem' or 'orphan' bears and were captured and sent to zoos around the world. Spunky and Ootec were two of these and they ended up in Dublin. They were placed in the polar bear exhibit on the west side of the lake. The council noted that they provided 'a very lively exhibit and are frequently found playing in the water.'[3]

Left: Spunky the polar bear being taken away from the rubbish dump in Churchill, Canada, 1979. Right: The lake and pelican bridge in the early 1980s.

Left: orang-utans, Sibu (left) and Leonie in 1984. Right: Riona, orang-utan, born 1996.

In 1981, two animals arrived on breeding loan from zoos in the United States. An eleven-year-old orang-utan called Annie was received from Brookfield Zoo, Chicago, and a female snow leopard called Sasha was received from the San Antonio Zoo in Texas. The movement of animals from one zoo to another for breeding purposes was becoming more frequent. The first notable breeding loans in the world had been in 1965 when Moscow Zoo sent its single, female giant panda to London Zoo, which had a single male.[4] Since then, structures to cater for such loans have been developed, making it easier for zoos to identify potential mates to ensure the health and diversity of the gene pool. In 1981 Dublin Zoo had two male orang-utans: Adam, who had been in the Zoo since 1958, and Tommy who had been there since 1987. Chicago-born Annie became ill shortly after she arrived; she was treated successfully but in 1983, it was announced that she 'has not proved an acceptable mate for Adam and is soon to be returned to Chicago'. In the end she was transferred to Dudley Zoo in England.[5]

Meanwhile Tommy died in 1983 and Sibu, a popular male Bornean orang-utan arrived in 1984. Sibu was born in Los Angeles Botanical Gardens in 1978 and lived in Rotterdam Zoo before being transferred to Dublin Zoo. Gerry Creighton (senior), the keeper-in-charge of the orang-utans for many years, said that Sibu was:

> A great character, hand-reared, up to all sorts and easily bored. He is very intelligent and very mischievous. He had a bucket that he threw around. He always had a few coins around him; we would search the place every morning looking for money but wouldn't find it all. He would put a few coins into the bucket and shake it at the visitors and they'd put money into it.[6]

A three-year-old female orang-utan, Leonie, arrived from Rotterdam Zoo at the same time as Sibu to form the nucleus of a breeding group. They were not expected to breed for some time. In fact they did not breed until 1996. In 1987, a four-year-old zoo-bred female called Maggie was introduced to the group and, in 1994, a zoo-bred male called Benjamin arrived at the Zoo. Not long afterwards, Sibu and Leonie mated and, in February 1996, Riona was born.

Siberian tigers

In 1972, the Siberian tigers were moved to a new, outdoor enclosure on the west side of the lake. The viewing area had an armoured glass front so visitors could have an unimpeded view of the animals. Three Siberian tiger cubs were born in 1978 and the tigress fed them herself.[7] By the early 1980s, the Siberian or Amur tiger was considered endangered and, in February 1982, Dublin Zoo initiated research with the intention of establishing a management plan for the species. However, that very same month, one of the Siberian tigers died of tuberculosis. George Burrows, a journalist and vice-president of the Zoological Society wrote a report that featured on the front page of *The Irish Times*: 'Dublin Zoo has had to destroy all its tigers and lions – two adult Siberian tigers and three cubs, and three adult lions and three cubs – because of an outbreak of TB that was first detected in the male tiger.'[8]

A post mortem on the male Siberian tiger indicated that he had died of tuberculosis of a bovine type. The tigers that shared the same space were put down, as were the lions in the

Above: Gerry Creighton (junior) with Alma, the male Siberian Tiger lent by the Chipperfield Organisation in England after the loss of the tigers following the outbreak of TB. Left: Zita, the female Siberian tiger donated by Marwell Zoological Park in Hampshire, England, in 1982, with one of the many cubs she bred with Alma.

adjacent enclosure. The putting down of the lions was a precautionary measure because there were no tests available for checking whether the lions had the disease while they were alive. It emerged that the tigers were infected but the lions were not. Quarantine procedures were stepped up, staff were checked, giraffes and zebras arriving to the country for the new Fota Wildlife Park went directly to Cork rather than via Dublin. The outbreak was successfully contained and, by July 1982, it was possible to lift the extra precautions.[9] The international zoo community responded rapidly with offers of replacement tigers and lions and, after a six-week period in which the paddock and dens were treated, two lions were donated. A pair of Siberian tigers was also acquired, one donated and one lent from British zoos. In 1983, much to the joy of the keepers, four Siberian tiger cubs were born. Gerry Creighton (senior), said:

> The loss of our tigers and lions in 1982 was devastating; I had to put them into the back of the van to send them up to Abbotstown[10], it was worst moment of my zoo life. Then we bred these four cubs a year later. They were the first tigers to be born after we lost all our tigers, that was why they were so special. The Amur tiger mother tends to be a great mother, and the male Amur, though the largest in the world, is the gentleman of the cats. Now we were back on track and we got a great response, it was very exciting.

Hippopotami

By the mid-1980s, many of the opportunities to interact with animals, which had provided previous generations with magical moments in the Zoo, had gone. Joe Byrne, who was now keeper in charge of the elephants and the hippos, allowed visitors to get close to the hippopotami in their pond. One of these encounters was reported by John Feeney in his 'Ad Lib' column in the *Evening Herald*; it related to the making of a piece for the popular television series, *The Live Mike*:

> Mike Murphy has landed in a hospital clinic. He was doing one of his home movies in the Zoo. The plan was to persuade passers-by that Murphy was a new keeper who had a special feel for hippos: in fact he could talk to them. With the RTÉ camera cunningly hidden in the prairie dog compound, Murphy had high

Henri, hippopotamus, with visitors.

jinks until he told a woman that he was going for a ride on the hippo. Up got Murphy on the broad and scaley [sic] back of the zoo animal but the seemingly sleepy animal was having none of it. It shook and flounced until Murphy was thrown, breaking a finger and severely straining another and his wrist. One hopes that producer Tom McGrath will not spike a home movie in which the butt of slightly sadistic humour is Murphy, not Sean citizen.[11]

Gilbert, the hippopotamus which had arrived in the Zoo in 1958, died in October 1986 while under anaesthetic for an operation on a tooth that was protruding through his upper lip.[12]

Clockwise from top left: Lion cubs; Clouded leopard cubs in the Roberts House. The medium-sized cat bred successfully in Dublin Zoo in the 1970s. In 1983, the four remaining adults in the Zoo, two of which had been bred in Dublin, were transferred to British zoos; Jaguar cubs with keeper Frank Burke.

Hippopotami Linda (left) and Henri with keeper Joe Byrne and his daughter Martina (aged 10).

A hippopotamus named Henri arrived on an exchange from Rotterdam Zoo in December 1986 to be a companion to Linda. Henri had a particular way of marking his territory in his new enclosure. Eoin Cooney remembers:

> I was about seven and I remember standing at the fence, looking at the pool with the hippos in it. There were a lot of people around it. We couldn't see the hippos properly because the water was brown and smelly; in fact the whole place smelt of pooh! Everyone was waiting for one of the hippos to stand up so that we could see it. Then one of the hippos came out, pointed his rear end at the crowd, twirled his tail very quickly and did a pooh at the same time. The dung went everywhere. Some landed on the ground close to me but it landed on other people. The adults were not happy but the kids loved it.[13]

The question of the water in the hippo pool had been discussed at a council meeting in 1969 and they had resolved that:

While the general cleanliness of the hippo pool was unsightly by human standards it reflected the biological requirements of the animals and that nothing should be done to alter this situation. On the contrary, the public should be allowed to see the animals in conditions which as far as possible, simulated natural conditions.[14]

The geese and horticulture

During this period, free-range geese were still a feature of Dublin Zoo. They roamed around the lawns and down by the lake, mingling with the visitors. Leah Benson described an encounter with the geese:

> We were on a day out with our school, the Dalkey School Project, and we had gone to the Zoo early in summer. A friend, Emma, and I were near the Children's Corner eating crisps, which I remember was a really big deal for us at the time. We were left behind by the group and were surrounded by geese. We were about seven years old and about the same height as the geese. The geese were vicious; they didn't bite but they were spitting at us. They wanted our crisps but I remember

Geese on the lawn by the lake.

clearly that we didn't relinquish them! We were completely surrounded for what seemed like an age until someone noticed and rescued us.[15]

The geese also made life difficult for the horticultural staff. They pecked the lawns down to 'bowling-green levels',[16] which allowed weeds and daisies to take over. Frank Burke, who worked as a pony boy while he was still at school and started as a member of the grounds staff in 1960, said that one of his first jobs was to poison the daisies on the lawn in front of the entrance lodge. Prior to the strawberry breakfast in May, the geese droppings were washed off the paths using a powerful hose, and the rose beds, tulip beds and other flowerbeds were prepared for the coming social season.[17]

While the garden beds and lawns were a source of pride, they were not practical in such a busy place. Crisp packets and other rubbish got caught in the rose bushes, and the many small patches of grass around the Zoo required constant attention. Stephen Butler, who trained as a horticulturalist in Kew Gardens in London, said:

When I joined the Zoo in 1981 it was a very bare and barren place. The animals were always visible. Most viewing areas had ordinary grass, which needed mowing all summer. The lake edges were very bare and muddy and the geese constantly grazed on whatever vegetation was there. There was no question of spending money

Tyson, a rare lion-tailed macaque with Gerry Creighton (junior) in December 1988. Dublin Zoo was very successful in breeding the macaque from the south of India and, in 1983, claimed to have the largest breeding group in Europe.

on mass planting and we propagated almost everything in our small nursery from cuttings and seed. Over several years we planted the lake edges with about 5,000 native Wood Sedge (*Carex pendula*) and New Zealand Satin Flower (*Libertia grandiflora*), both of which could resist the major problem of the geese. Many small labour-intensive grass areas were also removed and replaced with low-growing ground cover such as *Cotoneaster rotundifolia*. This helped reduce time spent on mowing.[18]

The pony and trap

The pony-and-trap ride had been available in the Zoo for a long time and was still very popular in the 1980s. But, in early summer, 1987,[19] there was an accident in which the driver, Helen Clarke, ended up injured in hospital, as did two children who suffered from shock. Helen Clarke[20] started helping in the Zoo in 1973 at the age of nine in Pets' Corner. She was known for having a natural ability with horses and began driving the pony and trap from the age of thirteen.[21] She described the incident:

> After I had been working weekends through the summer in the Zoo as a teenager, I left to work as a riding instructor for five years and came back in 1987. Taffey and Stoney were the two ponies that were used for the pony and trap rides and they were rock solid, strong and steady. But Taffey was knocked down and killed over winter. And it was difficult to get a pony to match Stoney. A pair called Rainbow and Festival was brought in that had already been trained. A supporter of the Zoo had bid for Festival in a charity auction against Charlie Haughey and had given him to the Zoo in exchange for a life membership. Festival was easily spooked and was afraid of balloons. Rainbow bit people.
>
> On the day of the accident, they had been going all morning and I was bringing them in at lunchtime. The normal route for the ride was to swing around in a small circle by the old parrot house but the director Peter Wilson was giving a lecture to veterinary students about the snow leopards so I had to go back around the restaurant [Haughton House]. A C&C lorry was making a delivery to the restaurant; the rattling bottles spooked the ponies and they careered out of control. I gave them rein but there was no place to turn. It was May and there were children everywhere and I tried to steer them safely into the yard where they

Staff member
Brian Stone and
the Bisto train.

Entrance to Pets'
Corner, with the
wishing chair in
the background.

Snow leopard and cubs in Dublin Zoo. The cat from central Asia has been breeding successfully in Dublin Zoo since 1988 when a young male cub, named Patrice, was hand-reared. In May 1993, three snow leopards were born and successfully reared. The Dublin Zoo snow leopards are part of a European Endangered Species Breeding Programme.

would have stopped. Two children were knocked down. I saw a building in front and turned them just in time but they hit a car. I was standing – the driver always stood on the trap – and I fell off and ended up under the car. I was in hospital for a week. There were no more pony rides after that.[22]

Restaurants

Although the social life of the Zoo had fallen away considerable by the mid-1980s, Haughton House members' restaurant was a popular place for lunch for people who worked nearby and for business lunches. The restaurant was often booked out well in advance for lunch on St Stephen's Day or Mother's Day. In March 1985, the restaurant was reviewed in the 'Table for Two' column in *The Irish Times*:

The restaurant reminds me of a middling hotel in a provincial town. It even has authentic touches like the whiff of Brussels sprouts that hits one at the door.

Left: Members' restaurant in Haughton House, mid-1980s. Right: African elephant Debbie, with Aoife Murphy, Zoo staff member from 1995 onwards, on her communion day in 1980.

Grown ups see things differently. They see the packet soup, undistinguished main courses, instant desserts and boring, but expensive, wine list. They also see the bill, £24.75 for lunch, with a half bottle of everyday wine for two parents and a two year old child. Yet I'll probably go back more than once during the summer. Everyone's so nice that it's one of the few places parents can go for a fairly formal lunch without feeling under pressure because they're accompanied by young children.[23]

In May 1985, a new fast-food restaurant and the new lakeside coffee shop were opened by Campbell Catering. A reporter in the *Evening Herald* noted, 'It's all a far cry from the old Royal Zoological Society of Ireland when sedate garden parties and private dining rooms made a clear division between those who belonged to the society and those who just paid their admission fee at the gate.'[24]

But at the Society's annual general meeting in January 1986, one of the members was not too happy. It was recorded in the minutes of the meeting that 'she had sampled the new chef's cooking at breakfast that morning and felt that the breakfast was not correctly cooked'.[25]

Fota Wildlife Park, Cork

In 1980, lack of space for the size of the collection in Dublin Zoo was a major obstacle in the way of modernising. In 1981 there were 1,020 animals.[26] The number dropped steadily during the 1980s but it was still cause for concern among staff and visitors. The council had been asking the Office of Public Works for extra land for the Zoo for many years and, while they were not going to give up the hope of an extension in the Phoenix Park, they decided to investigate the possibilities of purchasing a site within thirty miles of Dublin. Urban zoos around the world had taken the approach of splitting their collections between an urban site and a rural site with reasonable success. An overall zoo management body could arrange a collection of animals across an urban zoo and a wildlife park in a way that encouraged breeding, allowed for larger groups of animals to be kept, and provided its visitors with the

Young African elephants Judy (left) and Debbie, who were born in the wild in Uganda in the mid-1970s and arrived in Dublin in February 1980, after being purchased from the Chipperfield Organisation, Longleat. Council member, Margaret Sinanan (at rear of the group) is conducting a group of children on a tour of the Zoo.

option of seeing the animals in a natural-looking environment such as an open grassland with several species in one exhibit, or close up in the traditional zoo space. Often the wildlife park was within comfortable driving distance of the urban zoo but that was not always the case. The Dublin Zoo council looked at sites in Wicklow and Kildare. However, in 1979, following an offer from University College Cork to make a 70-acre portion of Fota Island available for a wildlife park, the decision was made to set up the new park there.[27]

The fund-raising was launched early in 1980 to take advantage of the anniversary celebrations. In light of the international developments, many urban zoos were creating wildlife parks and the 70 acres on Fota, which included

President Hillery at the opening of Fota Wildlife Park on 27 July 1983.

30 acres of parkland as well as woodland, grassland, a slight hill and a lake, were ideal. Terry Murphy, who 'conceived the Fota Wildlife Project as an essential part of the Society's programme of breeding endangered species',[28] was adamant that the collections in Dublin Zoo and in Fota should complement each other. Plans, fund-raising, organisation and management of the Fota Wildlife Park proceeded rapidly with the council discussing many details of its development. Principles concerning the species to be established in Fota focused on species which were rare, endangered or difficult to breed. The importance of Irish fauna was also stressed. The design of the exhibits was to be as open and natural as possible. Education was also to be an integral part of the management of the park, ensuring that the objectives of the modern zoo were incorporated into the new park. Sean McKeown, assistant to the director in Dublin Zoo was seconded to Fota and was later appointed its first Park Manager.

Giraffe, zebra and cheetah were amongst the animals acquired for Fota. In July 1983, it was opened to the public by President Hillery who described it as 'a most admirable and inspired idea'. For three years, the council had put a tremendous effort into developing Fota Wildlife Park and their efforts had paid off. It was noted with disappointment at the annual general meeting in January 1981, however, that of over 7,000 members of the Society, only 200 had made donations to date.[29] It is likely that Fota was too far away from Dublin for the average Zoo visitor or member to consider it in practical terms as an extension of Dublin Zoo or, indeed, as an alterative option for a day among wild animals. It also made little immediate difference in relieving the congested animal accommodation in the Zoo.

Strife

In the early 1980s, the council was running on an overdraft: £37,000 in 1980 suddenly jumped to £146,000 in 1982. All the major costs had escalated and, while revenue from admission and other sources also grew, it simply did not match the outgoings. In December 1980, the president and honorary officers of the Society had a meeting with the newly appointed 'staff union representatives' during which safety issues were raised and the question of staff representation on the council was discussed. During the meeting, the council also reassured the union that Fota would be run as a separate entity.[30] By then the conditions in Dublin Zoo had reached the stage where animal accommodation, visitor facilities and the general appearance of the Zoo was such that coats of paint and other low-cost maintenance were inadequate to fix them.

By 1982, the government grant was £5,000 and the Dublin Corporation grant was also £5,000, which paid the water rates and clothing for the staff and nothing else. Membership was steadily climbing but general admissions had started to fall. Members at the annual general meeting in January 1983 suggested 'many interesting and unusual methods of raising funds ... to reduce the Society's current deficit', which was now around £146,000. These included:

Members of council eating porridge standing up in the traditional way at breakfast prior to a council meeting in 1980. (L–r): Victor Craigie (president), Professor Edward Clarke, James Adam, Dr Niall Hogan and George Burrows.

'Pebbles', a hand-reared lemur, with keeper Charlie Stone.

An approach to Residents' Associations for donations to be sought through house-to-house collection, encouraging children to carry out fundraising projects, the building of a Dolphinarium in the Gardens . . . a mobile unit to promote the Zoo at public places such as supermarkets and the use of supermarket 'notice-boards' to carry items promoting the Zoo, and a suggestion that a hotel be built in the Gardens.

The president, Alex Mason, thanked the members for their contributions and pointed out that

While there was a deficit in the accounts for the year, the situation was not critical . . . he also pointed out that the Society is at present deeply involved in a public fundraising drive for the Fota Wildlife Park development.[31]

In April 1983, the *Sunday World* newspaper published a series of eight photos with the large headline, 'Ripped to Death'. In an article about 'mother nature at its most savage and bestial,' it described how a newborn chimp at Dublin zoo had been 'torn asunder, limb from limb, by its father only minutes after entering the world.' According to the report, the keepers had seen Betty, the mother, mating with Kongola up to a month beforehand, which suggested that she was not pregnant so she had not been separated from the male. The report continued:

> A spokesman for Dublin Zoo said yesterday that the phenomenon of parent animals killing their young 'occurs much more often than people might like to believe . . .' When asked whether it would have been dangerous for wardens [sic] to come to the baby's rescue he replied, 'no, it would have been suicidal. This father is a very elderly chimp, not like the younger ones you see at the tea parties. He is quite capable of tearing an adult human apart as easily as a baby chimp.'[32]

Industrial unrest was also a feature of the Zoo in the early 1980s, as it was in Ireland at the time. The council was in negotiation with the Federated Workers' Union of Ireland for a wage increase. In May 1983, George Burrows reported in *The Irish Times* about how serious the Zoo's financial situation was and referred to negotiations that were taking place with the union:

> The society is, of course, caught up today in negotiations for the next pay round and it is inevitable that if union demands are to be conceded at any point above the Government's guidelines, the future of the zoo certainly will be put in jeopardy. There is no other way to get money. It was put to zoo members on Saturday that if the gate receipts cannot generate enough funds to keep going then some sections might have to be closed off, leading to wage and other savings which in turn would lead to some staff layoffs or redundancies.[33]

A week later, Brendan Price, a keeper at the Zoo, responded in a lengthy letter, which was printed in *The Irish Times*:

> George Burrows, as a writer for your paper and as a one-time vice-president of the Zoo Council, should have known better than to write of possible 'lay-offs or redundancies'. To the staff and their dependents, this was the first indication that any such moves were under consideration.[34]

Brendan Price continued with a hint about tension in the Zoo at the time:

Honorary officers of
the council, Richard
Dennis (treasurer) and
Brian Blennerhasset
(secretary), at the
annual general
meeting of the Royal
Zoological Society of
Ireland, January 1985.

Keeper Brendan Price
at the annual general
meeting of the Royal
Zoological Society of
Ireland, January 1985.

Above: lion cub with Áine Duggan, daughter of Douglas Duggan, a photographer and frequent visitor to Dublin Zoo from the 1950s to 1980s; Left (top and bottom): polar bear in exhibit on west side of the lake. The barrels provided the bears with diversion.

I will not bore your readership with internal politics except to say these are hard times and there is much room for greater efficiencies, but they are not hopeless times. If your paper wishes to report further on Dublin Zoo, I'd welcome more thorough, in-depth investigation of the problems of a management structure, which is 'more old than venerable'.[35]

Several months later, a letter from another keeper, C. P. Gallagher, was published in *The Irish Times* with reference to the above exchange: 'As the two opinions expressed seemed to be at variance, I awaited further clarification of the matter by the RZSI in their Annual Report in respect of the official position with regard to the state of the Zoo's finances.' He queried the council's focus on asking members to fund-raise rather than to explore ways of incorporating 'policies pertaining to the conservation, education and, most importantly, animal care welfare and comfort'. He went on to say:

> I am responsible to a management allegedly more old than venerable (B. Price), they in turn to a Council whose greatest scientific achievement would seem to be the successful cloning of further prospective Council members to ensure that a lineage established under the patronage of Queen Victoria will continue unbroken, while they superciliously pose as the surrogate parents for the now easily bred Irish Lion.[36]

The public exchange between an honorary vice-president of the Zoological Society and two staff members opened the way for more criticism to be directed at the Zoo. The Donkey Society claimed that thirty-four asses a week were eaten in the Zoo. Terry Murphy, who was approaching retirement after forty years in the Zoo, denied it, stating that the meat was from an abattoir and he assumed it was horsemeat. The story attracted the headline in the *Irish Independent*, '"Slaughter" zoo claim is rejected'.[37] On 9 October 1983, the Zoo was closed for a one-day strike.[38] In February 1984, the *Phoenix* magazine wrote:

> The Zoo council ('Royal' as ever) seems to take a greater interest in the animals behind bars than its own employees. It's very much a gentleman and players situation in the zoo where the council now finds itself without either a director or even a head-keeper because they don't like promotion from the ranks. Replacements for these positions are now being advertised in the UK.[39]

Visitor figures in 1984 were proving disastrous as a prolonged bus strike and the visit of President Ronald Reagan over the Whit Sunday weekend made access to the Zoo very difficult. By the end of the summer, the council was anticipating an accumulated deficit of £260,000 and no way to pay it other than an unlikely surge in visitor numbers, members or their traditional method of a special appeal. To compound the council's difficulties, several newspapers reported that some staff members objected to the appointment of Peter Wilson, who had been selected to succeed Terry Murphy. The *Irish Independent* reported:

Young visitor in Pets' Corner.

> Staff have voted no confidence in Mr Wilson as director and have set up a 'save the animals' fund to help improve what they claim are seriously rundown conditions for many of the animals. During the negotiations – between Mr Wilson and two FWUI shop stewards – staff insist it was agreed that the redundancies sought should not be compulsory but on a voluntary basis.[40]

The *Sunday Independent* reported:

> Dublin Zoo is in a state of crisis. Part of the problem is financial, but not the most serious part. The crisis exists primarily because the animal keepers there are no longer prepared to be seen and not heard. Since they found voice, a virtual state of war has existed between them and those who run the zoo, members of the

Royal Zoological Society of Ireland, the inheritors of the zoo and its charter from Queen Victoria ... Part of the staff belief is that because of lack of long-term planning the society's aim to preserve rare and exotic animals and the requirement on it to provide an educational service are being defaulted on.[41]

The *Irish Press* said that threatened cost-cutting measures include the closure of Pets' Corner.[42] A report in the *Irish Independent* said that 'Dozens of cuddly children's pets may be under sentence of death as part of cash saving cuts at Dublin Zoo, according to angry staff'.[43] A letter to the *Phoenix* magazine, published in September 1984 read:

> Dear Sir,
>
> Oh, that Swift were still with us! What wouldn't he make of the strawberry-stuffed members of the Zoo Council who are now threatening to 'put down' the unfortunate 'pets' in pets' corner in order to balance their budget!!
>
> Thank goodness the lumpen lads who clean out the elephant droppings have called a halt to this madness and launched a 'save the animals fund' on their own initiative. Let's hope that this will bring the council members to their senses. If they can't at least keep the animals alive then they have no business running a zoo. The Zoo is one of the great amenities of this city but the running of it now seems to be in very strange hands indeed.[44]

In fact the Pets' Corner was closed for the winter and the animals were farmed out to people who looked after them for that period.

Peter Wilson, director

When Peter Wilson, veterinary surgeon, academic, a member of the Royal Zoological Society council since 1972 and Honorary Secretary since 1977, turned up to work on his first day as the new director, 1 October 1984, he was met by a union picket at the gate. The *Evening Press* reported it as follows:

> Workers mounted a token protest today at the entrance to Dublin Zoo as the new director of the zoo, Mr Peter Wilson, officially took up his appointment. The

Hippos Henri (right) and Linda with director, Peter Wilson. The problem of Henri's right tooth growing outwards is evident in this photograph. In September 2003, a specialist dentist sedated Henri and successfully carried out work on his teeth.

token picket was being maintained by FWUI shop steward Liam Fleming and zoo keepers Frank Dunphy and Colm Gallagher, but the animals will be fully looked after and the zoo is still open to the public as the protest is not an industrial action. On his first day on the job, Mr Wilson refused to discuss with reporters the objections of his staff to his appointment, their demand for more worker participation in decision making at the zoo, and for an independent inquiry in to the Royal Zoological Society's running of the zoo.[45]

Peter Wilson had a long association with Dublin Zoo. His father had been a member and he had visited the Zoo regularly as a child.[46] In the early 1970s, he was approached to join the council of Dublin Zoo. His uncle, Arthur Ganly, was a member, and his father-in-law, George Burrows, became a member in 1973. Other academics from Trinity College were encouraged to join the council around the same time in an attempt to bring some younger members onto the council.[47]

The Siamang gibbons being returned to their island in spring by Liam Reid and Gerry Creighton (senior). For many years the gibbons were removed from the island during winter because their elongated fingers are susceptible to frostbite and there was also the danger that they would mistake snow on thin ice as a solid surface.

Peter Wilson approached the job as director with vigour and, in February 1985, Gemma Hussey, Minister for Education, announced a government grant-in-aid of £250,000. As part of the discussion concerning this grant, 42,519 free admissions were arranged as the Zoo's contribution to International Youth Year.[48] This solved an immediate problem in the Zoo by eliminating the deficit that had accumulated by the end of October 1984 but there were no signs of the situation improving without major capital funding, which was not a likely prospect given the depressed economic condition of Ireland in the mid-1980s.

Criticism about the running of the Zoo continued at the annual general meeting in January 1985. Comments that were recorded in the permanent record of the Society included:

> One member who is also a member of staff, asked to have his comment that the animals were, in his opinion, nutritiously and behavourly [sic] deprived included in the minutes . . . [another member] complained of rubbish being thrown into animal cages, the fact that the Ladies' Committee was outmoded and that functions were elitist; the council was a self-perpetuating hierarchy and that ordinary members would volunteer for fund-raising activities if they were given more say in the running of the Zoo.[49]

Brendan Price put forward fourteen motions and very lengthy discussions took place. The president, Aidan Brady, thanked the members for their suggestions, saying that 'many suggestions made were already in the minds of council members, but it all came down to money'.[50]

Visit of the giant pandas

In 1986 two giant pandas, Ming Ming and Ping Ping arrived in Dublin Zoo with their keepers, on a goodwill visit from China. There was a huge response from visitors and the media. The giant panda was one of the last of the larger land mammals to appear in zoos; in 1936 a two-month-old male panda had been captured by trappers and taken on tour in the United States by Ruth Harkness, a New York socialite. It was then presented to Brookfield Zoo, Chicago. A few more were captured and sent to American and European zoos but, until the 1970s, most were held in Chinese zoos. In the 1970s, the Chinese government sent pairs of pandas as state gifts to several major zoos around the world but they were not available on the open market. Then, in the 1980s, in an unusual move, the Chinese government agreed to lend pairs of giant pandas to zoos in America, Australia and Europe.[51] The giant pandas, with their distinctive shape, markings and playfulness made them a huge attraction wherever they went. The giant panda is also the ubiquitous symbol for the World Wildlife Fund. Zoos, including Dublin, used the high-profile visit as an opportunity to spread information about the dangers facing animals in the wild.

In Dublin the arrival of Ming Ming and Ping Ping was also an occasion for celebration in bleak times as the country was deep in economic gloom with unemployment and emigration rising, and debates about abortion and divorce causing social conflict. The Zoo received sponsorship to help towards the cost of the visit, and the enthusiasm of the media gave the Zoo all the publicity it needed. At the opening ceremony on 15 June 1986, Tánaiste Dick Spring was interrupted by the hoots of the tree-top gibbons, a diversion that caused great amusement and added to the profile of the event. The giant pandas remained in Dublin Zoo for 100 days and it was estimated that over 350,000 people saw them, which contributed to very good gate receipts for that year.

Education

The question of developing formal educational programmes had been raised at council meetings for some time. In November 1980, there was discussion about creating a lecture hall and employing a full-time teacher. More tours for children were organised and such was the interest that many children could not be accommodated. It was still a small-scale programme and aimed at children of members.[52] Suggestions by the Education Committee that the keepers could be more involved with conducting the tours was not approved by the full council.[53] Jan Hatley, education officer at Paignton Zoo in Devon, was invited to meet the Education Committee for an informal discussion on education in other zoos. In March 1982, she met them at a council breakfast and provided a report that was summarised in the minutes as follows:

Clockwise from top left:
The giant panda exhibit on the west side of the lake in 1986 attracted an estimated 350,000 visitors; A sea lion being fed by Gerry Creighton (junior) in 1985 while trainee guides look on. The guides were sponsored by the government agency, AnCO, to work with school groups. AnCO also assisted with renovating Roberts House; Keeper Brian Stone at the chimpanzee enclosure addressing visitors.

Miss Hatley works with a staff of five, in an Education Department in Paignton Zoo which has been in existence for 21 years and is funded by the Devon County Education Committee. Two classrooms have been provided . . . Zoo tours take the form of a ten-minute lecture and a thirty-minute visit to exhibits, backed up by explanation booklets for teachers and attractive worksheets for children.

Jan Hatley suggested that the council ask the Department of Education for a primary school teacher rather than for the money. She also advised that an educational department in a zoo is not likely to be self-supporting.[54]

At the annual general meeting in 1984, the president, Alex Mason, said that 'the Society had been endeavouring for the past five years to obtain finances from the Department of Education in order to appoint an Education Officer, but the money was not available.[55] In terms of the national economy, it was very bad timing. Recruitment of teachers in the general education system was at a minimum. In the end, the council appointed its own education officer, Dr Elizabeth Sides, a zoology graduate from Trinity College Dublin who accepted the appointment in February 1986.[56] Using the limited resources available to her, she worked with teachers to develop ways of enhancing the children's visits to the Zoo and produced worksheets and other supports. A club called the Zoo Ark Club was created for children between the ages of six and fourteen and it held special activities during the summer months. She also established the volunteer programme whereby members would commit themselves to help with the delivery of talks to schoolchildren and would be available to talk to visitors in an informal way about the animals.

There was a good response to the idea of the volunteer programme in May 1987 with 100 people responding to the appeal for volunteers.[57] Maeve McDonald described the early days of the volunteers:

Three months later after a number of fascinating lectures, all given by Elizabeth herself . . . each volunteer was presented with a name badge, which identified the wearer as a Dublin Zoo Volunteer. The initial task was to stand on the driveway, between the Entrance Gate and the monkey house (now the South America House) offering newly arrived visitors the opportunity to take a guided tour, free of charge. Strangely, many visitors viewed such an invitation with deep suspicion, apparently fearing that there must be some catch . . . New badges were produced . . . volunteers were assigned positions around the zoo, where visitor questions could be answered. This was more effective than the tours but did invite some peculiar questions.[58]

The education department continued to grow into the 1990s as it took on the challenge of dealing with the thousands of primary school students who visited the Zoo between March and June every year. Una Smyth, who started as an assistant to Michelle Griffin, the Education Officer in 1994, said:

> The majority of schools would book in advance. Bus loads of kids (students!) would come into the Zoo with their teachers, and although they would have received worksheets in advance, they were very much left to their own devices, at that time, there was no fence around the lake and we were lucky that no one fell in. It was very difficult to give teachers and young students a worthwhile experience and whatever the students learnt was in the hands of their teachers.

Fiona Gartland, writing in 2003, said, 'My abiding memory of visiting the zoo as a child is of a class outing at the age of seven when two of my friends fell in the pond, another one got lost and the teacher had her purse stolen'.[59]

The Zoo's education staff introduced a system whereby a class of students would get a twenty-minute talk with a slide show in Haughton House before going around the Zoo. However, facilities were limited and, of the 41,264 school students who received worksheets and support from the Education Department in 1995, only 10 per cent could be accommodated for the slide show.[60] Arranging programmes for secondary school students was more challenging because there would have to be a direct link to the curriculum to make it worthwhile for the students and their teachers to participate. The introduction of the national Transition Year programme to the mainstream curriculum in 1994-1995 for students who had just finished the Junior Certificate was an opportunity that Dublin Zoo's education department seized with great effect. Una Smyth described the programme:

> Dublin Zoo's Education Department was one of the first institutions to respond in a structured and educational way to the needs of the transition year programme. We gave the students an introduction in the education centre in Haughton House and talked about conservation, why animals were endangered, and discussed the reasons why some of the species in the Zoo were endangered. We focused

Clockwise from top left: Dr Martyn Linnie, chief technical officer and curator of the Zoological Museum, Trinity College Dublin, holding the jaw of Tommy the crocodile. The body of the crocodile, which had arrived in the Zoo in 1938, was transferred to the Zoological Museum following its death in 1985; Chimpanzee Wendy with one of the young chimpanzees; Elephants Judy (left) and Debbie with Dr Elizabeth Sides, first full-time education officer appointed to the staff of Dublin Zoo.

Henri the hippopotamus, with keeper Joe Byrne (left) and education staff member, Aoife Murphy (right). The students were taking part in the Zoo Summer Camp, organised by the Education Department of Dublin Zoo.

particularly on the Siberian, or Amur tiger, and the rhinoceros, and talked about habitat destruction and poachers and how, in the case of the rhino, the animals are hunted for their horns, and so on. We tapped directly into the syllabus for transition year for the content. The transition year programme continues today and is one of the more sought-after modules we offer.[61]

Bertie Ahern, TD

The Zoo's troubles began to surface once more after the excitement of the giant panda visit began to wear off. Staff members, visitors and journalists were raising questions about the welfare of the animals in the Zoo. Even people who were supporters despaired; Eileen

Left: Orang-utan Sibu with Gerry Creighton (senior). Right: Chimpanzee Sunny with keeper Eddie O'Brien.

Cooper ran a kindergarten and brought the children to the Zoo on their annual visit: 'The animals weren't injured and the staff were doing their best but the animals simply did not have enough room. The polar bears were the most upsetting. But I knew that it was only by supporting the Zoo that things could improve.'

Her daughter, Alice Cooper, now an elephant keeper in the Zoo, said: 'When we came to the Zoo when I was fourteen or fifteen, I usually left in tears, particularly about the polar bears. I used to ask my mother why were we members of that place, it is so awful, it was horrible. She said that we had to be supporters at times.'

Margaret Sinanan, who joined the council in 1981, said that being a member of council in the 1980s was difficult at times. 'There was a lot of anti-zoo feeling about and I felt defensive; all I could say was that we understood and were trying to do something about it, but we simply did not have any money to do it.'

Helen Clarke said:

> When I returned to the Zoo in 1987, the place was very run down and looked
> tatty; it needed capital input, endless coats of paint were not going to solve the
> problems. Everyone was doing their best for the animals. The pandas had been
> very successful, the golden monkeys and koalas had also been successful. But the
> chimps were still in the pit.[62]

Paddy Woodworth, writing in *The Irish Times* in August 2000 said:

> Dublin Zoo, or simply the 'ah-zoo', has been one of the abiding pleasures of my
> life. I remember the reptile house, from which I used to emerge draped with
> pythons and boa constrictors, an impressive trick and one which must have infur-
> iated my parents since I was too scared to go to sleep if I could see a spider in
> my bedroom . . . Twelve years ago [in 1988] the zoo was still recognisable as the
> ah-zoo of my childhood, and many of its flaws were more obvious to me. Animals
> clearly driven neurotic by cramped and smelly cages and a general air of decay
> made it a depressing place. It was not that I had developed any objections to zoos
> as such . . . the educational and conservational benefits of good zoos surely out-
> weigh any cruelty inherent in confinement. Obviously, however, the conditions
> should be the best possible.[63]

In September 1986, Bertie Ahern, in his capacity as Lord Mayor, attended a breakfast meeting
with the council, which began as usual with eating porridge and drinking orange juice
while standing up. The alderman, who was also a TD at the time, had spent most weekends
as a child in the late 1950s and 1960s in or around the Zoo. His father managed the farm
at All Hallows College and he often walked up with him through Drumcondra to the
Phoenix Park. If his father was not available to take him to the Zoo, Bertie Ahern and his
sister, Eileen, would make their own way and walk around the perimeter looking at the
animals. 'You could see quite a lot then,' he said. Bertie Ahern continued to visit the Zoo
as a young adult and then as a parent: 'In the '70s, I watched the Zoo go downhill. There was
no money around and very little change, just the odd bit of paint and some wire, but they were
incidental changes. Then in the 1980s, the condition of the Zoo got worse and, as I wheeled
the girls around the Zoo, their prams would get stuck in the potholes in the paths.'[64]

Renovation of the Nesbitt Aviary in 1988, which was converted into the bat house. The Nesbitt Aviary was originally built in 1877 following a substantial donation by Miss Nesbitt of Leixlip, who thought it 'objectionable' that birds should be housed with monkeys, as was the case at the time. At her request, her donation funded an aviary. The Nesbitt Aviary was well known in the mid-twentieth century as the parrot house. It was finally demolished to make way for Kaziranga Forest Trail.

In 1987, Bertie Ahern was Minister for Labour and he sent in a FÁS team to undertake construction work in the Zoo. This was the first stage in Bertie Ahern's powerful intervention in the Zoo, which ultimately transformed it. There was 19 per cent unemployment in Ireland at the time. Many experienced tradesmen were unable to get work and apprentices were unable to complete their apprenticeships. A FÁS scheme called the Community Youth Training Programme (CYTP) organised the tradesmen and apprentices into construction crews and sent them to work on selected projects that would last for between six and twelve months. The Zoo, as a charitable organisation with no money, qualified for help from this scheme. Bertie Ahern said:

> I got FÁS to put the CYTP programme in. Tradesmen did major jobs around the
> Zoo, working with ten young people. And they worked their way through the
> Zoo. I knew a lot of the zoo keepers, they were constituents and they were in

my ear, suggesting projects and schemes. This was a cheap way of improving the Zoo and a very good way of helping to ease the unemployment situation.[65]

Dan Mahony was a construction supervisor with FÁS and started working in the Zoo in July 1987. 'We began work on the old bird aviary; we virtually demolished it. The walls were decaying, crumbling, and we left only some small base walls. We stripped the inside and effectively built a new house.'[66] The new building became the Bat House with bird aviaries on the outside. Sixty-three Egyptian fruit bats were acquired and information compiled by the Wildlife Service of the Office of Public Works about Irish bats was displayed, which stressed the importance of conservation of habitats for bats now under threat in Ireland and many areas of Europe.[67] The bat house was opened by Bertie Ahern in October 1988. In 1993, broadcaster, writer and environmentalist Dick Warner wrote:

> Probably the most useful thing you could do if you're a real conservationist . . . is to try and dispel all the prejudicial nonsense there is about bats. Tell people they don't get entangled in long hair, suck your blood, carry diseases or turn into Transylvanian mass murderers. I'm not exaggerating about this prejudice. I stood in the bat house in Dublin Zoo a couple of weeks ago and just listened to what people were saying. They treated the place as if it was the animal equivalent of the ghost train at a fun fair.[68]

When FÁS completed the bat house, there was turnover of personnel in the construction team but no question about FÁS moving out of the Zoo. They turned their attention to the monkey house and transformed that into the South American House. David Keane, of the architects Keane Murphy Duff, was a member of council and very involved in the design of this new house. Dan Mahony said:

> I came in believing I would be here for twelve months. In terms of the way FÁS operated, it was unusual to move smoothly from one project to another but in this case we did. We gutted the monkey house, leaving only the bare structure. I remember Mick Clarke and others lifting off the portrait of Jack Supple that was on the wall and the masses of cockroaches that were behind it.[69]

Work on the monkey house was halted in 1990 when the council could no longer afford the materials to complete the work.

Crisis

Criticism of the Zoo had been escalating in the late 1980s, and the budget deficit was growing once more to very worrying levels. The public campaign highlighting the cramped accommodation in which some of the animals in the Zoo were living continued. The number of animals in the Zoo in 1988 was 771 and had fallen since the early 1980s. Dorothy Kilroy, a member of council from 1989, said:

> The AGMs were always held on a Saturday morning and they were crammed. There was plenty of angst and argument. Apart from the fact that we had no money and everything was getting tatty, there was a real anti-zoo lobby. I remember being very hurt: this place meant so much to me as a child but I couldn't give up on it, I couldn't walk away.

In 1989, an RTÉ crew from *Today Tonight* came into the Zoo with a camera and took shots of Debbie the elephant looking emaciated and with sores on her skin.[70] The rhinos appeared to have very little space to move and the polar bears showed signs of repetitive behaviour. Bill Jordan, a veterinary surgeon, Bill Travers of Zoo Check and Brendan Price were interviewed. Peter Wilson responded. But the viewer was left with an indelible image of large animals in very small spaces looking distressed.

In 1988 a grant of £250,000 from the National Lottery fund was made to keep the Zoo going and a working party was established by the government to enquire into the affairs of the Zoo. Mick Doyle, a veterinary surgeon and former Irish rugby coach, chaired the working party. In the meantime, the situation in the Zoo continued to sink rapidly over the next year and gate receipts were the lowest since 1974. Business in the restaurant had fallen by nearly 75 per cent, the long tradition of providing the council with a cooked breakfast prior to meetings was dropped to save money, and the strawberry breakfast for 1 July 1989 was cancelled because of the postal strike. A grant was received in September from the Department of Education but that only helped the immediate situation. A debt of £320,000 was forecast and it was stated at a council meeting that 'legally speaking the responsibility for the entire deficit fell upon members of the council personally'.[71] In November 1989, Taoiseach Charles Haughey visited the Zoo and said that he was looking forward to receiving the government committee report.[72]

In December 1989 the council had only enough money to pay staff wages for two weeks and they began to investigate the 'best procedure for conducting an orderly winding up'.[73]

Zoo football team 1991–92. Back row (l–r): Noel Duffy, Anthony Ward, Willie Phillips, Joe Byrne, Phil, Paul Stone. Front row (l–r): Eddie O'Brien, Kevin O'Moore, Jim Quinn, Peter Phillips, John O'Rourke.

A council member wrote a cheque to cover staff wages if necessary.[74] Publicity about the crisis at the Zoo prompted Charles Haughey to say, in February 1990, that he was 'slightly tired of these panic statements from zoological quarters', and that he was waiting for the report from the Doyle committee.[75] Nevertheless in March 1990, the decision was made at a council meeting to close the Zoo after St Patrick's weekend if sufficient funds were not forthcoming.[76] Team-leader Eddie O'Brien remembers the reaction of staff to that news:

> Peter Wilson called a staff meeting and said that funds weren't going well and there was likely to be no money for wages. The staff got together. We made stickers saying, 'save our zoo', and used all of our contacts to get help. We got supplies of food for the animals for nothing. The Save the Zoo Pound Appeal was launched. A guy with a tape of a song called 'Save Dublin Zoo' was here every weekend

with a bucket collecting money. Visitors came to support us and to see the zoo for the last time. Around St Patrick's Day, the Zoo was very busy.[77]

Fund-raising campaigns received widespread, popular support. Schools, the banks, callers to *The Gay Byrne Hour*, the FÁS workers in the Zoo, Superquinn, Kodak, National Mutual, Kit Kat, the ESB, Shell, One Hour Photo, Xtra-vision, Ballygowan, Windsor Van Hire, Telecom Éireann and other companies organised events, gave sponsorship, promoted the Zoo and generally gave a degree of moral support to the society and the staff, which countered the continuing negative publicity.[78] Fortunately sufficient funds through gate receipts and fund-raising kept the Zoo going through the summer. In September, the council considered closing once more; the idea of going through another winter without support was too daunting. Yet they ploughed on, despite a miserable autumn and winter. Wolves had to be put down because of a disease outbreak. A raccoon killed one of the Chilean flamingos and there was bad publicity around the death of a polar bear cub and the euthanasia of the African elephant, Judy. Even the food at the candlelight dinner at Christmas, one of the few social events left for members, was poor.

In the meantime, staff members had made contact with Bertie Ahern, now Minister for Finance, and in December 1990 a supplementary estimate of £670,000 was made through the Department of Education. Debts were paid off and work on the South America House started up again. It was opened on St Stephen's Day in 1991 by Bertie Ahern, and the FÁS team moved on to work on the Reptile House.

Rejuvenation

In 1993, the Zoo hosted a major exhibition called Dino Live. It was a huge success with nearly 670,000 visitors coming to the Zoo that year. The exhibition included life-size or half life-size, moving models of dinosaurs and coincided with the release of the film *Jurassic Park*. It was created in a large marquee on the main lawn near Haughton House. The vegetation incorporated into the exhibition contributed to its success. Stephen Butler said:

> The Dino Live exhibition was a great challenge. It was completely designed and built in house and it showed what the garden and maintenance sections could accomplish given the funding and time. The densely planted background gave the pneumatic controlled dinosaurs a very lifelike appearance indeed.[79]

Clockwise from left: Chimpanzee Vicky with keeper Frank Burke and young visitor; Young visitors at the Dino Live exhibition; (l–r): Peter Wilson (director), with President of the Royal Zoological Society of Ireland, David McConnell, and then Minister for Finance Bertie Ahern at the Dino-Live exhibition.

Clockwise from top left: a squirrel monkey with visitors Anne Madden and Fiachra Ó Brolcháin in the South America House; exterior of the reptile house built by a FÁS team. The facade of the house is a copy of the original aquarium, later reptile house, built in 1868; Nile crocodile being observed by Heathcliff Maher and his nephew, John Moylan, in the reptile house.

The models arrived in five lorries and were unloaded beside the ring-tailed lemurs' exhibit. Stephen Butler remembers, 'When leaf-eating dinosaur models were being unpacked from one of the five lorries, the ring-tailed lemurs simply watched. But when the half-size T-Rex, a carnivorous dinosaur, was taken out, the lemurs went frantic, recognising it as a predator.'[79]

Bertie Ahern opened the exhibition in April and, such was the popularity of the exhibition that it was extended for several weeks.

Meanwhile the work by FÁS on the reptile house was moving ahead. Reptile expert Gerard Visser from Rotterdam Zoo helped with the design and the collection, which concentrated on East African reptiles. Facilities to promote breeding were incorporated into the design. During its construction, Bertie Ahern turned up unannounced to see how it was all going. Dan Mahony said,

> Halfway through construction of the reptile house, Bertie Ahern came in without warning. He had rung FÁS and told them he was on the way. He said that the Zoo was looking for a few bob and he wanted to see where it is going. FÁS was so pleased with his response to what he found that they gave the construction team lunch in the Zoo restaurant.[80]

The reptile house was opened by Bertie Ahern on 29 July 1994 and the FÁS team moved on to work in the Children's Corner, which was now called City Farm.

The structural problems in the management of the Zoo that had brought the institution to its lowest point still had to be resolved. The Doyle Report was completed in July 1990 but was not published for some years afterwards, although it was leaked in 1991. Its analysis on the role of Dublin Zoo was up-to-date and took into account the latest international thinking about the interlinking objectives of conservation, education, research and recreation. It also assessed all the exhibits in the Zoo and rated them from those that were satisfactory to those that should be closed down if conditions could not rapidly be improved. The bats, penguins and raccoons were among those that were satisfactory, while it was recommended that the polar bear exhibit be closed if major improvements were not carried out immediately. Half of the exhibits were listed as requiring major modification. The Doyle Report also stated:

> The role of Dublin Zoo is perceived as that of the National Zoo of Ireland. It appears to us to have been pure folly for the Royal Zoological Society of Ireland to have persisted with the word 'Royal' in its title and not to have amended the name of the Society. We hope that this small matter can be put right for it must be damaging the image of the Zoo for those from whom it should expect help and support.'[81]

In the early 1990s the council was going through a legal process to reform the Royal Zoological Society into a company limited by guarantee. Many of the council, who were active in business, the professions or academia, had become very concerned about the losses the Zoo was making on an annual basis. Joe McCullough, a consulting structural engineer, and Paddy Kilroy, a solicitor, both of whom had private practices, devised a new constitution that reflected modern business structures.[82] In August 1993, the council decided to drop the word 'Royal' from the title of the proposed new limited company, and to invite two senior civil servants to join the council. In November, the government announced that it intended to secure the future of the Zoo.[83] A £15-million development plan was approved by the government.[84] Sean Cromien, who retired as secretary general of the Department of Finance in 1994, and Barry Murphy, chairman of the Office of Public Works, joined the council, money was provided for redundancy and early retirement packages for staff and, for the first time since Henry Cole responded to a request from Samuel Haughton, Dublin Zoo had the money to create and implement a development plan that would complete its transformation.

The redevelopment

Martin Heffernan, an architect with the Office of Public Works, led the design team. Their first task was the installation of a ring sewer around the Zoo. Up until then, the enclosures for the rhinoceros, llamas, blackbuck, orang-utans, lions and others on the west side drained into the lake.[85] The ring sewer caused great disruption to visitors but was essential. In the circumstances, it was hardly surprising that visitor figures dropped to 370,000, the lowest number of visitors since 1962.

The design team visited zoos abroad to find out what worked and what did not. The result in Dublin Zoo was a mixture of themed areas based on classification of the animals or on geographical habitats. Principles incorporated into the designs included the concept of the successful zoo being 'devoid of the hand of the architect'. The architects wanted the visitor to be drawn to a glass wall where they might suddenly come face to face with a wild animal, which would be an unforgettable experience. The staff within the Zoo provided technical information, particularly about aspects of containment.[86]

Many of the exhibits built during this time are still in the Zoo today and the list of exhibits that were completed between 1996 and 1998 is remarkable. The World of Primates was completed in July 1996. In 1997, Bertie Ahern, now Taoiseach, opened the second phase of the City Farm, and the first phase of Fringes of the Arctic, which included accommodation for bears, arctic foxes and snowy owls and, in 1998, he opened the World of Cats. The jaguars, lions and snow leopards moved into the more spacious areas and visitors could now see the

Clockwise from top left: Grace, gorilla, with Liam Reid, who began working officially as a keeper in 1970. His father, Martin Reid, was appointed head keeper, or supervisor, in 1960 and moved into the house at the service gate of the Zoo in 1961 with his family including nine-year-old Liam. His uncle, Michael Clarke, was a keeper from 1949-1993. During the spring and summer, Liam and his sisters had plenty of friends. During the quiet winter months, Martin Reid encouraged Liam to help with the animals that were being hand-reared or treated for illness or injury in the off-limits areas. From the age of ten, Liam helped out with the pony rides; Architect Martin Heffernan with the gibbon island behind him. The island, which is in the deepest part of the lake, was created as part of the World of Primates. The dead beech tree was cut down from the vicinity of the old entrance to the Zoo in 2008 because it was heavily infected by fungus. It was transferred to the island by crane, which registered the trunk at twelve tons and the branch at seven and a half tons; Elephants Judy and Kirsty with keeper Joe Byrne and visiting girl guides.

animals through large, glass windows. They were also expected to look for the animals because such is the design of the exhibit, the animals could sometimes be hard to see.

The role of landscaping was now being recognised as a critical part of the enclosure design. External landscapers were used for the World of Primates but the Zoo's horticultural team did all of the landscaping for the World of Cats and Arctic Fringe. Stephen Butler said:

> Although there were disagreements as to how much money was available for plant purchase, we eventually spent ten times the original offer, and the effect was immediate. It was our first planting of bamboo, an expensive choice, but very quick to fill in. There was some themed planting, with all South American plants near the jaguars, mainly Himalayan plants near the snow leopards, and a jungle

Kepala, male Sumatran tiger, in the World of Cats habitat.

The Asian small-clawed otter in the Fringes of the Arctic habitat. Duck eggs, which are laid in City Farm, are hidden in the sand for the otters. The eggs are roughly the size of their mouths and the otters play with them until they crack them to get at the yoke inside.

263

appearance from the bamboo and tall grasses for the Sumatran tigers.

The Arctic Fringes were easier, we just used very bland non-showy plants with small flowers and small leaves, such as the birch and cotoneaster.[87]

Other exhibits completed in the Zoo in 1998 that year included the tapir exhibit and the penguin exhibit while another phase of the City Farm and the wolf exhibit neared completion.

African Plains

The question of extending the land occupied by the Dublin Zoo had been around since its earliest days. Bit by bit the Zoo had spread out around the original lake taking in a field here and a boundary there. However, in the twentieth century, the idea of a sizeable extension had been mooted several times. An extension into Áras an Uachtaráin, the President of Ireland's residence adjacent to the Zoo, had been suggested several times since 1968; the Hollow and the People's Garden had also been identified as potential locations for an extension. The Doyle Report had recommended that a major extension should be provided to the Zoo to allow a wildlife park to be created.

In 1997, during the interregnum period following the resignation of President Mary Robinson on 12 September and before the inauguration of President Mary McAleese on 11 November, the government agreed to grant 13 hectares of land around the lake in Áras an Uachtaráin to the Zoo.[88] President Mary McAleese, on taking up office, approved the grant of the land to the Zoo. Martin Heffernan once more headed the design team to develop this area. The decision was made to call it the African Plains and transfer the large African

Director, Peter Wilson (left) and President of the Royal Zoological Society of Ireland, Joe McCullough, at the unveiling of the plans for the African Plains in 1998. The new habitat was to be developed in the 13 hectares of land transferred from Áras an Uachtaráin the previous year.

animals to the new space. There was sufficient money to provide extensive open exhibits and good night facilities for the animals. There was also scope for a substantial mixed exhibit where giraffe, ostrich, zebra and oryx could share the same space. As each exhibit was completed, rhinoceros, hippopotami, lions, chimps, bongos and other animals were released into large, spacious exhibits.

Horticulture was a critical part of the design in the African Plains. Stephen Butler, the Zoo's horticulturalist since 1980, was challenged to provide plants that could be included in or around the exhibits but would not be eaten, trampled on or knocked over by the animals. He also had to select plants that were either native to the African plains or had a visual resemblance to African species. One of the plants he chose was the false acacia, a north American tree that looked like the African acacia but which would be viable in Ireland's climate. The similarity in appearance allowed the Zoo education staff to explain the story

The view at the
entrance of the
African Plains.

of the African Acacia and its relationship with the giraffe to groups of school students.

The African Plains habitat was opened in July 2000 by Taoiseach Bertie Ahern. By then the mixed exhibit with the giraffe and zebra was complete and the hippo exhibit was also complete. During the rest of the year, the remaining animals were transferred. Frank McNally in *The Irish Times* described the opening of the 'work in progress':

> The Zoo's hippos, Henri and Linda, were relaxing at their new lakeside property (featuring indoor and outdoor pools) when the Taoiseach's entourage arrived. Alarmed by the noise, however, they fled from the pool into a corner and turned their backs on the cameras for the duration for the visit. Proving that, thick-skinned as they may be, hippos will never be political animals.[89]

At the opening of the African Plains, Bertie Ahern announced a further £2 million a year for five years, to continue the development of the Zoo. The often stressful changes that the Zoo and its management and staff had undergone during the previous twenty years had ultimately proved very beneficial for Dublin Zoo. It once more had a solid base from which it could grow and take its place amongst the best zoos in the world. In 2009, council member Dorothy Kilroy said, 'We owe Bertie Ahern a huge debt of gratitude.'[90]

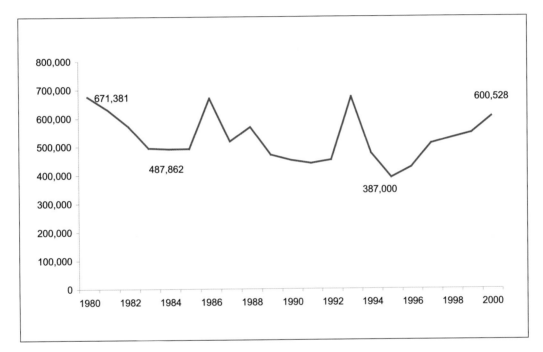

Diagram indicating visitor numbers from 1980–2000.

CHAPTER 7

INTO THE FUTURE
2000–2009

Introduction

By 2000, Dublin Zoo had changed fundamentally. With policies concerning animal acquisition, breeding and husbandry so heavily influenced by international guidelines, the daily activity of the Zoo team was realigned to take these into account. Staff were now expected to participate in specialist, global networks to share information and learn about new developments that would improve local animal husbandry practices. This involved everything from maintaining animal records in ARKS,[1] the international record database, to participating in on-line forums on specific species, making and hosting visits of fellow-professional zoo staff and attending conferences. Fortunately the Zoo continued to prosper during the Celtic Tiger years with the support of the Taoiseach Bertie Ahern and the resources to fund these expensive developments were available. By early 2009, at the time of writing, the Zoo had been transformed into a modern, international Zoo with over 930,000 visitors in 2008 and a structure that provides for further development.

The role of the council changed after the restructuring in the mid-1990s. When 'Royal' was dropped from the title of the Society, it finally marked the end of the nineteenth-century tradition whereby individual council members did everything from negotiating animal acquisitions and treating sick animals, to monitoring the size of the manure pile and throwing

Top: the refurbished Haughton House, view from the west side of the lake in 2009. Left: Matt and Sheila, African lions, in the African Plains. Matt and Sheila were the last representatives of the famous 'Irish lion industry' in Dublin Zoo. Matt was born in Dublin Zoo in 1983 and Sheila was born in 1987.

out the children who were caught jumping over the fence. The complexity of managing every aspect of a modern zoo with local and international responsibilities demanded that the council create a staff structure to do this work.

Today, the council meets every month and provides an anchor and support for the wide-ranging work that is being carried out by a professional Zoo team. The global campaign to preserve and conserve wildlife has great urgency to it and many international organisations are involved, including some who take an anti-zoo stance. The council strives to ensure that Dublin Zoo fulfils a practical role in that campaign. It is a challenging and pioneering task because it must involve the animals and visitors, both of which are at the heart of the Zoo.

The day out

The opening of the African Plains in 2000 provided a new dimension to a visit to Dublin Zoo by increasing the distance between the visitors and the animals and, of course, doubling the length of a full circuit of the Zoo. Everything was on a much larger scale, from the distance a visitor needed to cover to see the complete collection to the space in which many of the more popular animals roamed. The mixed exhibit was the first to be opened. Putting the giraffe, oryx, zebra, and ostrich into the same space required careful management to ensure that they would get used to each other and to the size of their new home. The giraffes were the only ones reluctant to venture out into the grass exhibit. Peter Wilson said:

> It is obviously not possible to force animals into this area and therefore animals were left with the gates open to explore in their own time. However right on cue as the Taoiseach [Bertie Ahern] walked toward the paddock after performing the opening ceremony [on 27 July 2000], the giraffes entered the large grass paddock for the first time and therefore the Taoiseach together with the guests were the first to enjoy the spectacle of all the large animals enjoying their mixed species exhibit.[2]

Members were invited to one of three special evening viewings of the new exhibit. By now, membership had risen to over 12,000. The exclusive breakfasts, dinners, dances and other social functions had gone, as had the reserved areas in the Zoo.[3] The value of modern membership was in the free entry, a regular magazine with news about the animals and forthcoming events, and occasionally some special events. In 2000, members were invited

The common zebra in the African Plains.

to an evening viewing of the African Plains and, much to the astonishment of staff who had expected about 500 people to turn up on each night, over 8,500 people attended.[4]

During the remainder of the year, the rest of the animals destined for the African Plains were transferred there. After the chimps moved into their new exhibit with an island, an adult female chimp and her baby arrived from Belfast. Not long afterwards, the baby fell into the moat and the mother went in after her to save her. Both drowned. The edges of the moat were modified.[5] In November 2002, three female chimps from Chester Zoo were integrated successfully. The council were told that 'the reshuffle of the chimp hierarchy resulted in only a few minor scratches. Good timing and sound judgement by animal care

Left: chimpanzee Lucy with her mother, Mandy.
Above: waldrapp ibis at the Ibis Cliff (above).

Elephants Judy (left) and Kirsty with keepers Ken Mackey (left) and Gerry Creighton (junior).

staff enabled this smooth introduction.'[6] In 2003 a young chimp was born. Called Lucy, she was rejected by her mother and had to be hand-reared.[7] A year later, she was successfully reintroduced to the adult group 'and is "unlearning" behaviours gained during her period of close contact with her human foster parents'.[8]

Two eastern bongos arrived in the Zoo in December 2000. This large antelope from remote mountain regions of central Kenya is classified as endangered with more specimens in zoos than in the wild.[9] On Halloween night in 2003, vandals got into the African Plains, damaged the glass viewing-window of the giraffe house and drove an electric vehicle around the area, frightening the female bongo so much that she ran into a fence, badly injuring one of her horns. She recovered from her ordeal and in 2004, she bred a young calf. The female calf named Kimba was initially hand-reared, before being successfully reintroduced to the mother.

Back in the old part of the Zoo, the hippo and giraffe houses were demolished to make more space for the elephants, Judy and Kristy. However, the vacant enclosures also gave the staff new opportunities to expand and in 2002, the old chimp enclosure, which had once been

DUBLIN ZOO – AN ILLUSTRATED HISTORY

A male eastern bongo being hand-fed by keeper John O'Connor in the African Plains.

the bear pit, became a cliff face for the critically endangered waldrapp ibis from northern Africa. With an estimated 220 left in the wild,[10] zoos were participating in their conservation by creating breeding groups and undertaking research. Twycross Zoo in England provided Dublin Zoo with six male and six female waldrapp ibis.[11] In 2004, the waldrapp ibis raised two chicks in Dublin.[12] In spring 2006, the vaccination of the birds against bird flu interrupted their breeding cycle but all the conditions remain positive for further hatchings and, in 2009, two chicks were successfully raised by their parents.[13]

Visitor facilities

In 2002, the restaurant in Haughton House was closed down for hygiene reasons.[14] For the previous fifteen years it had struggled to provide catering facilities in the Zoo and the rapid increase in visitors following the redevelopment along the west side of the lake and the

Clockwise from top: Ring-tailed lemurs with four of the five children of elephant keeper, Jimmy Kenny, in the Zoo in May 2009. (l–r): Paul, Mary, Pat and Anne Marie; Beau, a miniature Shetland pony in City Farm, and her foal with Daniel McEvoy and members of photographer Neil McShane's family; Vera Prendergast, staff member since 2006, in the Meerkat Restaurant.

Left: meerkat, Santa and Luke Kearney in the Meerkat habitat at the restaurant, November 2005. Right: Eurasian coot on the lake in winter.

opening of African Plains had put the old restaurant under even more pressure. Following an independent report, the council decided to build an entirely new complex rather than patch up the existing one. Alternative catering facilities were provided in a marquee on the lawn outside Haughton House for nearly three years while the new Meerkat Restaurant was built close to the original entrance of the Zoo.[15]

The new, 325-seater Meerkat Restaurant opened in January 2005. An exhibit of the small African mammals, made famous through a very popular film called *Meerkats United* by David Attenborough for the BBC in 1987, was attached to the restaurant. The exhibit was designed to create an impression of the semi-desert that is the habitat of the meerkat, which is a member of the mongoose family; electrical heating coils hidden in large concrete boulders provide a suitable temperature for the animals. The daylight feeding habits of the meerkat and the social system of the colony made them a very good species to have in the restaurant. Suzanne Yarker, visiting with a two-year-old boy, wrote in the *Evening Herald*:

> Coffee connoisseurs would probably turn up their noses, but for me the white coffee was purrfect. In fact, it was the first cuppa I've ever finished with the nipper in tow. He was mesmerised by the funky felines, so I actually got to enjoy my coffee.[16]

With increased resources, it was possible to tackle the chronic problem of litter in the Zoo. In August 2000, Paddy Woodworth wrote in *The Irish Times*:

In the 1990s Dublin Zoo made huge strides towards improving things for its captive primates on their impressive new island homes but failed pitifully to better the lot of the uncaged Homo sapiens who visits them.

After complaining about the quality of the food in the restaurants, he turned to the question of litter in the African Plains, noting:

> Among the rubbish which defaced its water margin on our recent visit was a floating uprooted sign. It read: 'Please do not throw your litter in the water.' No doubt the zoo staff sometimes feel like locking up the humans with some of the more carnivorous inmates.[17]

In 2001, Leo Oosterweghel, who had most recently been director of Melbourne Zoo, Australia, succeeded Peter Wilson as director of Dublin Zoo. He made it a priority to improve visitor facilities in order to 'maintain the good will of the public'.[18] In 2003, the Zoo team introduced a 'Clean Zoo' initiative. New bins that would not roll, shed rubbish in high winds or be too accessible to squirrels were placed around the Zoo. In addition, animal care teams assumed full responsibility for the cleanliness of their areas. There was more at stake in the battle with litter than the appearance of the Zoo: in 2006, Leo Oosterweghel said, 'If a plastic bag blows into the sea-lion pool, an inexperienced young sea lion might mistake that for something they can eat. Litter can kill.'[19] For much the same reason, drinking straws were no longer provided in the Zoo; notices telling visitors that such things 'are a danger to the animals', and that 'litter is harmful', are placed at intervals around the Zoo.

Stephen Butler, horticulturalist, with *Gunnera manicata*, a plant that grows quickly and well in Dublin Zoo. Thousands of very small flowers on each flower spike come out in spring. The leaves remain for the summer and, when they start to collapse with onset of winter, the horticulture team cut them down and use them to cover the crown of the plant to protect young buds from frost. During winter, neat formations of composting gunnera may be seen down by the lake.

The death of Linda, the hippopotamus

Birth and death are part of the natural rhythm in a zoo but occasionally, the careless, malicious or stupid behaviour of a visitor has caused the death of an animal. In 2002 Linda, the 28-year-old female hippo, who had been in the Zoo since 1975, died unexpectedly. Linda had come from Whipsnade Zoo, England, to replace Hilda as Gilbert's companion. Joe Byrne, her keeper for many years, remembered when she arrived: 'She was a very sweet animal.'[20]

The brilliant colour of Dublin Zoo's iconic Chilean flamingos is encouraged by including carotene in their diet.

Young tapir Diego, the sixteenth calf of Marmaduke and Hilary, is part of a European Endangered Species Breeding Programme. The spots and stripes camouflage young calves in the dappled sunlight on the forest floor of their native habitat in the South American rain-forests. The markings begin to fade after eight to nine months.

Clockwise from top left: Mark Prendergast (left) and Colm Smith, members of Dublin Zoo's very effective litter patrol; Paul Talbot, head of security (left) and Seán McMahon of the litter patrol outside Haughton House; Dan Mahony (left) and Dereck Clarke who started working in the Zoo in 1987 and 1977 respectively.

On 8 September 2002 Linda was observed lying in the corner of her outside enclosure behind the hippo house; she was very bloated and did not move. She died that afternoon. The post mortem found the tennis ball blocking her intestine and her stomach was full of food. Hippos had been killed by tennis balls in other zoos in the past: Adelaide Zoo in Australia had lost a hippo when it swallowed a tennis ball in

Robin with hippos Heidi (right) and Hoovie.

1929, and Melbourne Zoo lost two hippos to tennis balls, one in 1933 and the other in 1961.[21] Keeper Joe Byrne was surprised by the manner of Linda's death:

> Linda was intelligent and would not eat something that wasn't food; people would give her coke cans and stuff but she would just mess about with it. She would have known the difference between food and a tennis ball. It was very upsetting when she died. She was like an extension of my family because I was with her for so long.[22]

By the time she died, Linda had given birth to eight calves, five of which were reared successfully. She left a lonely calf called Hoovie who was only fourteen months old. News about the death went around the world and a search was made through the surplus list of the member zoos of the European Association of Zoos and Aquaria (EAZA). Basle Zoo in Switzerland had an available female hippo of similar size and age to Hoovie and, a few weeks after the death of his mother, Heidi arrived and bonded quickly with Hoovie. Henri now lives in a habitat adjacent to Hoovie and Heidi because two adult male hippopotami in the same space would not be compatible.

Polar bears

In a market survey on public attitudes to Dublin Zoo commissioned as part of the work undertaken by the government-appointed committee chaired by Mick Doyle in 1990, the polar bear was identified as the third most popular animal in the Zoo after the apes and the elephants. By then there were public concerns about the mental health of the bears and their repetitive behaviour.[23] In 1997, they had been moved to a new exhibit as part of the Fringes of the Arctic development.[24] In 1998, it was reported at a council meeting that the female, Spunky, was 'acting strangely by repetitive swimming'.[25] New behavioural enrichment techniques were introduced to deal with this but she continued 'showing stereotypical behaviour from time to time'.[26] In 2002, concern for Spunky's well-being grew. Sophie Sharpe, an animal behaviouralist from Oxford University spent two weeks studying the behaviour of the two polar bears to find a solution to the repetitive behaviour. Her study indicated that 'the repetitive behaviour of the female bear might well be caused by the constant presence of the male'.[27] A few 'hiding places' where she could get away from the male

One of the pools in the polar bear habitat in Sóstó Zoo in Hungary.

were immediately made in her enclosure to lower her stress levels while a search was made for alternative accommodation. Contacts in the international network identified a new facility for polar bears being constructed in Sóstó Zoo in Hungary; when completed, it would be much larger than the exhibit in Dublin Zoo and would have two separate but interconnected spaces where the bears could get away from each other if they wanted to. It would also have a large pool with underwater viewing facilities for the public. Sóstó Zoo agreed to take Spunky and Ootec when the exhibit was ready. They were transferred in April 2003 and their progress was monitored. The report came back that they had 'settled in well, making extensive use of their large pool'.[28] Spunky died in 2008 at the age of at least twenty-eight years.

Amur tiger

The Amur tiger, as the Siberian tiger is now known, was moved to the former polar bear exhibit at the northwest corner of the original Zoo in 2005 after a thorough redesign of the area.[29] Keeper Ciaran McMahon described the new tiger habitat:

> The space has its own beauty with the elevation, shade and sunlight. Tigers like to be up high; they like to see around them and, if you stand at the Flamingo Bridge and look at the exhibit from there, you will probably see them sitting, watching, under the redwood tree or on the rise of the ice house.[30] The wall at the base of the exhibit will be invisible from there. We also closed the Tundra Trail that went around the back of the tiger exhibit so that the tigers would not be surrounded by people and the high area would be fully theirs.
>
> When we did the conversion, we moved the viewing area into the exhibit and used 15-millimetre glass to separate the visitors from the animals. This allows the visitors to get a feeling of how big these tigers actually are.[31]

In July 2006, a nineteen-year-old woman and her partner climbed over a 1.80-metre-high timber gate into a service area and then over a security fence before pushing their way through dense vegetation in an apparent attempt to stroke a tiger. The woman stuck her arm through the mesh of a 6-metre-high tiger fence where one of the female tigers grabbed it and tried to drag her in. The tigress eventually released her and Zoo staff rushed to her aid. The report in *The Irish Times* stated:

Amur tigers Turlough and a female in Dublin Zoo in winter. The largest living tigers are from the mountainous forests of the far east of Russia in the Amur-Ussuri region. The Amur tigers in Dublin Zoo are part of a European Endangered Species Breeding Programme.

The woman (19), whom onlookers said appeared to be drunk, was seriously injured by the rare tiger . . . The director of Dublin Zoo, Leo Oosterweghel, said . . . 'The tigers obviously reacted the way tigers would, they are wild animals. The tigers will not be put down,' he added. 'They are beautiful animals and this was a natural reaction for the tigers if someone sticks their hand through the mesh.'[32]

A safety assessment was undertaken but concluded that Dublin Zoo could have done nothing to prevent this from happening.[33] It was not the first time a visitor had been injured by a tiger. In June 1950, a female visitor was bitten on the back of her right hand when she stretched her arm across the barrier rail in the Roberts House to pet the tigress. In this instance, she got away lightly, only requiring two stitches on the wound.[34]

Orang-utans (l–r) Sibu, Riona and Mujor.

Sibu, the male orang-utan

The degree to which the animals were now part of an international collection was evident through the orang-utan group in Dublin. When Riona was born to Sibu and Leonie, both the adults were on loan from Rotterdam Zoo in the Netherlands. Leonie was then donated to Dublin Zoo, while Sibu was transferred to Ouwehand Zoo in Rhenen, the Netherlands, in 2001 on breeding loan. He was of significant importance genetically to the European population of orang-utans because of his origins in the United States. At a meeting of the specialist orang-utan group of the EAZA, it was 'announced that Dublin's Sibu had successfully mated with Jewel [a female orang-utan in Rhenen]'.[35] It was a matter of pride and responsibility for a Zoo that one of its animals was contributing to the international breeding group; nevertheless the departure of an animal was a loss to those who knew him. Sibu had been particularly popular in Dublin and, in 2002, two of the regular visitors went to the Netherlands to see him there. Maeve McDonald, one of the Zoo's first volunteers,[36] said:

> Myself and Mary Neville, who is also a volunteer, went to visit Sibu in the Netherlands. We were very fond of him and he knew us: in Dublin, he would come over and say hello, he knew the regulars. Leo [Oosterweghel] gave us a letter for the director of Rhenen Zoo written in Dutch. Whatever the letter said, the keeper brought us in behind the scenes so we could see Sibu close up. Mary called him and he came over to us. He looked at us and, it might have been a coincidence, but we think he definitely knew us. The director of the Rhenen Zoo said that Sibu had been watching some construction work going on in the Zoo and had picked up the idea of throwing stones at the glass from the activities of the workers. Orangs are very intelligent and great mimics, but we reckoned that Sibu had brought some of his habits over to the Netherlands with him.

Dogs (l–r) Ruby, Kim and Honey with volunteers Daughne Uniacke (right) and Anne May at the Zoo lake. Ruby and Honey were trained to visit caring institutions as part of the Peata pet-therapy programme.

We were, of course, a bit sad that he had to be moved to the Netherlands, but it happens. He's part of the Zoo again and we were happy he was getting along very well over there. He fathered one baby when he was there.[37]

In 2008, Sibu returned to Dublin. Jenny Whilde, a PhD student from Trinity College, monitored the behaviour of Sibu, Leonie and Riona as a group. As she was watching them, she pointed out that 'Grooming is a good sign and they are in easy reach of each other, which suggests that they are at ease, and there is no apparent effort to get out of each other's way'.[38]

Leo Oosterweghel observed that '[Sibu] seems extremely happy to be back here now and reunited with his mating partner Leonie and their daughter, Riona'.[39]

Animal acquisition

Animal acquisition in zoos is a complex operation in the twenty-first century and involves international contacts, thorough record-keeping and up-to-date animal accommodation. Many of the most popular species in zoos are part of a European Endangered Species Breeding Programme or an American Species Survival Plan. Zoos could, of course, try to acquire animals without referring to the international studbook keepers but, were they to do that, they would find it very difficult to transfer zoo-bred animals out of their institution. They would also run the risk of losing the respect of the zoo community and could eventually find it very difficult to acquire popular species.

Breeding groups of animals are in particular demand in zoos for many reasons such as the good quality of life for the animals in a family group, the experience and knowledge gained by staff and the insight the groups contribute to formal and informal education programmes about their species in the wild. It is also satisfying for visitors and staff to be part of an international network

Sumatran tiger Sigra with her cubs Satu, Dua and Tiga. Many of the births in Dublin Zoo are now caught on infrared camera, providing vital information to the Zoo team.

that is endeavouring to preserve and conserve wildlife. And, most of all, adult animals with young offspring are a delight for visitors to watch as they interact with each other.

In 2004, Dublin Zoo used its own initiative to create a successful breeding group of the southern white rhinoceros in the African Plains.

The Southern White Rhinoceros

In 2004, Paul O'Donoghue, the newly appointed assistant to the director (animals and grounds) in Dublin Zoo, went to South Africa to acquire animals to start up a new breeding group of the southern white rhinoceros in Dublin. At the time, the Zoo had one male and two elderly female rhinoceros and their breeding potential was slim. In June 2004, Leo Oosterweghel advised the council:

It is predicted that in a few years' time Dublin Zoo will only have one female

The rhinoceros, which arrived from South Africa in 2004: (l–r) Chaka, Ashanti and Zanta.

Clockwise from top left:
Ring-tailed lemurs with Paul
O'Donoghue, assistant to the
director (animals and grounds);
The first picture of the southern
white rhinoceros calf, Zukiswa
(known as Zuki) who was born
on 28 May 2008, with her
mother, Ashanti; A female rhino
being rubbed down by keepers,
a procedure which the rhinos
enjoy and which keeps their
skin in good condition;
Glitter in the dung of the
rhinoceros, which allows the
keepers to match the dung
with the animals and carry
out tests on hormone levels.

rhinoceros left. To ensure that the Zoo has rhinoceros in the future and can contribute to the European zoo population, the acquisition of young animals must be considered. Unfortunately no surplus animals of breeding age exist within Europe but there is an opportunity to import directly from [National Parks in] South Africa, where a surplus does exist. The European studbook keeper is fully supportive of such an initiative from Dublin Zoo and the Assistant to the Director, Animals and Grounds, has started exploring the possibilities. This proposed importation will not be cheap but it would be a timely and wise investment in the animal collection of Dublin Zoo.[40]

Leo Oosterweghel discussed the ethics of importing and paying for the rhinoceros with Dr L. E. M. de Boer, the chairman of the EAZA. He informed the council that EAZA had no problems with this transaction. The following quote was included in his report: 'Occasionally opportun-ities arise where a direct importation of surplus animals from the wild is possible to improve the genetics of the European zoo population. We should not shy away from such importations.'[41]

The council agreed that the acquisition should go ahead and, in 2004, Paul O'Donoghue travelled to South Africa to select unrelated animals of breeding age. He said:

> We wanted animals that had been with their mothers for at least three years and who had left the group because they were now too old. These animals would have the sort of social experience required to breed and rear their young. We also wanted animals that looked healthy and who were part of the group and not out on their own. We wanted to make sure they had no physical problems, no wounds and no signs of bad feet.[42]

During his thirty years' experience working in zoos and with animals in the wild, Paul O'Donoghue had spent some time in the 1970s catching rhinoceros in Uganda for zoos in the United Kingdom. He had built up understanding about which animals would breed and which would not, and was part of the professional network of specialists who discussed breeding and other husbandry issues concerning rhinoceros. Drawing on his connections and experience, he made contact with two national parks and a private wildlife park in South Africa where rhinoceros of breeding age were available and where there was a high standard of management and care for the animals. He watched the animals, noting their characters, their social interaction with other members of the group and their condition. He selected one rhinoceros from each of the three parks and brought them together in the quarantine station in South Africa. Over thirty days, the one male and two female rhinoceros were introduced to each other and watched by local staff to see if they would get on.

They were kept together in South Africa and fed a diet that slowly adjusted them to the diet they could expect in Ireland. They were also trained to get into and out of the transport boxes, which would take them by air to Dublin. Once Paul O'Donoghue was satisfied they were ready and the quarantine period was completed, they were flown to Stansted Airport outside London, transferred to a Russian cargo plane and flown to Dublin. They underwent another quarantine period in Dublin. The old male already in the Zoo was separated from the group but the two old females integrated with the new arrivals easily. They were fed mostly hay and a dry feed concentrate containing vitamins. They were given fruit, vegetables and branches to chew on as behavioural enrichment rather than for nutrition.

The activity of the group was monitored for signs that one of the females might be pregnant. Their hormone levels were checked using samples of their dung. The difficulty in matching the dung to the female in their large, open space was solved by putting different colour glitter into their food. Harmless blue and silver glitter was added to their feed, allowing tests to be carried out successfully. In June 2008, the care with which the group was created paid off and after sixteen months of pregnancy a lively young female named Zukiswa was born to Ashanti. She soon became known as 'Zuki'.[43]

The Zoo Team

Following the restructure of the Society in the mid-1990s, the impact of the changes moved swiftly through the staffing structure. With the loss of experienced staff through redundancy and early retirement in the mid-1990s, the next generation found itself in senior positions. As in the past, many staff had started working in the Zoo as grounds staff but, with so many keepers leaving, there was a greater demand on everyone to assist with keeping duties. Traditionally staff training in zoos was localised with existing keepers training new members

Keepers (l–r) Yvonne Curtin, Bernie McDonnell, Anita Langstone, Julie Bevins and Gretchen Doyle.

Clockwise from top: The East-Side team (l–r):
Clair Aughy, Sandra Devaney, Louise Brennan,
Eddie O'Brien (team leader), Bernie McDonnell,
Ken Mackey, Peter Foley, Louise McDermott and
Brendan Walsh; Paddy O'Brien, who was on the
keeping staff from 1947 to 1949, with his
nephew, Eddie O'Brien, who helped in Pets'
Corner from the age of eleven in 1981, joined
the keeping staff in 1987 and is now team leader,
East-Side. His grandfather, father and uncles
were members of the Phoenix Park staff;
Michael Clarke, keeper from 1949 to 1993
and his daughter, Helen Clarke, team-leader,
African Plains.

of staff. This training had been augmented occasionally with Dublin Zoo staff visiting other zoos and experts from other zoos providing specialist advice to the Dublin team. In 1999 the Zoo established a link with Sparsholt College in Hampshire, England. Several members of the keeping staff were sponsored by the Zoo to undertake the Advanced National Certificate in Management of Zoo Animals, an initiative of the British and Irish Association of Zoos and Aquariums (BIAZA) and delivered by Sparsholt College to member zoos. New staff could undertake an internationally recognised training programme when they joined the Dublin Zoo team[44] and, in 2003, advertisements for several new keeping positions attracted hundreds of applicants. Three multi-skilled teams were created to cover every aspect of the work in designated regions of the Zoo. Team leaders were appointed and a formal career path within the Zoo was created. More women joined the keeping staff and work practices were introduced to ensure that muscle power was not required to handle even the largest animals. Helen Clarke, a keeper since 1987 and now the team leader in the African Plains, remembered the male environment of the Zoo when she started:

> Female keepers really only worked in the aviary or in Pets' Corner. Myself, Julie Staines and Gillian Steward used to gang up on the men and ask why we could not work with the larger animals. We were told we wouldn't be strong enough to open the gates and other nonsense. Gradually we started to branch out and I worked with the rhinos and Julie worked with the giraffes. Now the method of working has changed completely and so many things are mechanised. We also have training in manual handling, for example: the average weight of a bag of feed is twenty-five kilogrammes and if someone can't handle it, they get a second person to help them.[45]

Alice Cooper, who worked in the National Gallery education department before joining the Zoo team in 2003, commented on being a female keeper:

> It was a very male environment but Leo addressed the gender balance. I had lived in Borneo from 1998 to 1999, working in Sepilok Orang-utan Wildlife Centre as a volunteer. I left with a bigger picture of conditions in the wild for animals, which is much more bleak and complicated than I imagined. In Dublin, I worked with big cats and now the elephants. Historically it was a male environment but I get on very well with the men; they can be outrageous but there's no chauvinism.

Keeper Ciaran
McMahon speaking
at the Association of
British and Irish Wild
Animal Keepers, held
in Dublin Zoo in
March 2009.

> I started with five or six other women. Health and safety standards have helped
> women and allowed significant openings for women to do the job. Besides, men
> aren't allowed to lift large bales of hay any more than the women are.[46]

As the demand on staff to participate in international networks increased, attendance at
conferences and other meetings was no longer confined to the directorate. In 2004, Dublin
Zoo was represented at the EAZA annual conference in Sweden by the director, the assistant
to the director (animals and grounds), Paul O'Donoghue, and the three team leaders, Helen
Clarke, Gerry Creighton (junior) and Eddie O'Brien. In October 2005 several keepers spoke
at the British Association of Science Festival hosted by Trinity College Dublin.

As more requests to attend conferences, undertake research and participate in conservation
projects came through from the Zoo team to the director, in October 2005 the council
decided to set up a budget for staff development.[47] In May 2006, two of the elephant team
attended the International Congress of Zoo Keepers in Australia.[48] In 2008, Gerry Creighton's
(junior) paper entitled 'Giant Footsteps' about the development of Dublin Zoo's new elephant
habitat, the Kaziranga Forest Trail (opened in 2007), was voted by delegates to the British

and Irish Association of Zoos and Aquariums (BIAZA) conference as the best paper of the conference. And at Bristol Regional Environment Enrichment Conference in 2008, delegates selected the paper about the enrichment programme for elephants presented by elephant team members James Creighton and Alice Cooper as the best paper.[49]

New staff facilities were also completed in 2005. Besides improving conditions for the staff, the new facilities provided easy access to the computerised, complex, record-keeping system and to international resources such as Zootrition, which provides up-to-date information on nutrition for the animals. Computer courses were provided for staff, as were courses in public speaking for those who were happy to address the public during a scheduled 'meet the keeper' session.

Education

Life in the Zoo has changed for the visitors also. The traditional access to most of the animals by touching or feeding has ceased. Now visitors can only watch the animals but the more they know about the subtle interactions, the more interesting a visit to the Zoo can be. Substantial formal and informal education programmes have been created for school students by the Zoo's Education Department. Many of the students are primary age but the success of the transition year programme in the 1990s prompted the education staff to pursue this approach further. In 2009, Dublin Zoo offers a range of modules that link directly to the secondary school curricula in biology and art. In the case of the ecology module in Leaving Certificate and Junior Certificate biology, students have the option of looking at a habitat, such as a grassland and woodland. After a theoretical introduction, the students are taken to a site in the Phoenix Park to look at a natural environment. Una Smyth, the education officer in Dublin Zoo, said:

> The Phoenix Park Authority gave us access to a site down in the Victorian gardens to carry out the practical elements of the ecology module. However, because of its location, the Park staff had to keep it mowed neatly and we were then given a site opposite McKee barracks and they don't touch it; it's under trees and it is allowed to grow naturally so it's perfect for the practical element of our very popular ecology module.[50]

In 2005, Dublin Zoo was accredited as a Discover Science Centre[51] as part of a national

programme to assist primary school teachers in delivering science-related subjects to school students. In one programme run by the Zoo called 'Mini-Beasts', young students examine earwigs, caterpillars, centipedes, woodlice, zoo-bred stick insects, cockroaches and other insects and fill in worksheets that teach them how to identify and classify the insects. Through graded worksheets, they identify, for example, how many legs an insect has, or how it moves, or whether it lives in wet or dry habitats. Stephen Butler, the horticulturalist, provided logs to assist in the creation of habitats so that the Education Centre has plenty of insects to work with. Such is the popularity of the programme that a full-time and a part-time teacher plus Zoo volunteers now assist Una Smyth with the Zoo's education programmes.[52]

Dublin Zoo runs many other hands-on educational programmes to provide excitement and interest to young visitors in a semi-formal or informal way. Days and events are organised all year around and include such themes as 'Springtime on the Farm', or 'Craft in Action', which includes sheep-shearing and milking demonstrations, 'Native Species Weekends', 'Young Zoologist Days' and art competitions. In 2007, nearly 1,000 girl guides visited the Zoo in April and raised €600 towards the Zoo's Rhinoceros Campaign, which was part of the EAZA-coordinated campaign to raise money for rhinoceros conservation.[53]

Casual education for visitors has been promoted through Dublin Zoo keeper talks, signage or chats with a volunteer. Dublin Zoo staff have always been known for their approachability and willingness to provide information about the animals to visitors when queried. In recent years, the Zoo invested in a portable microphone to allow keepers to speak to a crowd during the scheduled feeding of some animals. The daily, scheduled feeding of the sea lions with a commentary by the keepers has become one of the more popular events in the Zoo. This innovation tied in well with the sea lion training, which the keepers developed with the help of sea lion expert Peter Bloom of Flamingo Land in Yorkshire. Eddie O'Brien, team leader in charge of the sea lions, said:

> The veterinary side of looking after the sea lions was always difficult because we would have to chase them around or even empty the pool to catch the animals to carry out routine checks. In 2006 we started training the sea lions to follow a red target. The animals know that if they touch the target and hear a whistle, they get a reward. We do this every day so that the animals are used to it and we include it in the public performance but it is essentially for veterinary procedures. With this training, we can guide the sea lions into separate pens where we can look at them and carry out any veterinary work when necessary.[54]

A small natural history museum has also been created in the Learning and Discovery Centre. Many of the skulls, skins and other parts of dead animals are now being kept in the Zoo to be made available for visitors to look at and, in many cases, touch. A team, formed by the Zoo's volunteers, prepares 'biofacts', which are artefacts such as skulls and eggs, for the Learning and Discovery Centre. Maeve McDonald, a volunteer and member of the Biofacts Team, described the development of the Centre:

> Volunteers acquired some basic animal artefacts, shed camel hair, deer antler etc., to show to visitors. For a time a small table was set up beside the now defunct fish tank in the Roberts House. Then there was a space assigned in the Education Centre, which in those days was based in Pets' Corner . . . Over the years the Discovery Centre was relocated . . . Most recently [it] moved to join the Education Department in the Society House . . . There is always a need to add to the collection of animal artefacts . . . These days the director himself leads a biofact team, whose task it is to clean and prepare these items for display. Despite being gory and at times smelly, definitely not a task for the faint-hearted, there is a waiting list of volunteers willing to join this team.[55]

Clockwise from top left: drawing of a lion by Max Tormey (aged five); Kate, Max, Issy and actor Paul Tormey, with keeper Donal Lynch at the elephant habitat; boys examining tiny aquatic animals at Native Species Weekend, April 2009, with insectivorous plants in the tray at the front of the picture; Native Species Weekend in Dublin Zoo, April 2009.

In 2007, nearly 90,000 people visited the Learning and Discovery centre; most were casual visitors who wandered in to touch the tiger skin on the wall, feel the size of a hippo skull or look at the snake skin. A recent acquisition was the professionally mounted skin of Matt the lion. He was the last of Dublin Zoo's male African lions. Dublin Zoo had not bred lions since 1988 when a litter was bred in honour of the Dublin's millennium and a female, called Millie, was hand-reared and declared the Zoo's animal of the year. In 2008, Matt was euthanised. He was twenty-five years old and suffering from malignant tumours; he had been given palliative care for some time and, finally, the distressing but necessary decision to euthanise him was made.[56] Dublin Zoo now plans to switch to the highly endangered Asian lion.[57]

Sheila, a lioness born in Dublin in 1987, is now the last remaining hybrid African lioness in Dublin Zoo. Under the rigid studbook rules for the Asian lion, a zoo cannot have both in the collection to ensure there is no spread of disease or cross-breeding. The purity of the bloodlines in animals that are part of internationally managed breeding populations is a critical factor in their management and success. The temptation that she might be put down to make way for the new animals was resisted. Leo Oosterweghel said, 'A breeding group of Asian lions is waiting to be transferred to Dublin Zoo and there is a danger that they will go somewhere else as the zoo that is holding them at present is short of space. But, while Sheila might be old, she is in perfect health and content.'[58]

Conservation

In 1999, the assistant director (animals and grounds), David Field, was invited to become a member of the international recovery and management group for golden lion tamarins. At the time Dublin Zoo was acting as coordinator for the European Endangered Species Breeding Programme for this small, highly endangered primate, which is native to Brazil's Atlantic coastal forest.[59] In the early 1970s, there were fewer than 200 golden lion tamarins. Zoos, international conservation organisations and the Brazilian government have been working to conserve this monkey and estimates of the wild population now range from 562 to 1500.[60] In 2006, Dublin Zoo adopted a family of golden lion tamarins in the União Biological Reserve near Rio de Janeiro where there are large tracts of primary and secondary rainforest and a wild population of about 120 of the monkeys. Sandra Devaney, Dublin Zoo's Registrar and Research Coordinator said:

> With the money we donate to the União Biological Reserve, they can pay for someone locally to track families of golden lion tamarins in this reserve and also in Poço das Antas Biological Reserve and on private lands. Golden lion tamarin families normally include a male, a female and their offspring – they usually have twins. They can see what trees they use, where they sit, eat and sleep. All of this information is then put together to produce reports on the species and the more we understand about the species, the better equipped we are to conserve them.
>
> In the past, we had a male and a female in the Zoo and we bred them. Then a recommendation was made to move the animals around. The new male that we received in the place of our original male was hand-reared and unfortunately hand-reared tamarins don't breed well. The animals get on really well but they haven't bred yet.[61]

A local researcher monitors each group of wild golden lion tamarins for at least one day every week and compiles a report on their activities. Dublin Zoo receives a copy of this report. The entry from Paula Procopio de Oliveira for 19 February 2006 read:

> The group today was very difficult to follow. They went inside a horrible swamp and I couldn't follow them. I lost them for one hour and I had to use the radiotelemetry to find them again. They were in a big tree eating flowers. They love to eat the nectar from this flower during this time of the year. They just jumped from one tree to another eating these flowers and finally they left the swamp.[62]

Clockwise from top left: Biofacts team working on the lower jaw of a hippopotamus in the director's garden, which was built over when the Meerkat Restaurant was constructed. Volunteers Nora McDowell (left) and Ritamary Bolton are preparing the jaw for display in the Learning and Discovery Centre with the help of director, Leo Oosterweghel; the tiger skin and children in the Learning and Discovery Centre; An elephant tooth from the Learning and Discovery Centre being examined by council member Sean Cromien; Matt, the African lion, who was euthanised in 2008, in the Learning and Discovery Centre with volunteer Thomas Davis.

This is one of several conservation programmes to which Dublin Zoo currently contributes money and resources. As one of the conditions for maintaining a licence under a European Union Zoo Directive, the Zoo is obliged to support research and conservation and the council takes this commitment very seriously. Currently, approximately 10 per cent of the Zoo's annual surplus is dedicated for research and conservation.[63] In 2004, an all-Ireland Research and Conservation Committee was created with representatives from Dublin Zoo, Belfast Zoo and Fota Wildlife Park. Together they coordinate the conservation and research activities of their respective zoos. They also take a national approach to support native species conservation. Meanwhile, Dublin Zoo has provided support to programmes involving the red grouse, the red squirrel and the chough, and has also donated funds to help the work of Birdwatch

Female golden lion tamarin in Dublin Zoo.

Ireland at Black Ditch Reserve in Wicklow. Since 2007, a Native Species Weekend has been organised in the Zoo each spring. Sandra Devaney explained:

> We invite different wildlife organisations from all parts of Ireland to come to the Zoo for that weekend to help us host the event. They set up stands and hold workshops and organise games and other activities. It highlights the wealth of our own biodiversity but also highlights that if we don't look after it, we could lose a lot. Organisations like coming here because the people they meet in the Zoo are interested in the animals and it is a very good way of getting their messages across. It also allows us to meet people who are working with wildlife in Ireland and strengthens our links with them. With all the activity, it's a great weekend.[64]

The Zoo also donates money and resources to several other international programmes such as the West African Primate Conservation Action, which was started by eleven European Zoos including Dublin Zoo. The white-crowned (or white-naped) mangabey is one of the world's most endangered primate species and is part of this programme. Dublin Zoo holds

The entrance, as seen from the west side of the Zoo through Gibbon Island.

a small breeding group. The scimitar-horned oryx is another animal that Dublin Zoo actively supports. They once lived in north Africa but due to drought, human encroachment on their habitat for agriculture and hunting, regional wars and other reasons, they are now extinct in the wild.[65] Zoo populations of this desert antelope are doing well and the scimitar-horned oryx in Dublin Zoo are part of the international breeding project. Sandra Devaney said, 'A reintroduction programme in Tunisia got under way in 2007 and animals were hand-picked from European and North American zoos based on health, age and gender. Fota Wildlife Park gave a male to this programme and Dublin Zoo contributes through sponsorship.'[66]

The Zoo donates money to several other programmes, including one organised by German zoos, which supports Chilean activists who are trying to save the Humboldt penguin from extinction. In 2009, it donated money to the Snow Leopard Trust, which is working with communities close to the snow leopards' habitats in mountainous central Asian countries to conserve the wild populations of the endangered cat.

Conservation was identified as an objective of zoos in the 1960s but was slow to take shape as zoos went through major periods of change and their efforts were concentrated on improving accommodation for animals and developing educational programmes. In the past fifteen years, however, the practical ways in which zoos can contribute to the preservation and conservation of wildlife have been increasing in number and diversity. It is probable that the programmes relating to the conservation of wildlife will become a more prominent part of the experience of visitors to zoos including Dublin Zoo, in the future.

Vision for the future

In 2005, the World Association of Zoos and Aquariums produced a conservation strategy called 'Building a Future for Wildlife', which was a common philosophy for zoos and aquaria around the world. It provided a level of detail that was designed to assist zoos establish local standards, policies and practices in a very practical way. In 2006, the council endorsed a document called 'A Vision for Dublin Zoo', which echoed the principles contained in this strategy. In his introduction, Leo Oosterweghel stated:

> There have been two plans, the first beginning in 1994 and ending in 2001, the second beginning in 2001 and being completed at the end of 2005 . . . At the heart of both plans was a commitment from the Zoo that it would become a centre

Clockwise from top left: Dublin Zoo Registrar/Research coordinator Sandra Devaney (left) with researcher Jenny Whilde, a PhD student from Trinity College Dublin, at the wolf habitat. Jenny is studying the interactions of animals after a change in their social group, such as the introduction or removal of an animal to the group for her thesis entitled 'Changing social groups of zoo populations'; The wolf pack in Dublin Zoo; Scimitar-horned oryx in Dublin Zoo; Humboldt penguins being fed by keeper Garth de Jong, with actor Jim Bartley by the penguin habitat.

for learning about wildlife and conservation, where new generations could come, see and learn about the many animals and plants with which we share this planet . . . The foundations are strong. Now is the time to build on these foundations and to complete the job.[67]

Celtic Tiger Ireland in 2006 was still going strong, as was the interest of the then Taoiseach, Bertie Ahern, in the fortunes of the Zoo. Earlier that year, Bertie Ahern had announced another €20 million over five years for further redevelopment.[68] The 'Vision for Dublin Zoo' included a master plan for the entire Zoo that would create several geographical zones along similar lines to the African Plains. The zones included an Asian and an African rainforest and Irish wildlife habitats in the old part of the Zoo, and additional African habitats

in the African Plains area. The historical part of the Zoo dominated by Haughton House and the Roberts House would remain. At the launch of the Vision, Bertie Ahern said:

Humboldt penguin in the pool in Dublin Zoo.

> I am lucky to have witnessed at first hand the tremendous work, the vision and commitment of Peter Wilson, Leo Oosterweghel and all their team over the years. They were enthusiastically assisted by the staff of the Office of Public Works and FÁS since the first development plan began twelve years ago. The development plans have been animal centred. They have been conservation centred. And remarkably they have been visitor centred too. And I say remarkably, because at the best of times, it is difficult to realise a vision in which you have so many strands dovetailing with each other with one ultimate goal in mind.[69]

The council invited Jones and Jones, a Seattle-based landscaping and architectural firm specialising in zoo design to draw up the master plan. They had pioneered the design concept for animal habitats in zoos that had become known as 'realism and landscape immersion'. In these habitats, the visitor is immersed in an environment in which the vegetation, twisting pathways, enclosure design and features all contribute to an experience that provides an impression of the natural habitat of the species. Several different viewing locations are provided and it is up to the animals as to which location they are visible from.[70] Implementation of the 'Vision for Dublin Zoo' began with the creation of the Kaziranga Forest Trail for the elephants and the restoration of Haughton House.

Sulawesi crested macaques, which are part of a European Endangered Species programme.

The Kaziranga Forest Trail

Plans to improve the space for Dublin's elephants had been discussed for some time. Alan Roocroft, an internationally renowned elephant expert from San Diego, came over to Dublin twice in 2002 to work with the Dublin elephant team and assist with improvements to the old elephant house. Behavioural enrichment in the form of three, large, tree-root balls was provided for the animals. The inadequacy of their space became all too evident when, in 2004, they became highly stressed due to loud explosions associated with Halloween fireworks. They had been locked into their house overnight to prevent a nocturnal stampede but in the morning, they had numerous scratches and Judy's tusks were snapped off while Kirsty had received a bite wound to her tail. The decision was made to give the elephants access during the night to their daytime exhibit area but it was an interim measure only.[71]

Meanwhile, Rotterdam Zoo was splitting up its herd of Asian elephants, which had become too large as a result of years of successful breeding. It offered Dublin three Asian

elephants, which were part of the EAZA regional collection plan. Two of the elephants, sisters, Bernhardine and Yasmin, were of breeding age; with them was Anak, the daughter of Yasmin. An opportunity like this, where a major elephant-breeding institution decides to split their herd because they have reached capacity, was rare and it was a true indication of how highly respected Dublin Zoo and its team were that this offer was made. For their part of the deal, Dublin Zoo had to provide accommodation for the elephants that was designed to the very best husbandry principles. Also, a new home had to be found for Judy and Kirsty. After a major international effort involving the assistance of the Asian elephant studbook keeper in Rotterdam Zoo and the inspection of potential homes by the Dublin Zoo team, the two elephants were moved to Neunkirchen Zoo in Germany, where an elderly female elephant had recently lost her companion.[72]

Jones and Jones, the Office of Public Works, the Dublin Zoo team, Martin van Wees of Rotterdam Zoo and Alan Roocroft started work on the design of the new elephant habitat in Dublin Zoo. The Nesbitt Aviary, more recently the bat house, was among the buildings demolished to make way for the new habitat. The landscape of the elephant habitat was based on the Kaziranga Forest in India, a place with which Leo Oosterweghel was familiar from his travels. It is described in Dublin Zoo's draft master plan as follows:

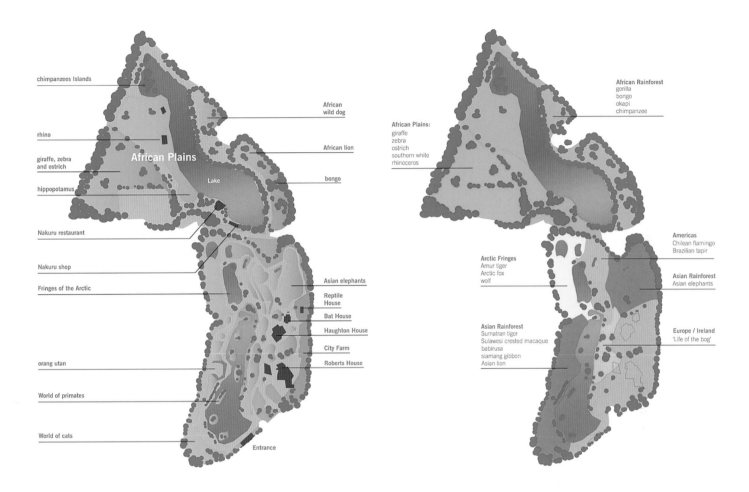

In the heart of Assam [on Brahmaputra river], this park is one of the last areas in eastern India undisturbed by human presence. It is inhabited by the world's largest population of one-horned rhinoceroses as well as many mammals, including tigers, elephants, panthers and bears, and thousands of birds.[73]

The Kaziranga Forest Trail was opened by the then Taoiseach, Bertie Ahern, in June 2007. Visitors enter through lush plantings and walk along a winding path, by a waterfall and past a stream with tall plants on either side. At several points, the plants thin out and viewing spaces have been created. The elephants have about 8,000 m² and their area is curved with

Vision for Dublin Zoo 2006: map on the right indicating an overall plan for the Zoo based on geographical zones. By 2009, the Asian Rainforest and the African Savanna had been completed, while the Arctic Fringes had been completed in the 1990s.

Director Leo Oosterweghel (left) with then Taoiseach Bertie Ahern at the opening of the Kaziranga Forest Trail, in June 2007.

artificial rock and mud banks behind which they may vanish from the sight of one viewing location and appear at another. Within the space, there is a wide variety of enrichment, with which the keepers constantly work. Elephants spend about 70 per cent of their time foraging for food, so the keepers supply them with food throughout the habitat. Hay, browse branches, fruit and vegetables are placed in the open space or in high rope baskets that need some effort to shake out. There are two large pools, one 5 metres deep, the other 3.5 metres deep for the elephants to swim in, and a power hose to shower them with cold water on warm days.

The night quarters and facilities in the elephant house are exceptional and specialists from all over the world have come to look at them. The facilities allow the keepers to undertake routine medical checks and to remove dead skin from the elephants' feet in what is known as a 'protective contact' environment: this means that at no time are the elephants and the staff in the same space without a barrier. The staff are protected from dangerous encounters, and the elephant can choose whether to present itself for a medical check or not. It also means that physical strength on the part of the keeping staff is no longer a requisite and therefore makes it easy for women to work on the elephant team. The Dublin Zoo elephant habitat is one of the first in Europe to be fully operated with 'protective contact'.

Protective contact also means that elephants that might be considered dangerous can be kept here successfully. Bernhardine, who was born in 1984, was once considered 'an animal

(L–r): Budi, Asha and Anak playing in the elephant house at night.

with no future'.[74] She was born in Rotterdam Zoo and sent to a German zoo, where she was trained in an old-fashioned way to give rides to children. Some months later, she was returned to Rotterdam Zoo where she was taken on regular walks and later integrated into the herd. However, as she grew up, she became more difficult and it became dangerous for keepers to work too closely with her. But in Dublin Zoo, in 2009, she is the calm, relaxed matriarch in the herd, which includes her sister Yasmin, her daughter Asha, niece Anak and nephew Budi. And, as the keepers do not go into the same space as the herd, safety concerns are minimal.[75]

Unlike many other zoos, the elephants in Dublin Zoo stay together at night. Traditionally, elephants were put into separate stalls. Here, the interior of the elephant house is a 300-m² space; the ground consists of 2-metre-deep sand. It is monitored by CCTV linked up to the

computers of the Zoo team. The solid waste is collected in the morning when the animals are out in their outside habitat, and sprinklers spray water onto the sand to clear the liquid waste. Periodic checks on the cleanliness of the sand have revealed that the liquid waste is broken down in the deep sand. Throughout the night, the elephants continue their forage for food and vegetables. Leaves, branches and so on are hidden in specially designed places around the elephant house. Holes in the walls lead to containers in which hay is placed. The doors to the containers are on timers and are opened at intervals during the night.

Several times a week, keepers encourage each elephant to go into a separation den and to put its feet one by one into a cradle. The health of their feet, which is a major concern for elephants in zoos, can be closely monitored and their nails filed if necessary. This process also provides keepers with an opportunity to carry out other routine veterinary checks. If an elephant is being trained for an injection to take a blood sample, for example, a keeper will rub the disinfectant on the spot from which the blood sample will eventually be taken and press a key or other metal item on that spot. When the time comes to take the sample, the elephant will be so used to having that point of its body touched, it will not react to the needle. Such is the level of detail in the design of this elephant house that the hydraulics used to open and close the huge metal doors of the separation dens are lubricated with vegetable oil, which is harmless to the elephants if eaten in the case of a leak.

Horticulture

A key factor in the success of the Kaziranga Forest Trail is the vegetation, which was treated as an integral part of the design, with the horticulturalist being part of the design team.

Grant Jones, who assisted with the design of the Kaziranga Forest Trail said, 'Dublin Zoo is like San Diego Zoo in that they are among the few zoos in the world where the key horticulturalist is equal to the key animal curator.'[76]

Stephen Butler was the key horticulturalist. Gradually he and his team have transformed Dublin Zoo into a lush botanical garden where evergreen trees and shrubs are used in and around the animal exhibits, replicating where possible the natural habitat of the animals. The vegetation also creates shelter and protection for the animals and sometimes provides environmental enrichment for the animals. Unusual plants can be found around the Zoo; the *Puya chilensis*, which had been planted in three different places, was moved to Society House garden in June 2008 when it started to blossom. It blossoms irregularly, as the plant has to build up enough energy to develop and sustain a flower with a stem that grows up to 2 metres.

The biggest challenge for horticulturalists in selecting plants for a landscape immersion habitat is to provide plants that can share the space with the animals but which will not poison or be torn up by them and which do not grow so densely that the visitors cannot see the animals. Stephen Butler communicates with horticulturalists around the world to identify which plants work and which do not.

The birth of the elephants

When Bernhardine and Yasmin arrived in Ireland from Rotterdam, they were both pregnant. Bernhardine's calf was due in early summer 2007. As the expected arrival date drew closer, the elephant team prepared for the event. CCTV and infrared lights were installed in the elephant house and the director, assistant to the director (animals and grounds) and the elephant team followed the elephant's behaviour on their laptops. The intention was to allow the birth to be completely natural and leave the herd to manage it themselves. The deep sandy surface of their communal night quarters ensured that the environment would be close to a natural one for them and that when the newborn tried to find its feet shortly after it was born, it would not slip on a concrete floor that was wet from the fluids associated with birth. The following description of the event is by Gerry Creighton (junior), the team leader for the elephant team:

> We had a hint something was happening. [Bernhardine] was lifting her tail up, walking backwards and doing everything [the elephant expert] Alan Roocroft had told us she would do. I couldn't really sleep, I kept going and glancing at my

laptop, which was relaying the CCTV from the elephant house. At midnight I realised something was happening and rang Alan, who was having dinner with friends in San Diego but was watching on his laptop too. I picked up [keeper] Alice [Cooper] on the way in. [Keeper] Ciaran [McMahon] was already here. We were all in Leo's office at two in the morning – Leo, Paul [O'Donoghue], John Bainbridge [the vet]. There was tension in the room: is everything all right? Every time her tail twitched we reacted. We kept going with coffee. Alan was on the other end of the phone: 'Here she goes, baby entering the birth canal.' There was a large swelling under the tail but it still could be twenty-four hours before the baby arrives. Anak, the five-year-old, was following her around, sniffing Bernhardine. Then the baby came out. There was no movement for two minutes. It felt like an eternity. Mam was doing everything great, ears flapping in excitement. But there was no movement. We had to make decision: do we go up?[77]

Bernhardine and her calf, Asha, born in Dublin on 7 May 2007.

Above: Budi, born on 17 February 2008, rolling in the sand during his debut for the nation's press.
Left: The Asian elephant calves Asha and Budi with Anak, going into the 5-metre pool to play. Keeper Ciaran McMahon said: 'Budi and Asha get into the pool quickly and then encourage Anak to join them by splashing her and pushing her in. Once she is in, the three play together. The adults, Bernhardine and Yasmin, let them play in there on their own and go swimming when the young ones are in a different part of the habitat.'

Thirty-nine minutes after Bernhardine came into labour, she gave birth to a healthy female calf. The entire birth took place in total darkness with Yasmin and Anak nearby. The new-born was on her feet and moving within eight minutes and took her first steps ten minutes after her birth. She was named Asha, meaning 'Hope' in Hindi following a public competition; nine entrants had nominated that name and Clare Creegan, a twelve-year-old school girl from Raheny, was selected randomly as the winner of the competition.

The publicity generated by the birth of Asha was widespread and contributed to the increase in the number of visitors to the Zoo from 750,000 in 2006 to 907,000 in 2007. The birth in 2008 of Budi to Yasmin received plenty of attention also. Once more the birth was during the night and captured on CCTV with the elephant team, director and assistant to the director watching and biting their fingernails to the bone![78]

The Kaziranga Forest Trail Learning and Discovery Centre

The Kaziranga experience was further extended by opening an elephant-themed learning and discovery centre in the refurbished Haughton House in 2008. The building had been returned to its original footprint and the open-air balconies restored. European white oak, a sustainable wood, was used; although it was more expensive than tropical hard woods, it adhered to an integrated philosophy that is designed to make every aspect of Dublin Zoo environmentally friendly. Haughton House was opened by the former Taoiseach, Bertie Ahern, in the presence of Dr Martin Mansergh, Minister for State with responsibility for the Arts, in November 2008. The upper floor is an elegant meeting or lecture space and the balconies on the west side look out over the Kaziranga Forest Trail. The interpretative centre is on the ground floor and displays the skeleton of a full size elephant alongside a model skeleton of a human and a real skeleton of a common mouse for comparison purposes. Around the room are exciting ways in which children can learn more about elephants.

As part of Dublin Zoo's research programme, which focuses on learning more about the animals in order to improve their lives in the Zoo, Meike Artelt from the University of Vienna spent two weeks studying the elephants in Kaziranga Forest Trail and recording the vocal communication within the group. *Zoo Matters*, the members' newsletter, explained:

> The trumpet call is most often associated with the elephant but they can also rumble, chirp, squeak, cry, scream, roar, snort and groan. 'Dublin Zoo's mature female elephants make a squeaking noise when they are excited, that I haven't

Clockwise from top left: Haughton House 2009. The Kaziranga Forest Trail Learning and Discovery Centre is on the ground floor; skeletons of an elephant, a human and a mouse in the Learning and Discovery Centre; One of four stained-glass panels in Haughton House by Peadar Lamb; former Taoiseach Bertie Ahern with volunteers at the opening of the refurbished Haughton House in November 2008. Front row (l–r): Betty Cottuli, Mary Neville, Bertie Ahern, Daughne Uniacke; middle row (l–r): Maeve McDonald, Avril Bannister, Patricia Pickett; back row (l–r): Kay Marren, Patsy Barron, the late Olive Regan, Mary Timbs (obscured), Rachael Martin, Tom Kilmurray, Catherine McGuinness and Claire Meade.

heard anywhere before, that was a highlight,' says Meike. A fairly recent discovery is that some elephant language exists in a low frequency range known as infrasound that humans can't even hear.

When asked what conclusions she drew from studying Dublin's elephants, Meike Artelt said:

> They are the quietest herd I have studied so far. This is a good sign because it means they are a closely bonded, small, happy and relaxed family unit who communicate more in non-verbal ways. They seem to experience little or no stress and so the panic and scared sounds are not in their repertoire.[79]

The African Savanna

Implementation of the master plan described in the 2006 Vision for Dublin Zoo continued rapidly and, in April 2009, President Mary McAleese opened the new African Savanna habitat, which transformed the west side of the African Plains. Created by Jones and Jones, the Office of Public Works and the Zoo team, the ambitious undertaking incorporated rock escarpments, sand, grasses and isolated trees in an expansive landscape. It was designed to allow giraffe, ostrich, zebra and oryx as well as the southern white rhinoceros to mix in an environment that resembled the dry savanna conditions of their natural habitat. Visitors are drawn into the world-class habitat along a winding path that takes them up a high escarpment faced with Donegal sandstone boulders. Looking out over what was once a flat field, visitors can watch the animals interact with their surroundings and with each other. Trees, plants and a themed playground contribute to the visitors' sense of immersion in an exotic environment. At the opening ceremony, President McAleese said:

> If you live in the Park it is hard to avoid noticing how popular the zoo is. It is remarkable how its popularity has never waned, just grown stronger year after year, drawing each new generation into its own special magic, its own unique world. That world has kept changing, offering something new and fresh and it was that spirit of progress and devotion to animal welfare that set the scene for this new Savanna habitat.[80]

Into the future

The World Association for Zoos and Aquariums state that, 'Urban children are the conservationists and opinion-formers of tomorrow'.[81] Vivid memories of a short encounter with a wild animal in Dublin Zoo linger on in visitors' minds decades after the event; it is an extraordinary thing that the touch of an elephant's skin or the feel of the weight of a snake on young shoulders can be so memorable even if, after careful deduction, it emerges that the encounter probably took place when the visitor was only four or five years old. Singer, actor and Dubliner, Keith Duffy, has been visiting the Zoo for many years and now visits the Zoo with his young family:

> As a kid, my imagination ran wild. You can see animals, like the tigers, right up close beside you. I remember the penguin den, which was magical. I remember having dreams about what might be happening there. There was a little cave and I imagined there was a separate world in that cave. I didn't go to the Zoo for years from the age of sixteen or seventeen. I was away with the band or living abroad. I went back once, years ago, and the place was not looking great. The penguin den was

President Mary McAleese with the director, the animal care and horticulture teams at the opening of the African Savanna. Front row (l–r): Garrett Glynn, Tina Tumulty, Lynsey Lynch, Jimmy Prior, Ken Mackey, President McAleese, Bronagh Timmons, Helen Clarke, Bernie McDonnell, Julie Bevins, John O'Connor; middle row (l–r): Darren Scott, Pat Kane, Chris Fusco, John McGuinness, John Meade, Gretchen Doyle, Sean Duffy, James Maloney, Yvonne Curtin; back row (l–r): Joxan Garcia, Mark Mooney, Stephen Butler and director Leo Oosterweghel.

Left: President Mary McAleese with the president of the Zoological Society, Derek McCleane (left), and director Leo Oosterweghel at the opening of the African Savannah habitat in April 2009. The *Libertia formosa* planted along the edge of the path will grow in clumps to cover the lower third of the fence. Right: African Savanna.

Left: Jade Pepper (aged seven) from Ballyhaise, County Cavan, in the playground in the African Savanna habitat. Right: playground at the African Savanna, Kuba Ewartowski on zebra.

upside down and there weren't any penguins in it. For a while I was reluctant to go back because it had been pretty awful and only a shadow of what I remembered.

But I have really noticed the change on recent visits and the penguins are back in a renovated den. My daughter Mia will stare intently at various animals. She has autism and there are times you would think that she has eye contact with the animals and that they are aware of her. It is unpredictable which animals she will respond to on a given day. She gives the animals her own names and remembers all the names from one visit to the next. It is a special place where she can escape herself.[82]

Brother and sister James and Kate McGowan, and Max Tormey are young members who visit the Zoo frequently for short visits. When asked in 2009 what they liked about the Zoo, James McGowan, aged seven and a half, said:

I like how the people care about the animals and let you see them feeding them, like the sea lion. I love the African Plains and the giraffe and the zebra. The giraffe

Left: Giraffe Sandy with Keith Duffy and his daughter Mia. Right: stick insects being examined by James and Kate McGowan with help from director Leo Oosterweghel.

is tall and yellow with spots and the baby is as small as a human. The zebras are stripy and strange and you can only find them in Africa. I like to see the elephants and I hope they are where people can see them. I felt elephant skin in the museum. And I love the meerkats in the farm, and the house where the bats and the parrots are. It's like a museum but with animals.

Kate McGowan, aged six, said:

I like the sea lions because I like it when I see the people feeding them. I like the museum too, with the elephant and the bones of the humans and the things you have to feel and guess what it is. I like the playground as well where I can see the elephant if I stand up on something. I like to see the baby and if the baby isn't there I look at the adult because the mother elephant knows where the baby is, so if she goes over to a corner, I'll know the baby is there. I like the meerkats in the restaurant, too, because they often dig a big pile and go in to rest.

And five-year-old Max Tormey said:

I like the elephants because they have a trunk and they make me laugh. And I like the penguins because I like the way they dive into the water and their walk.[83]

Dublin Zoo is now firmly established as an influential member of the international zoo community and is expected to join other good zoos in taking a leadership role in the global preservation, conservation and educating about wildlife. Since 1831, Dublin Zoo has provided generations of visitors with an opportunity to experience the smells, sounds, behaviours and magic of wild animals. As economic recession once more becomes a reality in Ireland, the council will again be challenged to maintain the Zoo on a steady course while ensuring that its complex responsibilities are fulfilled. It is supported by a committed, professional team and has been bolstered by fifteen years of generous government support. The combined forces of the council, the Zoo team and visitors have kept Dublin Zoo going through tough times in the past. Future generations of animals and visitors will be relying on them to continue to develop into the future. Ultimately Dublin Zoo and the entire community that supports it have an important role to play in the global campaign to conserve the world's wildlife.

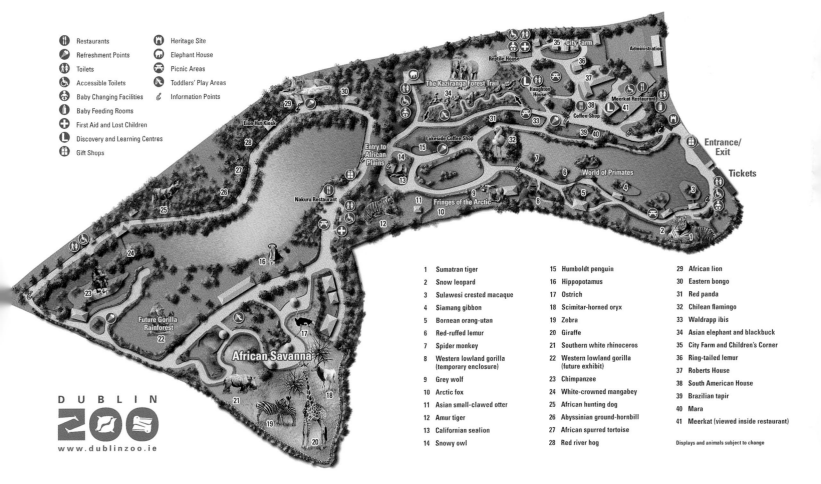

Restaurants
Refreshment Points
Toilets
Accessible Toilets
Baby Changing Facilities
Baby Feeding Rooms
First Aid and Lost Children
Discovery and Learning Centres
Gift Shops

Heritage Site
Elephant House
Picnic Areas
Toddlers' Play Areas
Information Points

1	Sumatran tiger	15	Humboldt penguin	29	African lion
2	Snow leopard	16	Hippopotamus	30	Eastern bongo
3	Sulawesi crested macaque	17	Ostrich	31	Red panda
4	Siamang gibbon	18	Scimitar-horned oryx	32	Chilean flamingo
5	Bornean orang-utan	19	Zebra	33	Waldrapp ibis
6	Red-ruffed lemur	20	Giraffe	34	Asian elephant and blackbuck
7	Spider monkey	21	Southern white rhinoceros	35	City Farm and Children's Corner
8	Western lowland gorilla (temporary enclosure)	22	Western lowland gorilla (future exhibit)	36	Ring-tailed lemur
9	Grey wolf	23	Chimpanzee	37	Roberts House
10	Arctic fox	24	White-crowned mangabey	38	South American House
11	Asian small-clawed otter	25	African hunting dog	39	Brazilian tapir
12	Amur tiger	26	Abyssinian ground-hornbill	40	Mara
13	Californian sealion	27	African spurred tortoise	41	Meerkat (viewed inside restaurant)
14	Snowy owl	28	Red river hog		

Displays and animals subject to change

DUBLIN
ZOO
www.dublinzoo.ie

The Dublin Zoo Team, May 2009

Back row (l–r) Tony Kearney, Dan Mahony, Dereck Clarke, Mark Bowes, James Creighton, Joxan Garcia, Donal Lynch, Leo Oosterweghel, Craig Wolfe, James Gleeson, Colm Smith, James Maloney, Stephen Butler, William Phillips, Darren Scott, Michael Shaughnessy. **Second last row (l–r)** Declan Harmon, Chris Fusco, Patricia Pickett, Tony Rudenko, Marie Bannon, Noel Duffy, Paul O'Donoghue, Craig Clarke, John Meade, Garth de Jong, Mark Mooney, Yvonne Curtin, Gretchen Doyle, Pat Kane, Garrett Glynn. **Middle row (l–r)** John Bekema, Sheila Murphy, Mary O'Dowd, Claire Meade, Agnieszka Czerniawska, Suzanne O'Donovan, Sofie Rogge, Anita Langstone, John McGuinness, Aoife Keegan, Brendan Walsh, Aoife Murphy, Deirdre Colgan, Helen Clarke, Bernie McDonnell, Nora McDowell, J. P. Cranny, Albert Henderson, Christel Sudway, Val Lynch. **Second row (l–r)** Daughne Uniacke, Kathleen Molloy, Jennifer Nolan, Linda Kehoe, Avril Bannister, Sandra Devaney, Thomas Davis, Una Smyth, Paul Kelly, Veronica Chrisp, Jim Quinn, Joe Byrne, Jane Almqvist. **Front row (l–r)** Maeve McDonald, Michelle Murphy, Barbara Murphy, Audrey Jacquin, Julie Bevins, Mary Neville, Paul Talbot, Mark Prendergast, Jimmy Prior, Louise McDermott, Thérèse Malone, Pamela O'Brien, Melanie Sheridan, Yvonne McCann, Rose Capitano, Rachael Martin. **Dogs (l–r):** Honey, Kim, Ruby.

Insert: Back row (l–r) Anne May, John O'Connor, Liam Reid, Aoife McQuinn, Helen Clancy, Ronan Murray, Tara Lacey, Aisling Greene, Sean Duffy, Peter Phillips. **Centre row (l–r)** Gerry Creighton (junior), Florica Rascau, Catherine Doggett, Lise Jorgensen, Adam Koziak, Laura Keaver, Patricia Kennerk, Alan Kelly, Frances Quinn. **Front row (l–r)** Alice Cooper with her son Turlough Rooney, Doris Holland, Susan O'Brien, Ciaran McMahon, Eddie O'Brien, Ken Mackey, Breda Dillon, Fiona Scally.

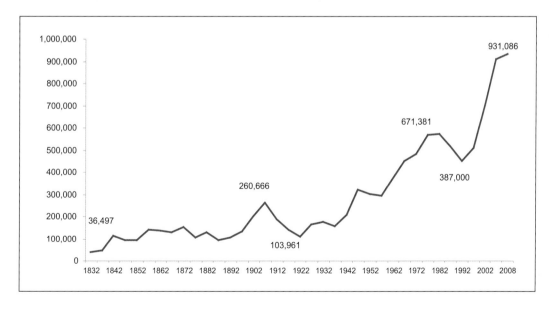

Clockwise from top left: Council of
the Zoological Society of Ireland, May
2009. (l–r) Michael O'Grady, Paul
Burke-Kennedy, Michael MacNulty,
Derek McCleane (president), Sean
Cromien, Dorothy Kilroy, Joseph
McCullough and Dermot MacDonald;
Chris Kane and Margaret Sinanan.
(missing from the picture: Tom Dunphy);
Diagram indicating visitor numbers
from 1832–2008.

Sigra, Sumatran tiger
in Dublin Zoo, 2009.

APPENDIX A

Presidents of the Zoological Society of Ireland, 1833 to 1837, and 1994 to date; and the Royal Zoological Society of Ireland, 1838–1993.

Information taken from the president's chain of office and verified, where possible, from the annual reports.

1833	Sir Philip Crampton	1916	Mr W. E. Peebles
1834	The Duke of Leinster	1917–1921	Sir Frederick Moore
1835–1836	Captain Portlock R.E.	1922–1926	Sir Robert H. Woods
1837–1838	Sir Philip Crampton	1927–1931	Professor A. Francis Dixon
1839–1840	The Archbishop of Dublin	1932–1933	Sir William Taylor
1841–1842	Sir Philip Crampton	1934–1942	Lord Holmpatrick
1843–1844	The Archbishop of Dublin	1942–1943	Dr R. Lloyd Praeger
1845–1846	Sir Philip Crampton	1944–1950	Captain Alan S. Gordon
1847–1848	The Duke of Leinster	1951–1953	Professor John McGrath
1849–1850	Sir Philip Crampton	1954–1958	Dinnen B. Gilmore
1851–1852	The Marquis of Kildare	1959–1961	George F. Mitchell
1853–1854	Sir Philip Crampton	1962–1964	N. Hamilton Lambert
1855–1856	Lord Talbot de Malahide	1965–1967	George Shackleton
1857–1858	Sir Philip Crampton	1968–1970	Professor Patrick N. Meenan
1859–1863	Dr D. J. Corrigan,	1971–1973	Professor John Carroll
1864–1869	Viscount Powerscourt	1974–1976	Arthur E. J. Went
1870–1871	Earl of Mayo	1977–1980	Victor Craigie
1872–1874	Earl Spencer	1981–1983	Alex G. Mason
1875–1878	Mr J. Murland	1984–1986	Aidan Brady
1879–1884	Sir John Lentaigne, C.B.	1987–1989	John D. Cooke
1885–1889	The Reverend Dr Haughton, F.R.S.,	1990–1991	Padraig O'Nuallain
1890–1892	Sir Robert Ball, F.R.S.	1992–1996	Prof David J. McConnell
1893–1897	Dr Samuel Gordon	1996–1999	Joe McCullough
1898–1902	Field Marshal Earl Roberts	1999–2001	Sean Cromien
1903	Prof D. J. Cunningham, F.R.S.	2001–2004	Michael O'Grady
1904–1905	Earl of Dudley	2004–2005	Brian Murphy
1906–1910	Rt Hon Jonathan Hogg, D.L., P.C.	2005–2008	Michael MacNulty
1911–1915	Sir Charles Ball	2008–	Derek McCleane

APPENDIX B

Superintendents and directors of Dublin Zoo

Information is taken from the Zoological Society of Ireland minute books and full names have been listed where available. During the period when the minute books are missing, little precise information is available. From about 1858 to 1879 Robert J. Montgomery worked as assistant secretary and undertook many of the tasks of a modern director. In 1966 the title of the position was changed from 'superintendent' to 'director'.

c. July 1832	Francis Buckley
1833–1839	R. Drewitt
1839–1840	Mr Underwood
1840 to *c.* 1847	Mr Scott
c. 1847 to unknown date	Mr Buckley (possibly Francis Buckley)
Unknown date to 1862	Mr Lowe
October – November 1862	James Henry Lowe
November 1862 – *c.* July 1865	William Smith Batho
c. August 1865–1880	Edward Carter
1880–1890	Edward Sinclair Snow
July 1890 – February 1891	Francis John Guy
1891–1907	Thomas Hunt
1907–1911	Captain L. C. Arbuthnot
1911–1938	Benjamin Banks Ferrar
February 1938 – October 1938 (leave of absence);	
February 1939 – March 1939	Lt Col A. G. Doherty
October 1938 – February 1939 (acting superintendent);	
March 1939 - 1952	Cedric Flood
1952–1956	Cecil Webb
1956–1984	Terry Murphy
1984–2001	Peter Wilson
2001 onwards	Leo Oosterweghel

ENDNOTES

Most of the information in this book is based on information contained in the minutes and annual reports of the Zoological Society of Ireland (ZSI) as it was known from 1831–1838 and from 1993 onwards, and the Royal Zoological Society of Ireland (RZSI) as it was known from 1838–1993. Rough minutes only exist from May 1830 to July 1840 and May 1860 to September 1865. No minutes are extant for the period August 1840 to April 1860. The minutes from 1830 to 1953 are in Trinity College Dublin Manuscripts Department.

Annual reports have been located for 1833, 1838, 1847, 1854–55, 1858 and from 1860 onwards. Records of the RZSI annual general meetings from 1840 to 1860 in the contemporary newspapers were compiled by the council in 1908 and published as *Proceedings of the society as reported in Saunders's News-Letter, the Dublin Evening Post and the Freeman's Journal.*

In the nineteenth century, unidentified newspaper cuttings were often inserted in the minute books; these are cited here by the date of the meeting to which they are attached. Letters from Robert Ball to the Zoological Society of London are held in the library of the Zoological Society of London.

All conversations with current and former members of staff and visitors took place between May 2008 and May 2009. In the case of Zoo staff, positions mentioned are those held at the time of the conversation.

Preface
1. *Building a Future for Wildlife*, World Association of Zoos and Aquariums, Berne, 2005.
2. *Encyclopedia of the World's Zoos*, Fitzroy Dearborn, 2001, p. 559.

Chapter 1
1. Philip Crampton in 'A report of the proceedings at a meeting held in the Rotunda convened by advertisement on Monday 10 May 1830 in order to establish a Zoological Society. His Grace the Duke of Leinster in the chair'. Dublin, Joshua Porter, 1830, p. 5.
2. The lake that is central to the Zoo was often referred to as 'the pond' in the nineteenth century. The name lingered on in the twentieth century but it is commonly known as 'the lake' now.
3. Philip Crampton, *op. cit.*, p. 20.
4. *Ibid.*, p. 20.
5. *Ibid.* p. 26. The cruel sport of bull-baiting, in which a bull is tied to a post, provoked, then attacked by trained dogs, was the subject of much discussion at the time; the Cruelty to Animals Act outlawing this blood sport was passed in 1835.
6. The co-founder of the Zoological Society of London was Nicholas Vigors, an Irishman who was to provide material support to the Zoological Society of Ireland. For a comprehensive history of zoos, see *Zoos and Aquarium History: Ancient Animal Collections to Zoological Gardens*, Vernon Kisling, ed., CRC Press, Boca Raton.
7. From 1847, the general public could enter London Zoo for a shilling on Monday and Tuesday. In the following years, public entry was gradually extended and cheaper days were introduced; Sundays remained exclusively for members and guests until the 1940s. Information from the staff of the library, Zoological Society of London.
8. In December 1830, the Duke of Northumberland was replaced by Henry William Paget, first Marquess of Anglesey

in the office of Lord Lieutenant. The letters involved in this negotiation were transcribed in the RZSI minutes in September 1894.

9. ZSI rough minutes, 28 May 1831. Their surname was sometimes spelt 'Goden' in the Society's records.

10. Precise information about the arrival of the boar is not available but it may have been donated by a member listed only as Eaton Esq of the Rifle Corps.

11. The Goddens moved to the deer keeper's lodge at the edge of the Fifteen Acres. Information from John McCullen, author of a forthcoming history of the Phoenix Park.

12. Reference to the running battle between the council and Mrs Rourke (sometimes spelt Rorke in the minutes) in ZSI minutes, 5 October 1831, 20 April 1832, 13 December 1833, 28 November 1834, 3 April 1835.

13. Minutes of the ZSI Committee, 25 June 1831. London Zoo donated duplicate animals to Dublin and to private zoos in Britain. Some of the animals had been transferred from the Royal Menagerie, which had been housed in the Tower of London since the thirteenth century and was disbanded by King William IV when he ascended the throne in 1830. Information from the minutes of the Zoological Society of London, April 1831; and Reports of the Auditors of the Accounts of the Zoological Society for the year ... 1831; and 1832; and Day record of the Zoological Society of London 12, 13 August 1831 and 16 October 1831.

14. ZSI minutes, 24 September 1831.

15. *Dublin Penny Journal*, vol. 1, no. 1, June 1932, p. 4.

16. *Dublin Penny Journal*, December 1832, p. 181-182.

17. ZSI rough minutes, 19 November 1832. Once a very common species, the world's last passenger pigeon is thought to have died in 1914 in Cincinnati (a passenger pigeon named 'Martha'), (*Encyclopedia of the World's Zoos*, Fitzroy Dearborn, 2001, p. 255). Dublin Zoo's passenger pigeons were donated by London Zoo.

18. ZSI rough minutes, 30 August 1830 (reference to Drewitt's experience) and 30 November 1832 (Drewitt's appointment).

19. Information about Burton's plans are contained in a transcript of his report, dated 27 October 1832, in the ZSI rough minutes, 19 November 1832; drawings of the plans are not in the ZSI records.

20. At the time of writing, the spa is believed to be in the White Owl exhibit, near the Penguin exhibit. Information from John McCullen, *op. cit.*

21. ZSI rough minutes, 11 March 1833 and 26 April 1833.

22. In October 1870, the entrance lodge was patched up until 'sufficient funds can be raised to replace it'. In 1876, it went on fire and was repaired. In 1971, it was fully restored and the cost was borne by the Educational Building Society.

23. These societies, which included the Linnean Society, the Geological Society and the Astronomical Society, formed a network in which the study of science flourished in Britain.

24. At the RZSI meeting, 9 April 1983, the council agreed that reference to 'proposer' and 'seconder" be dropped from the membership application, but left the line, 'your application will be considered for election at the next council meeting'.

25. *Dublin Penny Journal*, 9 April 1836, p. 322.

26. 1831, population of Dublin exclusive of the county of the city of Dublin, 176012; (www.oldtowns.co.uk /Ireland/Dublin). The population was c.182,000 in 1800, and 258,369 in 1852 (Jacinta Prunty, 'Improving the urban environment' in *Dublin through Space and Time*, Four Courts Press, Dublin 2001, p. 170).

27. ZSI rough minutes, 31 May 1833 (the keepers' uniform) and 24 December 1835 (the grounds staff uniform).

28. *The Humours of Donnybrook*, by Séamas Ó Maitiú, p. 22.

29. Miss Edworth may well have been the writer Maria Edgeworth who was a friend, confidante and patient of Philip Crampton.

30. Letter from Robert Ball, honorary secretary of the Zoological Society of Ireland, to the Zoological Society of London, 5 July 1839.

31. *The History of Science*, Macmillan Press, 1981, p. 378.

32. Kevin Bright, *The Royal Dublin Society, 1815–1845*, Four Courts Press, Dublin. 2004, p. 104-110.

33. *Evening Freeman* 13 August 1835, p. 3.

34. *Evening Freeman*, 13 June 1835, p. 3, for story on wapiti; Information concerning Crampton's tracheotomy on the waiter from an unpublished paper on Philip Crampton by Robert Mills, librarian at the Royal College of Physicians, Kildare Street.

35. The ZSI records do not indicate whether the rhinoceros was Asian or African but the illustration in the *Dublin Penny Journal*, 29 August 1835, suggests that it was Asian.

36. *Dublin Penny Journal*, 29 August 1835, p. 69.

37. Reports of the council and auditors of the Zoological Society of London, 1836, p.15-16.

38. This may be the skeleton in the Natural History Museum, Dublin. Information from Sylviane Vaucheret, documentation officer in Natural History Museum: ' "The skeleton of an elephant" was registered on the 5th of March 1842 from the Royal Zoological Society of Ireland. The mounted full skeleton on display was listed in Mark Holmes' catalogue as being "possibly" this one. Any other elephant material that we have come across so far have nothing to indicate that they could match the description better.'

39. ZSI rough minutes, 25 November 1837.

40. A very busy day in Dublin Zoo in 2009 would register about 10,000 visitors in a single day.

41. Report of the proceedings, 1830, *op. cit.*, p. 50. p. 52-53. The names of the members were listed in the proceedings.

42. Letter from Robert Ball to the Zoological Society of London, 23 December 1838.

43. Letter from Robert Ball to the Zoological Society of London, 5 July, 1839.

44. RZSI rough minutes, July 1838.

45. Robert Ball to the Zoological Society of London, 14 August 1839.

46. *Memoir of James Haughton: with extracts from his private and published letters*, by his son, Samuel Haughton, Longman, Green and Company, Dublin, 1877, p. 46.

47. *Saunders's News-Letter and Daily Advertiser*, 1 January 1940.

48. Report of the RZSI annual general meetings held on 5 May 1841 and on 3 May 1842, both reproduced in *Proceedings of the society as reported in Saunders's News-Letter, the Dublin Evening Post and the Freeman's Journal*, Royal Zoological Society of Ireland, 1908.

49. Zoological Society of London minutes, 5 June 1844, 3 July 1844, and RZSI annual report 1902.

50. The minute books from this period of the Zoo are not extant and much of this information is gleaned from the daily transaction books, the annual report for 1847 and the extracts from the *Saunders's News-Letter and Daily Advertiser*.

51. RZSI annual report 1854, p. 3.

52. RZSI annual report 1854 and 1855.

53. RZSI annual report 1854, p. 6.

54. RZSI annual report 1855, p. 5.

55. In 1858-59, for example, some of the school groups given free entry included girls and boys from the South Dublin Union, children from the Portobello Military School, boys from Cabra Deaf and Dumb Institute, boys from the Christian Brothers' school on Capel Street, boys from St Vincent-de-Paul's school, and Girls from the Female Orphan House, North Circular Road. (RZSI annual report 1854-55. p. 3; and annual report 1858-59, p. 16.

56. RZSI annual report 1864, p. 37. At the time the Royal Dublin Society owned the Botanic Gardens and, despite a proposal from James Haughton in 1851 to open the Gardens on Sundays after divine service, the Royal Dublin

Society did not open the Gardens on Sundays until 1861. Following Haughton's proposal, a petition with 16,000 names and the support of William Gregory, MP, was also added to put pressure on the RDS to open the Glasnevin Gardens, as the Botanic Gardens were sometimes referred to. Information from: 'The development of museums and galleries as places of learning in Ireland 1700-2005', Marie Bourke, PhD, NUI, Maynooth, 2006.

57. RZSI annual report 1858-59, p. 14. In the RZSI annual report 1893, Valentine Ball, the honorary secretary of the council, reported that the lions of Dublin Zoo had given birth to 169 cubs, of which 125 had been successfully reared for sale or stock.

Chapter 2

1. Philip Crampton donated the plesiosaurus fossil in 1853. It had been presented to him by the Marquess of Normanby. A special building 36 feet long was constructed for the exhibition of the delicate fossil, which was described in the RZSI report in *Saunders's News-Letter and Daily Advertiser*, 4 May 1853, as 'this most interesting relic of one of "the great sea dragons".'

2. Haughton had joined the council in 1860, became a vice-president in 1862, honorary secretary in 1864 and served as president from 1885 to 1889. He remained on the council as an ex-president until his death in 1897.

3. Purchasers of dead animals between 1860 and 1895 included Trinity College Dublin, the Royal College of Surgeons, Dr Steeven's Hospital, the Catholic University, Carmichael, The Ledwick, The Royal Dublin Society and private individuals with an interest in anatomical studies.

4. RZSI visitors' notebook, March 1859; the initials of the author of this entry are indecipherable.

5. *Ibid.*, 13 September 1860.

6. *Ibid.*, 19 April 1859, signed by J. Good.

7. *Ibid.*, 1 October 1859.

8. *Ibid.*, 12 April 1859, 14 July 1860, 8 November 1860, 18 June 1861, 20 June 1863.

9. *Ibid.*, 23 February 1859, November 1863.

10. There is no accurate record of when Robert Montgomery commenced working for the Zoo.

11. In 1860, there were twenty-nine members of council including ex-presidents, five vice-presidents, the honorary officers and fifteen council members. Council members attended frequently because those with the fewest attendances were liable to be replaced.

12. Report in the *Saunders's News-Letter and Daily Advertiser* of the RZSI AGM held 14 May 1861. Until now the Zoo was open for a penny at 6.00 p.m. on weekdays.

13. *Ibid.*

14. RZSI visitors' notebook, 7 July 1861.

15. *Ibid.*, June 1861.

16. RZSI annual report 1862-63, p. 14; RZSI annual report 1863-64, p. 16-17. James Haughton was, at this stage, lobbying for Sunday opening with the founders of the National Gallery of Ireland. Marie Bourke, PhD thesis, *op. cit.*

17. RZSI visitors' notebook 1863; the emphasis is Montgomery's.

18. *The Irish Times*, 17 September 1859, p. 2.

19. *The Irish Times*, 14 August 1860, p. 2.

20. Information from various *Irish Times* reports, 17 September 1859; 14 August 1860; 20 May 1863.

21. Letter from Robert Ball to the Zoological Society of London, 5 July 1839.

22. Floating islands had been placed on the lake in 1861 to encourage wild birds to nest there.

23. RZSI visitors' notebook, late August, early September 1864. 'Lockspitting' is a term used to describe a way of surveying land by digging trenches beside a peg or post along survey lines.

24. The fence line remains although, of course, the fence has been replaced.

25. RZSI visitors' notebook, 21 January 1865. Hundreds of people continued to skate on the lake in the days after this incident; for example, on the following Wednesday, over 300 men, women and children enjoyed the ice without incident.

26. Minutes of the RZSI annual general meeting, 25 May 1867, in RZSI minute book. Edward Carter was superintendent from August/September 1865 to 1880.

27. RZSI minutes, 8 January 1864. An additional fee for skating was later charged; and the right to suspend members' privilege of bringing in guests free of charge was introduced in 1867 (RZSI annual report for 1867, p. 15).

28. RZSI visitors' notebook undated entry around March 1865 and 6 June 1863.

29. RZSI visitors' notebook 29 December 1862, 14 January 1865, 8 December 1864 and 7 January 1865. Mrs Batho was the superintendent's wife; her husband, William Batho, was appointed after the sudden death of Mr Lowe in October 1862.

30. Unidentified printed document in RZSI minutes, 1 July 1876.

31. RZSI visitors' notebook various entries including 6, 30 and 31 August, 1864, and 9 December 1864.

32. RZSI visitors' notebook series of entries April 1865.

33. *Ibid.*

34. *Ibid.*

35. RZSI rough minutes, 15 April 1865; report signed by Samuel Haughton.

36. Prior to the report of Patrick Supple's death in the RZSI annual report, 1913, there was no reference to a retirement date in the minutes or annual report and it was probable that he was still a member of staff at the time of his death.

37. This was a time of expansion in the sciences and arts in Dublin and Sir Henry Cole, Secretary to the Department of Science and Art, was making capital funds available to Irish institutions; however, no money was provided for ongoing expenses.

38. Society House has been extended and is now the Education Centre and the director's home. The site of the monkey house is now the South America House.

39. The aquarium, built in 1868 and opened in 1869, was altered in 1897 to become the reptile house; after several renovations, it was finally demolished and a new reptile house was built that retained the design of the original facade. The new reptile house was opened in 1994. The carnivore house, also known as the lion house, was demolished and rebuilt in 1909 and attached to the Roberts House. It is now an open aviary.

40. Unidentified newspaper clipping in the RZSI minute book, 8 May 1869.

41. RZSI minutes, 26 August 1876 contain a reference to the fact that the omnibus company had ceased to run a bus to the Zoo. Population in Dublin city in 1881 was 249,602, Brady, *op. cit.*, p262.

42. *The Irish Times*, 31 May 1870, p. 2.

43. Unidentified newspaper article in RZSI minutes, 6 May 1871.

44. Unidentified newspaper article in RZSI minutes, 7 October 1871.

45. Unidentified newspaper article in RZSI minutes, 25 May 1872.

46. RZSI minutes, 8 June 1872.

47. Unidentified newspaper article in RZSI minutes, 7 June 1873.

48. RZSI minutes, 13 September 1873.

49. Unidentified newspaper report in RZSI minutes, 11 January 1882.

50. Unidentified newspaper article in RZSI minutes, 4 March 1876. 'Zoophilus' was probably the nom-de-plume of Arthur Foot, a council member.

51. By the 1860s, zoos had been established in numerous cities around the world, including Amsterdam, Antwerp, Berlin, Marseille, Calcutta, Melbourne and New York; and by the 1880s, urban zoos were commonplace. This provided Dublin Zoo with a network for selling, purchasing and exchanging animals.

52. Quote in unidentified Irish newspaper in RZSI minutes, 27 August 1870.

53. Unidentified newspaper article in RZSI minutes, 28 December 1878.

54. RZSI annual report for 1873, p. 16. The rarity of the pygmy hippopotamus is such that Carl Hagenbeck, the famous animal dealer, is credited with the first successful capture and transportation to Europe of the small creature, which looks like a miniature hippo, from Liberia in 1912 (Nigel Rothfels, *Savages and Beasts*, Johns Hopkins University Press, Baltimore, 2002, p. 219).

55. RZSI minutes, May 1880.
56. *The Irish Times*, 17 July 1874, p. 7.
57. Unidentified newspaper article in RZSI minutes, 6 April 1878.
58. RZSI minutes, 22 August 1885.
59. RZSI minutes, 7 November 1889.
60. RZSI annual report 1889, p. 14.
61. RZSI minutes, 30 October and 6 November 1880, and unidentified newspaper articles in RZSI minute book at these meetings.
62. Letter from Samuel Haughton to the *Freeman's Journal*, 10 March 1882, p. 5.
63. Unidentified newspaper article in RZSI minutes, 8 April 1882.
64. Unidentified newspaper in newspaper clippings book, c.1883
65. RZSI annual report 1890, p. 15-17.
66. RZSI minutes, 15 October 1881.
67. Unidentified newspaper article in RZSI minutes, 22 April 1882.
68. RZSI minutes, 13 May 1882; *Encyclopaedia of Ireland*, Gill & Macmillan, Dublin, 2003, p. 869.
69. The fossil had been in the museum of the Royal Dublin Society since 1861. Ownership of the RDS museum was transferred to the state and the new Natural History Museum (www.museum.ie). The letters in this exchange are transcribed in the RZSI minutes, December 1877. The fossil is now part of the collection of the Natural History Museum.
70. Unidentified newspaper article in RZSI minutes, 12 October 1878.
71. *Daily Express*, Report of the RZSI AGM, 9 January 1884, p. 2.
72. RZSI minutes, 14 July 1888.
73. Record of the AGM from an unidentified newspaper article in RZSI minutes, 13 January 1880.
74. *Daily Express*, Report of the RZSI AGM, 9 January 1884, p. 2.
75. *Daily Express*, 31 July 1884, p. 6.
76. *Evening Telegraph*, 5 February 1891, p. 2.
77. *Daily Express*, 28 January 1891, p. 7.
78. *Freeman's Journal* and *Daily Commercial Advertiser*, 10 February 1891, p. 6.
79. *Evening Telegraph*, 5 February 1891, p. 2.
80. *Daily Independent*, 1 February 1893.

Chapter 3

1. Field Marshal the Right Honourable Lord Frederick Sleigh ('Bobs') Roberts, VC, KP, was born in 1832. He was awarded a Victoria Cross for action during the Indian Mutiny in 1857-58, and had been commander-in-chief of the army in India from 1885-1893.
2. The 1911 census recorded the population of the city of Dublin as 304,802; Joseph Brady, 'Dublin at the Turn of the Century' in *Dublin through Space and Time, op. cit.* p. 263.
3. Report containing recommendations for renovations and improvements inserted after the minutes of the RZSI meeting 12 October 1895.
4. The full possibilities of the changes became apparent when Carl Hagenbeck opened his zoo near Hamburg in 1907; Hagenbeck was a major German animal dealer and exhibitor and is credited with developing the concept of the bar-less enclosure. (See also endnote 31, chapter 4.)
5. RZSI annual report 1896, p. 10-11.
6. RZSI annual report 1898, p. 19-20.
7. For example, Col. G.T. Plunkett, who joined the council in 1896, was very impressed by the famous concert hall in Antwerp Zoo that could cater for 2,000-3,000 people; the concert hall had a very large restaurant and cafe attached, as well as a substantial playground, which was open to children of members of the society. It was, Plunkett said, a chief inducement to many people to pay the members' subscription. He also pointed out that the

Gardens were not open at all to the general public except on certain holidays (RZSI minutes, 17 October 1896). Plunkett contributed to the design brief of Haughton House.

8. Roberts' comments were reported at the following meeting, RZSI minutes, 27 May 1899.

9. RZSI minutes, 23 December 1899.

10. RZSI minutes, 3 March 1900; J. B. Yeats was a visitor at this meeting.

11. James Kenny was elephant keeper in the Zoo from 1903 to his retirement in 1940. His son, Jimmy Kenny, succeeded him to become the famous elephant keeper until his retirement in 1976. In a conversation with the author, Paul Kenny remembers his grandfather James as 'ramrod straight and wiry. I remember him on Christmas Day sitting by the fire in a pinstripe suit in his house on Infirmary Road. On that occasion, he was gripping a bottle of stout between his knees and very closely and gently, he drew the cork out of the bottle. He was a very kindly man who always had time for the children.'

12. The address to the Queen reprinted in the RZSI annual report 1897, p. 31-32. In RZSI minutes, 14 January 1899, the council 'raised no objection to the request of the Royal Dublin Society for permission to apply to the donors to have the donations towards erecting a statue to the Queen handed to them for the purpose of erecting a Jubilee House in honour of the Diamond Jubilee of Her Majesty'. A herbivore house was built but not called 'Jubilee House'. RZSI annual report, 1899, p. 16.

13. RZSI annual report 1901, p. 8.

14. Professor D. J. Cunningham speaking at the opening of the Roberts House, quoted in *The Irish Times*, 21 May 1902, p. 5.

15. *The Irish Times*, 21 May 1902, p. 4 and 5.

16. The revolt against the Egyptian rulers of Sudan by a sheik who took the title of Mahdi disrupted the supply of giraffes from this region between 1881 and 1899; in 1899, the area came under the control of an Anglo-Egyptian condominium and supplies were resumed. *The Hutchinson Dictionary of World History*. Helicon, Oxford, 1993, p. 492.

17. RZSI annual report 1902, p. 14.

18. RZSI annual report 1903, p. 5-6.

19. RZSI minutes, 13 February 1897. The official report of the accident on the 16 May 1897 in the RZSI minutes, May 1897.

20. *The Irish Times*, 10 June, p. 5; *The Irish Times*, 12 June, p. 3; RZSI annual report, 1903 p. 12-13. The record in the RZSI minutes, 13 June 1903 states that the incident happened on the evening of Wednesday 10 June; however the report on the death is carried in *The Irish Times* on 10 June.

21. Unidentified newspaper in RZSI minutes, 22 June 1912.

22. *Evening Herald* 19 January 1924; and information from Frank Burke, Dublin Zoo keeping staff, 1960-1995; Patrick Supple married in about 1886, according to the census record of 1911.

23. *The Irish Times*, 6 March 1914, p. 2; RZSI minutes, 28 March 1914.

24. According to the RZSI minutes, 2 May 1914, 395 rats were destroyed in the first four months of the year.

25. RZSI annual report 1914, p. 7.

26. RZSI annual report 1914, p. 11.

27. RZSI annual report 1914, p. 13.

28. Letter dated 29 January 1915 in RZSI minutes, 13 March 1915.

29. Mrs Ferrar's first name is not on record despite the significance of her role during the Rising.

30. *Freeman's Journal* and *Daily Commercial Advertiser*, 4 May 1915, p. 10.

31. These may have been the rhesus, patas, bonnet, pigtail, macaque and capuchin monkeys, which were donated that year by the Lister Institute, now the Lister Institute for Preventive Medicine. In 1917, the Surgeon General, Sir David Bruce asked that zoos should abstain from purchasing rhesus monkeys as there was difficulty in getting a supply of these species for purposes of research work in connection with the study of tetanus especially in regard to the wounded in the war (RZSI minutes, 16 March 1917).

32. RZSI minutes, various references including 3, 24 March and 7 April 1917 (hay supply problems); 16 December

1916 and 21 April 1917 (plans for growing potatoes); (21 July 1917 and 27 July 1918 (problems with supplies of coke); April 1917 (declining pythons); 27 July 1918 (discussion about pigs).

33. Various references including annual report 1914, and RZSI minutes, June, July and August 1917. Reference to handbills, RZSI minutes, 3 June 1916. At the time the admission charge was one shilling for the general public on Mondays, Tuesdays, Thursdays and Fridays, sixpence on Wednesdays and Saturdays, and twopence on Sundays.

34. RZSI minutes, 17 February 1917; the invitation was sent to the acting commandant of the Royal Hospital; no address was given.

35. RZSI minutes, 4 August 1917.

36. Several of the adjectives used to describe the cages that required work in the report of the Reconstruction Committee, RZSI minutes, 12 April 1919.

37. The gorilla in the Breslau Zoologischer Garten, now the Wroclaw Municipal Zoological Garden in Poland, lived from 1897 to 1904. *Encyclopedia of the World's Zoos, op. cit.*, p. 807.

38. RZSI minutes, 6 December 1919.

39. RZSI minutes, 6 March 1920. The periscope had been given to the Society by the Royal Navy War Trophies Committee in February 1920.

40. Professor Carpenter, a council member, objected to this development and stated that he wished to resign his position. RZSI minutes, 4 June 1919.

41. The Ladies' Committee was established in 1903 to improve the quality of the refreshments in Haughton House. They ran the restaurant very successfully for three years and then announced their wish to pass the responsibility over to a manager. RZSI minutes, 7 July 1906.

42. RZSI minutes, 3 January 1920.

43. RZSI minutes, 6 November 1920.

44. RZSI minutes, 27 November 1920.

45. RZSI minutes, 12 February 1921.

46. RZSI minutes, 10 September 1921

47. RZSI minutes, 25 March 1922.

Chapter 4

1. RZSI annual report, 1923, p, 5.

2. RZSI annual report, 1923, p. 6.

3. The ministers joined the society in 1924; RZSI minutes, 22 March 1924 and 29 March 1924.

4. The *Dublin Evening Mail*, 3 April 1923, p. 2. On 27 April, de Valera ordered the suspension of the Republican campaign and, in May 1923, the republicans dumped their arms, thereby officially ending the Civil War.

5. RZSI minutes, 9 June 1923.

6. Belfast Zoo was opened in March 1934. In 1932, the council arranged additional advertising in association with the Eucharistic Congress. On 26 November 1938, the superintendent Cedric Flood informed the council that he had talked to the city engineer about putting up notices to advertise the Zoo at key locations around the city. The engineer agreed to the erection of twenty of these notices provided they were not painted in the following colours: red, white and blue, blue and white, red and white, black and yellow, or green and white.

7. RZSI annual report, 1924, p. 17, 'By permission of *The Irish Times*'.

8. The letter is in the RZSI minutes, 7 March 1925. All other references are taken from the lists of donations and the list of corresponding members in the annual reports.

9. RZSI minutes, 1 March 1923. The council noted that Lord O'Shaughnessy took an interest in the Irish Free State (RZSI minutes, 20 January 1923). This consignment of animals came from the Canadian National Parks in Ottawa.

10. *The Irish Times*, 28 February 1924, p. 5.

11. *The Irish Times*, 8 October 1923, p, 4.

12. RZSI minutes, 22 October 1932. According to one report, Slats, the first lion used in the MGM logo from 1924 to 1928, was born in Dublin Zoo in March 1919. There is no record in Dublin Zoo or at MGM to indicate

whether this is the case. Two strong, male cubs were born in September 1919; one remained in Dublin and was called Conn II; the other was probably sold before it was named. According to the entry on the MGM lions in Wikipedia.org, there were five MGM lions and Slats was born in Dublin. It gives no provenance for the three lions used in the logo between 1928 and 1958. Stephen, a Dublin lion, was filmed by MGM in 1947 (minutes, 3 May 1947) but there is no record to suggest that the footage was ever used. There are no available records in MGM on the provenance of their lions during this period. In July 1949, George Emerson, a famous Hollywood animal expert, asked the council if he could hire fifteen lions for the production of the film *Quo Vadis* in Italy. The council refused, 'particularly in view of quarantine regulations'. RZSI minutes, 23 July 1949.

13. *Sunday Independent*, 23 July 1933.

14. *The Irish Times*, 14 June 1919; army championships were referred to in the RZSI minutes, July–August 1923, and *The Irish Times,* 3 September 1923. The Leinster Amateur Swimming Association also planned to hold a swimming gala in the lake in summer 1923 but, despite planning and negotiation with the council, it may not have gone ahead that year. References to the Tailteann Games and other swimming galas include receipts referred to in RZSI annual report 1924, p. 6 and RZSI annual report 1925, p. 5.

15. The pike fishing competitions were organised by Dublin Trout Anglers Association, and held several times in the 1930s. For example, in 1931, fourteen pike were caught (RZSI minutes, 24 October 1931). In 1932, the heaviest pike caught was 4½ lbs and twenty-six fishermen competed (RZSI minutes, 30 January 1932). The pike fishing competitions continued until at least 1944 (RZSI minutes, 22 January 1944).

16. RZSI minutes, 8 October 1938.

17. Various incidents were recorded regarding the elephants around this time; the elephants were not identified but neither was likely to be Sarah. The incident with Dr Ferrar was reported in the RZSI minutes, 13 August 1938.

18. RZSI minutes, 13, 20 and 27 April, 11 May 1940, and 8 June 1940.

19. Letter to *The Irish Times*, 25 April, 1940, p, 9.

20. *Evening Mail*, 30 April 1940.

21. Unidentified newspaper dated 4 April 1940 in the Dublin Zoo archive.

22. *The Irish Times*, July 26 1940, p. 4.

23. RZSI minutes, 21 November 1925.

24. *The Irish Times*, 13 March 1952, p. 7; quote from an appreciation following the sudden death of Cedric Flood in his home in the Zoo. His grandson, Michael Ward, said in conversation with the author that Cedric Flood had a bullet lodged in his shoulder and the family believed it may have moved and caused his death.

25. RZSI minutes, 3, 17 and 31 December 1938; RZSI minutes, 2 March 1940.

26. RZSI annual report, 1940, p. 5; RZSI minutes, 12 June 1943. Michael Ward believes that it was his mother, Yvonne Ward's idea to create the Children's Corner. Yvonne Ward had been living in the south of England with her husband and two sons, Michael and Patrick, at the start of the Second World War. When the German bombers began to fly overhead, Yvonne Ward and her sons were evacuated to Dublin and spent the remainder of the war living in the Zoo.

27. *Belfast Telegraph*, 8 September 1942; and RZSI minutes, October 1945.

28. Terry Murphy, *Some of My Best Friends are Animals*, Paddington Press, London, 1979, p. 209

29. RZSI minutes, 19 July 1952.

30. RZSI minutes, 9 March 1940. The council also invited Hugo Flynn to accept an honorary membership but he refused this (minutes, 28 January 1941). However, he said he would be delighted to join them for breakfast if he were in Dublin some weekend. His name was variously spelt Flynn and Flinn in the RZSI records.

31. Carl Hagenbeck, animal dealer and trainer, opened Tierpark Hagenbeck in Hamburg in 1907. Drawing on his knowledge of the natural capabilities of a species, he used natural features such as moats and dykes to contain the animals; consequently visitors were provided with the excitement of seeing the animals without having to look through metal bars. When making his calculations about the containment features, Hagenbeck added extra height, distance or depth to allow for an animal's increased ability under stress. Bears and other animals had long been kept in bar-less spaces but, in the case of bears, their pits were so deep as to make them relatively safe from the danger of escape.

32. RZSI minutes, 20 July 1940, and 22 February 1941.

33. RZSI annual report for 1941, p. 4.

34. The famous Stephen, the lion who was filmed by MGM in 1947 with a view to using him as part of the logo, fell into the water but succeeded in getting out again. Later it was observed that another lion, Larry, was wet and may have been in the moat. A cub, which was one of the litter allowed into the arena under staff supervision, ended up in the moat also but was rescued by its mother. In 1952, the lion arena was converted into an exhibit for the polar bears.

35. Michael Ward in conversation with the author.

36. RZSI minutes, 13 September 1941.

37. The Dolphin Hotel was a famous Dublin hostelry on Essex Street; the building has a Victorian exterior with a dolphin over the corner entrance; it has now been converted to office space for the courts service (information from www.irish-architecture.com).

38. *The Irish Times*, 18 June 1942, p. 2.

39. *The Irish Times,* 17 January 1942, p. 4.

40. *Evening Herald*, 16 February 1942.

41. *The Irish Times,* 6 September 1941.

42. RZSI minutes, 17 November 1945.

43. A 'pony' is bookmakers' slang for £25, and a 'monkey' is slang for £500. Information from website: www.online-betting.me.uk/betting-a-to-z.html.

44. *Sunday Independent*, 30 June 1946. 'Any water?' was the name of a famous cockatoo in Dublin Zoo, which died in 1950.

45. Report dated 4 May 1946 in RZSI minute book.

46. *Ibid.*

47. RZSI annual report 1947, p. 5.

48. Throughout the 1940s, there had been discussions about providing electricity to the Zoo. A temporary electrical supply was provided in June 1942 for the fete and the superintendent was given permission to wire his house for electricity in August 1942. A temporary supply was made available for the June fete in 1944; plans to provide electricity to the switchroom, superintendent's house and Haughton House were mentioned in the minutes, November 1947 and in the RZSI annual report, 1947, p. 5, it was announced that electricity had reached the Zoo for the first time in December 1947. Electricity was extended to other houses in the following years.

49. RZSI minutes, 6 December 1947 and annual report 1947, p. 6. Reduced admission price on Wednesdays was abolished in 1939; half price on Saturdays was suspended in 1940; in 1945, half-price admission (sixpence for adults and threepence for children) was shifted from Sunday to Wednesday because of the large crowds on Sundays. Half-price bank holidays were abolished at RZSI council meeting on 22 March 1947 and the tradition of cheap days finally abolished in December 1947.

50. RZSI minutes, 6 July 1948 and 29 January 1949.

51. *Evening Mail,* 29 January 1949; *Irish Press* in July 1948, and RZSI annual report 1949, p. 4.

52. RZSI minutes, 25 March 1944.

53. *Carlow Nationalist*, 1 July 1946.

54. 'Visits to Dublin Zoo during the Second World War: transcribed from notes and diaries written at the time,' an unpublished paper by Sean Cromien.

55. *The Irish Times,* 4 January 1947, p. 9.

56. Sean Cromien, *op. cit.* and RZSI minutes, 18 January 1947.

57. RZSI minutes, January 1947 and 10 May 1947. The BCG is the Bacillus Calmette-Guerin vaccine, which was available to Irish children.

58. *The Irish Times*, 19 April 1946, p. 5.

59. The keeper in question may well have been James Kenny senior, who retired in 1940.

60. Anne Madden le Brocquy, *Seeing His Way: Louis le Brocquy – A Painter,* Gill & Macmillan, Dublin, 1994, p. 11-12.

61. References to the injuries to the children from the RZSI minutes, 21 August 1943, 21 August 1948, 9 July 1949, 19 March 1949.
62. Report on this exchange was in *The Irish Times*, 8 December 1949, p. 1. When the Society's patron, King George V had died in 1936, the council had sent a message of condolence via the Department of External Affairs. A blank space was left under the heading 'patron' in the annual report until 1943.

Chapter 5

1. Early initiatives in formal international cooperation were in Germany in 1928. *Encyclopedia of the World's Zoos, op. cit.* p. 1328. (See also chapter 5 endnote 60.)
2. The population of Dublin county and borough fell from 551,555 in 1951 to 537,448 in 1961; Census of population 1956, p. 55, Central Statistics Office, 1957; and Census of population 1966, Central Statistics Office, 1967.
3. Until 1957, the names and addresses of members were published in the annual report. During the 1950s, there were an increasing number of people from the growing suburbs of Terenure, Dundrum, Mount Merrion and Stillorgan, for example.
4. 'An Irishman's Diary', *The Irish Times*, 4 May 1955, p. 8.
5. By 1970 there were 5,255 memberships, and by 1980 there were 7,074.
6. Martyn Linnie, Chief Technical Officer and Curator of the Zoological Museum in Trinity College, in conversation with the author.
7. The RZSI minutes, 9 September 1944 record that Terry Murphy's three-month probation period was completed. In his book, Terry Murphy said that he joined the Zoo in 1943 (*Some of My Best Friends are Animals, op. cit.*, p. 25). Annual report 1956 for information about the trip to the continent. *Official guide to the Dublin Zoo*, by Edward Terence Murphy, Royal Zoological Society of Ireland, undated but published in 1952 or 1953.
8. RZSI minutes, 3 July 1954.
9. The dance floor was stored between functions but on one occasion in 1956, it was used to form a passage corral between two enclosures allowing the zebras to walk to their new home.
10. Tom McGrath, electrician and general maintenance man, in conversation with the author.
11. RZSI minutes, 1 February 1964; the issue was raised at the council meeting following a question asked at the AGM.
12. The Zoo fell into the Parish of St James for the purposes of granting bar licences.
13. RZSI annual report 1950, p. 8.
14. Retired keeper Michael Clarke in conversation with the author.
15. *Ibid.*
16. RZSI minutes, 29 March 1952. During this period, Dublin Zoo had close contacts with Chipperfields, a British animal dealership. It was owned by Jimmy Chipperfield, an animal trainer, circus owner and showman. In 1966, Chipperfield was involved in opening Longleat Park in Wiltshire, England, a safari park initially designed for fifty lions in a 100-acre reserve (www.goodzoos.com).
17. RZSI council, finance committee minutes, 5 July 1955.
18. RZSI minutes, 25 May 1957
19. The chimpanzee enclosure is now the waldrapp ibis habitat.
20. RZSI minutes, 8 June 1974; ARKS, the official record of animal births and deaths in Dublin Zoo, records the first chimp born in the Zoo as June 1974.
21. RZSI minutes, 15 September, 1973, and 21 May 1983.
22. RZSI minutes, 13 August 1955.
23. RZSI annual report, 1960, p. 9.
24. RZSI minutes, 12 April 1958, and RZSI annual report, 1958, p. 5.
25. Murphy, *op. cit.*, p. 129.
26. *Ibid.*, p. 130
27. RZSI annual report 1969 in 'Director's animal report'.

28. The black rhinoceros is now highly endangered and considered to be one of the world's fastest-disappearing large mammals (*Animal Factfile*, Kingfisher, London, revised ed, 2005. p. 285).

29. RZSI annual report, 1965, p. 12; annual report, 1969, in 'Director's animal report', and information from Gerry Creighton (senior) in conversation with the author. Information about the cost of feeding Bim in Murphy, *op. cit.*, p. 105. By way of contrast, fete receipts in 1966 after expenses came to £1,218 and membership income came to £10,836.

30. At first, a section of the sea lion pond was cordoned off for Bim. When he became too large for this enclosure, he was moved to what is now the penguin enclosure. Information from Gerry Creighton (senior).

31. RZSI annual report, 1966, and Murphy, *op. cit.*, p. 105-106.

32. In September 1951, the council noted that there was 'no hope of getting an increased grant from the Government'. RZSI minutes, 22 September 1951.

33. Paul Kenny in conversation with the author.

34. Micheál Ó Nualláin in conversation with the author.

35. Jim Bartley in conversation with the author.

36. Visitors in conversations with the author, including Olwyn Lanigan, Margaret Sinanan, Mary de Courcy, Ann Murphy, Paddy Halpin and Dorothy Kilroy.

37. Paul Kenny in conservation with the author.

38. RZSI minutes, 5 July 1958.

39. RZSI minutes, 17 January 1959.

40. RZSI annual report 1950, p. 8, and RZSI minutes, 1 and 8 July 1950.

41. Olwyn Lanigan in conversation with the author.

42. RZSI annual report 1963, p. 11.

43. Terry Murphy, *op. cit.*, p. 153.

44. RZSI minutes, 24 April 1976.

45. Tony Tormey in conversation with the author.

46. RZSI minutes, 2 February 1952, 1 March 1952 and 6 December 1952.

47. Gerry Creighton (junior) had begun working as an official member of the keeping staff in 1985 but had been coming to the Zoo with his father, Gerry Creighton (senior), since he was a child. He was very familiar with the Zoo because, 'We could go anywhere we wanted to go, in around the backs of the enclosures. There was great sense of freedom. Other staff members' children used to come to the Zoo also and they would help Teasee [Irene] Craigie in Pets' Corner. It was like a little club.' (Gerry Creighton [junior] in conversation with the author.) Public feeding of the lions ended in the 1970s.

48. Margaret Sinanan in conversation with the author. In 1971, Tommy Kelly retired after fifty-eight years in the Zoo (RZSI annual report, 1971, p. 5).

49. RZSI minutes, 11 June 1960.

50. RZSI minutes, 21 March 1959; 2 January 1960.

51. Brian O'Reilly in conversation with the author.

52. RZSI minutes, 20 April 1963; RZSI minutes, 11 July 1964.

53. The reptile house had been built as an aquarium in 1868, and renovated in 1896; at that stage, the fish tanks remained while additional accommodation was made for reptiles and diving birds. RZSI annual report, 1896, p. 11. The reptile house was demolished in winter 1992-93 and replaced with a new building, the facade of which replicated the facade of the original.

54. RZSI annual report 1963, p. 5; RZSI annual report 1965, p. 6.

55. Margaret Sinanan in conversation with the author.

56. RZSI annual report, 1969, p. 2; RZSI annual report, 1970, p. 5.

57. RZSI minutes, 26 June 1976; RZSI minutes, 4 September 1976.

58. RZSI annual report 1966, p. 5.

59. Pam McDonough in conversation with the author; statistics from RZSI annual report 1965, p. 16; RZSI annual report 1970, p. 14.

60. The first attempt to create an international zoo association was in Germany in 1928, arising out of which the International Union of Directors of Zoological Gardens was created in 1935. Progress was interrupted by the Second World War and, in 1946, J. Kuiper, director of Rotterdam Zoo, invited zoo directors to a meeting. Six directors attended. The Zoological Society of Ireland initially accepted the invitation to the first meeting of the Union from 23-25 September 1946 after ascertaining the views of 'other zoos in England' on this matter but, in August, decided not to go (minutes, 11 May, 1 June, 31 August 1946). The International Union met the following year and drew up a constitution. The establishment of the professional body marked the beginning of the international approach to shaping the role of zoos in modern societies.
61. RZSI minutes, 8 October 1966 and annual report 1967, p. 11.
62. One young gorilla had arrived in 1967 but died shortly afterwards (RZSI annual report 1967, p. 12). Two gorillas arrived in 1972 (RZSI annual report 1972, p. 3).
63. The Catholic hierarchy ban on Catholics attending Trinity College Dublin was lifted in June 1970. There were Catholic students at undergraduate and postgraduate level in Trinity at the time, some of whom had applied for permission from the archbishop to attend (*The Irish Times*, 26 June 1970. p. 1 and 15).
64. RZSI annual report 1980, p. 4.

Chapter 6

1. RZSI minutes special council meeting, 16 December 1989.
2. J. Barrington-Johnson, *The Zoo – the Story of London Zoo*, Robert Hale, London, 2005, p. 181-182. The Emir of Kuwait intervened with a gift of £1 million from the children of Kuwait to the children of London as a way of thanking the British people for support during the First Gulf War.
3. RZSI annual report, 1980, p. 10.
4. RZSI annual report, 1981, p. 12; *Encyclopedia of the World's Zoos, op. cit.*, p. 2. Sasha, the snow leopard, had several cubs over the following years but most died shortly after birth; one lived for just over three months. Another snow leopard, acquired from Helsinki Zoo in 1978, bred a male cub in 1988, called Patrice, who was successfully reared. Information from ARKS, Dublin Zoo's record system.
5. RZSI minutes, December 1983; RZSI minutes, May 1984.
6. Gerry Creighton (senior) in conversation with the author.
7. RZSI minutes, 7 October 1978. The Siberian tiger or Amur tiger had been the subject of an international studbook since 1966. *Encyclopedia of the World's Zoos, op. cit.*, p.1238.
8. *The Irish Times*. 20 February 1982, p. 1.
9. Information from *The Irish Times*, 20 February 1982; RZSI minutes, 20 February, 6 March, 17 April, 17 July 1982, and RZSI annual report 1982 (p. 7).
10. Gerry Creighton (senior) in conversation with the author. Abbotstown was the location of the Veterinary Research Laboratory, Department of Agriculture and Fisheries, where post mortems were carried out.
11. *Evening Herald*, 23 December 1982.
12. RZSI minutes, 4 October 1986.
13. Eoin Cooney in conversation with the author.
14. RZSI minutes, 17 May 1969.
15. Leah Benson in conversation with the author.
16. Dublin Zoo horticulturalist Stephen Butler in conversation with the author.
17. Retired keeper Frank Burke and Stephen Butler in conversation with the author.
18. Stephen Butler in conversation with the author.
19. RZSI minutes, July 1987 contain a reference to a 'recent' accident; no date is given for the accident.
20. Helen Clarke is the daughter of retired keeper Michael Clarke; she is now the Team Leader in charge of the African Plains.
21. Michael Clarke in conversation with the author
22. Helen Clarke in conversation with the author.

23. *The Irish Times*, 16 March 1985, p. 12.
24. Mary Glennon, in the *Evening Herald,* 9 July 1985.
25. Minutes of the AGM, 1986, in RZSI annual report, 1985, p. 3.
26. By way of comparison, there were about 620 animals and two colonies of invertebrates in the Zoo in 2007.
27. RZSI annual report 1980, p, 8.
28. RZSI annual report 1984, p. 20.
29. RZSI annual report 1983, p. 19; minutes of the AGM 24 January 1981, in RZSI annual report, 1980, p. 2.
30. RZSI minutes, 20 December 1980. According to Dereck Clarke, one of the union representatives referred to in this minute, the union in question was the Federated Workers' Union of Ireland and their chief concerns at this stage were issues regarding health and safety. A staff safety committee was formed with the director as an ex officio member of the committee.
31. Minutes of the AGM held 22 January 1983 in RZSI annual report 1982, p. 2-3; statement of the cash account for the year ending 31 October 1982, p. 12-13.
32. RZSI minutes, 9 April 1983, and *Sunday World*, 10 April 1983.
33. *The Irish Times*, 9 May 1983, p. 1.
34. *The Irish Times*, 16 May 1983, p. 11.
35. *The Irish Times*, 16 May 1983, p. 11.
36. *The Irish Times,* 27 July 1983, p. 9.
37. *Irish Independent,* 4 October 1983.
38. RZSI minutes, 15 October 1983.
39. The *Phoenix*, 3 February 1984.
40. *Irish Independent*, 24 September 1984.
41. *Sunday Independent,* 4 November 1984.
42. *Irish Press*, 11 September 1984.
43. *Irish Independent,* 6 September 1984.
44. Letter signed by Stephen Canning, Mt Merrion, in the *Phoenix*, 1 September 1984.
45. *Evening Press*, 1 October 1984.
46. Shortly after graduating as a veterinary surgeon from Trinity College in 1968, Peter Wilson joined the staff of the School of Veterinary Medicine in Trinity and subsequently the Faculty of Natural Science in Trinity. Information from Professor Peter Wilson in conversation with the author.
47. Peter Wilson in conversation with the author. RZSI annual reports, 1972, 1973, 1974 and 1984.
48. RZSI annual report 1985, p. 10.
49. Minutes of the AGM, 26 January 1985, in RZSI annual report 1984, p. 2.
50. *Ibid.*, p. 4-9.
51. *Encyclopedia of the World's Zoos, op. cit.*, p. 952-953.
52. RZSI minutes, 3 October 1981, Report of the Education Committee: 330 children from 136 families registered for the tours but 150 children could not obtain places.
53. RZSI minutes, 3 October 1981.
54. RZSI minutes, 15 May 1982. Paignton Zoo is now called Paignton Zoo Environmental Park.
55. Minutes of AGM, 21 January 1984, in RZSI annual report, 1983, p. 2.
56. RZSI minutes, 8 February 1986 and RZSI annual report 1986, p. 14.
57. RZSI minutes, 2 May 1987.
58. From 'Dublin Zoo Volunteers – 1987-2007 & Going Strong' by Maeve McDonald. Unpublished paper.
59. Information from Una Smyth, Dublin Zoo education officer, in conversation with the author. Una Smyth succeeded Michelle Griffin as education officer in January 1999. Fiona Gartland's article in unidentified newspaper from around September 2003 in the Dublin Zoo archive.
60. Una Smyth in conversation with the author.
61. *Ibid.*

62. Alice Cooper, Eileen Cooper, Margaret Sinanan and Helen Clarke in conversation with the author.
63. *The Irish Times*, 30 August 2000.
64. Bertie Ahern TD in conversation with the author.
65. *Ibid.*
66. Dan Mahony in conversation with the author.
67. RZSI annual report 1988, p. 9.
68. RZSI minutes, October 1988; the bat house has since been demolished to make way for the Kaziranga Forest Trail. Dick Warner's article was in the *Evening Press*, 21 April 1993.
69. Dan Mahony in conversation with the author.
70. Dorothy Kilroy in conversation with the author. The *Today Tonight* programme was broadcast on 14 March 1989.
71. Information concerning breakfast from Council member and past president Michael O'Grady, in conversation with the author. Quote from RZSI minutes, 24 October 1989.
72. RZSI minutes, 9 December 1989.
73. RZSI minutes, special council meeting, 16 December 1989.
74. Information from council member Dorothy Kilroy in conversation with the author. The council member who offered the cheque remains anonymous.
75. *The Irish Times*, 26 February 1990.
76. RZSI minutes, 3 March 1990.
77. Eddie O'Brien, now a team leader, in conversation with the author.
78. Various RZSI minutes 1990. The Ladies' Committee was no longer as active as it had been and, on 21 March 1992, Dorothy Kilroy advised the council that 'the present ladies' committee wished to disband and to form a social events committee and sought approval from council'. The council welcomed the announcement.
79. Horticulturalist Stephen Butler in conversation with the author.
80. Information from Eddie O'Brien, whose responsibilities now include the reptile house, and from Dan Mahony in conversations with the author,
81. 'Report of the government-appointed committee to advise on Dublin Zoo', Dublin Stationery Office, July 1990, p, 49-50. It is known as the Doyle Report.
82. Michael O'Grady in conversation with the author. The new constitution was introduced in 1994. Under this constitution, which continued until 2008, the council devolved its power and authority to an executive committee, which had only ten members and continued to meet on a monthly basis. The council, which continued to have a membership of about twenty-four, met five times a year. In 2008, given the status of the Zoo as a limited company and the fact that all the members of the council were de facto company directors, it was decided to amend the memorandum and articles of association to bring them more in line with best corporate practice. These changes dissolved the council, changed the executive into a new council and created an advisory board. For the sake of clarity, the governing authority of the Zoo during this period is referred to as 'the council' in this book.
83. ZSI minutes, 6 November 1993.
84. *The Irish Times*, 22 June 1994, p, 11.
85. Stephen Butler in conversation with the author.
86. Martin Heffernan in conversation with the author.
87. Stephen Butler in conversation with the author.
88. Bertie Ahern, TD in conversation with the author; Michael O'Grady in conversation with the author; and Dublin Zoo annual report, 1997, p. 4.
89. *The Irish Times*, 29 July 2000.
90. Dorothy Kilroy in conversation with the author.

Chapter 7
1. ARKS stands for the Animal Record Keeping Software, which was produced by ISIS, the International Species Information System.

2. Dublin Zoo annual report, 2001, p. 20.

3. The club licence, which permitted the sale of alcohol to members and their guests, expired with the end of Haughton House as a restaurant and bar. When the Meerkat Restaurant was opened, a 'special restaurant licence' was granted, which permits the sale of alcohol at events in the Zoo. Information from Tony Kearney, Chief Financial Officer, in conversation with the author.

4. Dublin Zoo annual report 2000, p. 20.

5. Dublin Zoo annual report 2001, p. 20.

6. Director's report to the executive committee, November 2002.

7. ZSI minutes, 12 June 2003.

8. Dublin Zoo annual report 2004, p. 5.

9. The eastern bongo is part of a Species Survival Plan of the Association of Zoos and Aquariums in America in 2000; Dublin Zoo's eastern bongos are part of a European Endangered Species Breeding Programme, which links with the American Species Survival Plan.

10. Dublin Zoo annual report, 2006, p. 14, and information about the waldrapp ibis, from Twycross Zoo, www.twycrosszoo.com.

11. Director's report to the executive committee, May 2002.

12. Dublin Zoo annual report 2004, p. 4.

13. The waldrapp ibis received the first part of the avian flu vaccination on 6 April 2006. The same year, Barry Brogan, a PhD student from Trinity College, examined the differences in behaviour between the flock of waldrapp ibis in Dublin Zoo and a semi-wild flock in Austria. The results of his research provided information on enrichment techniques that could be employed by Dublin Zoo and other zoos, which would ultimately increase the chances of successfully reintroducing this species to the wild (Dublin Zoo annual report 2006, p. 14).

14. ZSI minutes, 17 July 2001. Reference to the spot check by Eastern Health Board in ZSI minutes, 18 December 2001; also a report in *The Irish Times*, 10 April 2002.

15. ZSI minutes, 18 December 2001 and 12 March 2002.

16. *Evening Herald,* 29 April 2005.

17. *The Irish Times*, 30 August 2000.

18. ZSI AGM minutes, 9 September 2004. Leo Oosterweghel had worked in zoos in his native Netherlands and in Australia; he was director of Melbourne Zoo prior to taking up the appointment in Dublin Zoo in October 2001.

19. Dublin Zoo annual report 2003, p. 8 and *Irish Independent*, 25 September 2006.

20. Keeper Joe Byrne in conversation with the author.

21. Royal Zoological and Acclimatisation Society of Victoria minutes, July 1933. Zoological Board of Victoria minutes, October 1961. The diameter of a tennis ball is similar to the diameter of a hippo's intestine.

22. Keeper Joe Byrne, in conversation with the author.

23. 'Report of the government-appointed committee to advise on Dublin Zoo', *op. cit.*, p. 138. For example, in *Today Tonight*, on RTÉ television, 14 March 1989, Bill Jordan said that the polar bears were showing 'psychotic behaviour'; the polar bears were shown walking up and down, and comparisons were made with the polar bear facilities in Bristol Zoo.

24. Dublin Zoo annual report, 1997, p. 4.

25. ZSI minutes, 14 April 1998.

26. ZSI minutes, 16 June 1998 and 15 September 1998.

27. Dublin Zoo annual report 2002, p. 7.

28. Director's report to the executive committee, April 2003.

29. Director's report to the executive committee, August 2004; annual report, 2005, p. 16. The Siberian tiger is now known as the Amur tiger.

30. The 'ice bank' is formed by the old Ice House, which predates the establishment of Dublin Zoo.

31. Keeper Ciaran McMahon in conversation with the author.

32. *The Irish Times,* 12 July 2006.

33. *Irish Independent*, 25 September 2006.
34. RZSI minutes, 3 June 1950.
35. The announcement was made at the Orang-Utan TAG group, i.e. Taxon Advisory Group, and is referred to in the director's report to the executive committee, September 2002.
36. The volunteer programme was established in 1987.
37. Volunteer Maeve McDonald in conversation with the author.
38. Jenny Wilde, a PhD student from Trinity College, is collecting data on changing social groups in the Zoo in order to come up with guidelines on how to manage these changes successfully. Jenny Wilde in conversation with the author, and Dublin Zoo annual report 2007, p. 18.
39. *Zoo Matters*, (members' magazine published by Dublin Zoo), winter 2008, p. 4
40. Director's report to the executive committee, June 2004.
41. Director's report to the executive committee, September 2004.
42. Assistant to the director, animals and grounds, Paul O'Donoghue, in conversation with the author.
43. Paul O'Donoghue in conversation with the author; various newspaper articles, including the *Irish Examiner*, 20 December 2007 for information on the glitter, and *The Herald AM*, 5 June 2008 for information on the birth.
44. Information from Andy Beer, Sparsholt College Hampshire, in conversation with the author.
45. Team leader Helen Clarke in conversation with the author.
46. Keeper Alice Cooper in conversation with the author.
47. Director's report to the executive committee, September 2005 and ZSI minutes, 7 October, 2005.
48. ZSI minutes, 20 December 2005.
49. Team leader Gerry Creighton (junior) and keeper Alice Cooper in conversation with the author.
50. Education officer Una Smyth in conversation with the author.
51. Part of a Discover Science and Engineering programme run by Forfas, a government body. The Discover Primary Science held their first Awards for Excellence in the Meerkat Restaurant in 2005.
52. In 2008, 3,478 students participated in the Mini-Beasts programme.
53. Dublin Zoo has been involved in successive fund-raising campaigns approved by EAZA: in 2004, for example, it raised over €15,000 for 21st Century Tiger, a wild tiger conservation partnership between Global Tiger Patrol and the Zoological Society of London.
54. Eddie O'Brien in conversation with the author.
55. Unpublished paper 'History of the volunteers' by volunteer Maeve McDonald.
56. Director's report to the executive committee May 2007. Matt the lion was euthanised on the 5 June 2008.
57. Leo Oosterweghel in conversation with the author.
58. Leo Oosterweghel in conversation with the author.
59. ZSI minutes, 1 June 1999 and Dublin Zoo annual report 1999, p. 7. Dublin Zoo was also coordinator for the Moluccan cockatoo. In 2009, it is still coordinator for the Moluccan cockatoo and for the citron-crested cockatoo. Information from Sandra Devaney, Dublin Zoo Registrar/Research coordinator.
60. Smithsonian National Zoological Park website suggests there are 1,500, while the National Primate Research Center at the University of Wisconsin suggests 562 in the wild.
61. Sandra Devaney in conversation with the author.
62. Mico-Leao Dourado Associacao, 'Adopt a group report – Dublin Zoo: golden lion tamarin translocation program', prepared by Paula Procopio de Oliveira for Dublin Zoo. In 2009, on the recommendation of Mico-Leao Dourado Associacao, funding from Dublin Zoo was transferred to monitor a golden lion tamarin group in Poça das Antas Reserve: Golden Banana.
63. Sandra Devaney in conversation with the author.
64. *Ibid.*
65. Smithsonian National Zoological Park website: http://nationalzoo.si.edu/Animals/AfricanSavanna/fact-oryx.cfm
66. Sandra Devaney in conversation with the author.
67. 'A vision for Dublin Zoo', published by the Zoo, 2006. The strategy 'Building a Future for Wildlife' is an update

on the 1993 World Zoo Conservation Strategy, which defined a future for zoos. The 2005 document further refined the earlier one, taking into account the rapidly changing environment.

68. Dublin Zoo annual report, 2006, p. 1.

69. Speech by then Taoiseach, Bertie Ahern, on Monday 25 September 2006 in Dublin Zoo at the launch of 'A Vision for Dublin Zoo'.

70. The company, led by Grant Jones and Ilze Jones, had developed this concept when designing new habitats for Woodland Park Zoo in Seattle in the mid-1970s. It was considered revolutionary in its emphasis on naturalistic design to organise the Zoo's exhibits. The expertise of ecologists, researchers and other scientists was incorporated to ensure the development of the exhibits drew on studies of natural habitat and animal behaviour (*Encyclopedia of the World's Zoos, op. cit.*, p.1354–55). Jones and Jones have contributed to the creation of habitats worked in zoos all over the world, including the Trail of the Elephants in Melbourne Zoo; their ideas have been picked up and used worldwide.

71. Director's report to the executive committee, October 2004.

72. Leo Oosterweghel in conversation with the author.

73. From notes on the draft master plan for Dublin Zoo. Ironically, Dublin Zoo's relative poverty since its foundation was a major advantage when it came to 21st-century development. Wealthier zoos such as London Zoo have buildings that are considered to have historical interest and demolition is prohibited. This has been a major difficulty for many zoos as contemporary zoo habitats require a lot of space and these buildings are very difficult – and often impossible – to incorporate into a modern design.

74. Gerry Creighton (junior), team leader with responsibility for the elephants, in conversation with the author.

75. Gerry Creighton (junior) and Leo Oosterweghel in conversations with the author.

76. Grant Jones in conversation with the author; the references are to Stephen Butler and Paul O'Donoghue.

77. Gerry Creighton (junior) in conversation with the author. The team in question included keepers Alice Cooper and Ciaran McMahon, director Leo Oosterweghel, assistant to the director (animals and grounds) Paul O'Donoghue, the vet John Bainbridge, and the expert on Asian elephants, Alan Roocroft.

78. Leo Oosterweghel in conversation with the author.

79. *Zoo Matters*, winter 2008, p. 6

80. Speech by President Mary McAleese at the opening of the African Savanna, 9 April 2009.

81. 'Building a Future for Wildlife', the World Zoo and Aquarium Conservation Strategy. Berne, WAZA executive office, 2005.

82. Keith Duffy in conversation with the author.

83. James McGowan, Kate McGowan and Max Tormey in conversations with the author.

PICTURE CREDITS

Most of the pictures used the book are from the Dublin Zoo archive, which includes substantial collections of glass slides and prints. Few of the photographers are identified on the casing of the slides or on the prints and, where they have been identified, every effort has been made to contact all copyright holders. The publisher would be happy to hear from any copyright holder not acknowledged and undertakes to rectify any omissions or errors in future editions.

Information used in the captions was taken, in most cases, from the casing of the glass slide or the back of the print, for from the lender. Animals in pictures in chapters 5–7 have been identified with the help of current and former staff members.

Pp ii, 215 (right), 273 (left), 274, 285, 288, 289, 294 (top), 307 (bottom right), 328 courtesy of Mark Hogan; pp. vi, 263, 272, 277 (right), 280, 290 (top right), 307 (top right) 313 © Fran Veale; pp. 2 (left and right), 34 (from *Ireland's Eye*, 21 November 1874; J.A. Galbraith was his Haughton's colleague in TCD and Lord Cairns was Lord Chancellor in Disraeli's conservative government at the time), 35 courtesy of the Royal College of Physicians of Ireland; p. 3 © ZSL (Zoological Society of London); pp. 4, 8, 15; 1833: 5, 13; 1834: 20; 1835: 10, 16, 17; 1836: 7 (left), 11, 14 (left and right), 21 (right), 23 (bottom), 26 (left and right), 27 1832: images from the *Dublin Penny Journal*; pp. 6, 42, 52, 55 photographs by Damien Maddox, courtesy of the Department of Zoology, Trinity College Dublin; pp. 7 (right), 10, 20, 38, 84 courtesy of the National Library of Ireland; pp. 9, 28 (top), 60 (right; Quote from *The Life and Work of Sarah Purser,* by John O'Grady, 1996, p. 42), 111, 117, 197. 247 (top left), 254, top right), 258 (all), 261 (top right), 264 (right), 270 (top), 275, 276 (top and bottom left), 278, 281 (all), 290 (top left), 293, 294 (bottom left and bottom right), 300 (top right), 301 (right), 303 (bottom left), 304, 305, 307 (top left), 307 (bottom left), 310, 317 (bottom), 319 (top left, top right and bottom right), 322 (top and bottom left), 323 (top left and top right), 324 (top right), 326, 327 (all) photographs by Damien Maddox; pp., 22, 33 (right), 48 (bottom), 40, 56, 60 (left), 62 (top), 62 (bottom), 105 courtesy of The Board of Trinity College Dublin; p. 45 courtesy of the National Museums Northern Ireland; p. 51 courtesy of Grellan D. Rourke; p. 57 (information from RZSI annual report, 1874, p. 14, and RZSI annual report, 1895, p. 14) from the Dublin Zoo collection; p. 68 courtesy of the National Museum of Ireland; pp. 130, 132, 146, 188 (top, middle and right) courtesy of Paul Kenny; p. 138 (caption from the RZSI annual report, 1941, p. 15) Dublin Zoo Collection; pp. 140, (all pictures), 203 (top) courtesy of Michael Ward; pp. 141 (bottom left), 142, 151 (right), 156, 162, 166, 168 (bottom) 179, 185 bottom, 187, 223, 225, 266 (Photo by Dara MacDonaill) courtesy of *The Irish Times;* p. 150 courtesy of Butlins, Bourne Leisure; p. 151 (left) courtesy of Eddie O'Brien; pp. 152, 177, 195 (Liam Reid Collection) courtesy of the *Irish Independent;* p. 163 (bottom left) courtesy of Nora McDowell; p. 163 (top left) courtesy of Olwyn Lanigan; p. 163 (top right) courtesy of Sheila de Courcy; pp. 163 (bottom right), 168 (top left), 173 (right), 189, 249 (left) courtesy of Gerry Creighton (senior); p. 168 (top right) courtesy of Tom McGrath; pp. 170 (bottom left), 186 courtesy of Liam Reid; pp. 170 (top), 247 (bottom left; photo by Colin Riordan) courtesy of Irish Press Archives; pp. 171 (left and right), 174. 191, 196, 201 bottom right, 209 (top left), 236 (right and bottom left), 241, 247 (right) courtesy of Douglas Duggan; p. 172 courtesy of Frank Burke; p. 173 (left) courtesy of Fáilte Ireland; p. 176 photo by Bill St Leger, courtesy of Joe St Leger; p. 178 courtesy of Mary Neville; p. 180 drawing courtesy of Micheál Ó Nualláin; pp. 182 (left and right), 193 (right) images reproduced with the kind permission of the Guinness Archive, Diageo Ireland; p. 183 (left and right) courtesy of *The Irish Times* and Micheál Ó Nualláin; pp. 185 (top right), 200 (left) courtesy of Dorothy Kilroy; 188 (top left) courtesy of Paul Burke-Kennedy; p. 190 (left) photo © John Hinde Ltd; pp. 190 (right), 201 (bottom left) courtesy of Maeve McDonald; p. 194 photo by Bobby Coleman, courtesy of Bobby Studio; pp. 198 (right), 287 courtesy of Anne May; p. 200 (right) courtesy of Brian O'Reilly; p. 204 courtesy of Pam McDonough; pp. 205, 222 (right) by Jill Breivik; p. 206 (bottom) by JJ Holly, Wicklow; p. 206 (top) by Deegan Photography, Dublin; p. 209 (top left) by Edward Moss, Terenure; pp. 214 (top), 232 by Pat Sweeney; pp. 215 (bottom), 222 (top left) by Reilly, Clondalkin; p. 216 (left) © Dan Guravich /PolarBearsInternational.org; pp. 217 (left, photo by John Carlos), 228, 233 (photo by Tony Gavin), 235 (top and bottom, pictures by Bob Hoby), 240 (photo by Ann Egan), 249 (right, photo by Tony Gavin), 252 (right, photo by Ann Egan), 257 (left, photo by John Carlos) courtesy of the *Sunday Tribune;* pp. 217 (right), 265 by Frank Fennell; p. 219 (top) by Jonathan Pratschke; p. 229 (right) courtesy of Ann and Pat Murphy; p. 231 courtesy of the *Irish Examiner;* p. 252 (left) courtesy of Brendan Price; p. 257 (top right) by Liam Kennedy, Cork; p. 261 (bottom) by Photostyle, Dublin; p. 261 (top left) by Bill Matthews; pp. 262, 270 (bottom), 276 (bottom right), 291, 308, 309, 316 by Neil McShane; pp. 273 (right), 282 by Keith Arkins; pp. 277 (left), 279, 312, 314 (right), 317 (top) by Robbie Reynolds; pp. 286, 290 (bottom right), 319 (bottom left), 320 by Suzanne O'Donovan; p. 290 (bottom left) by Sharppix; pp. 296, 324 (top left) by Frank Malone; p. 300 (top left) courtesy of Max Tormey; p. 314 (left) photo by Fred Nordheim; reproduced by kind permission of Rotterdam Zoo.

INDEX